EYEWITNESS ANTHOLOGIES

AMERICAN PEOPLES

A DORLING KINDERSLEY BOOK

Chapter One
Project editor Marion Dent
Art editor Vicky Wharton
Managing editor Simon Adams
Managing art editor Julia Harris
Research Céline Carez
Picture research Sarah Moule
Production Catherine Semark
Editorial consultants Laila Williamson, Department of Anthropology, and Scarlett Lovell, Director of Special Publications, American Museum of Natural History, New York; and Mary Ann Lynch

Chapter Two
Project editor Christine Webb
Art editor Andrew Nash
Managing editor Helen Parker
Managing art editor Julia Harris
Production Catherine Semark
Picture research Cynthia Hole
Research Céline Carez
Additional photography Andy Crawford & Dave Rudkin

First American Edition, 1996
2 4 6 8 10 9 7 5 3 1

Published in the United States by
DK Publishing, Inc., 95 Madison Avenue
New York, New York 10016

Visit us on the World Wide Web at http://www.dk.com

Distributed by Houghton Mifflin Company, Boston

ISBN 0-7894-1410-4

Reproduced in Italy by G.R.B. Graphica, Verona
Printed in Singapore by Toppan

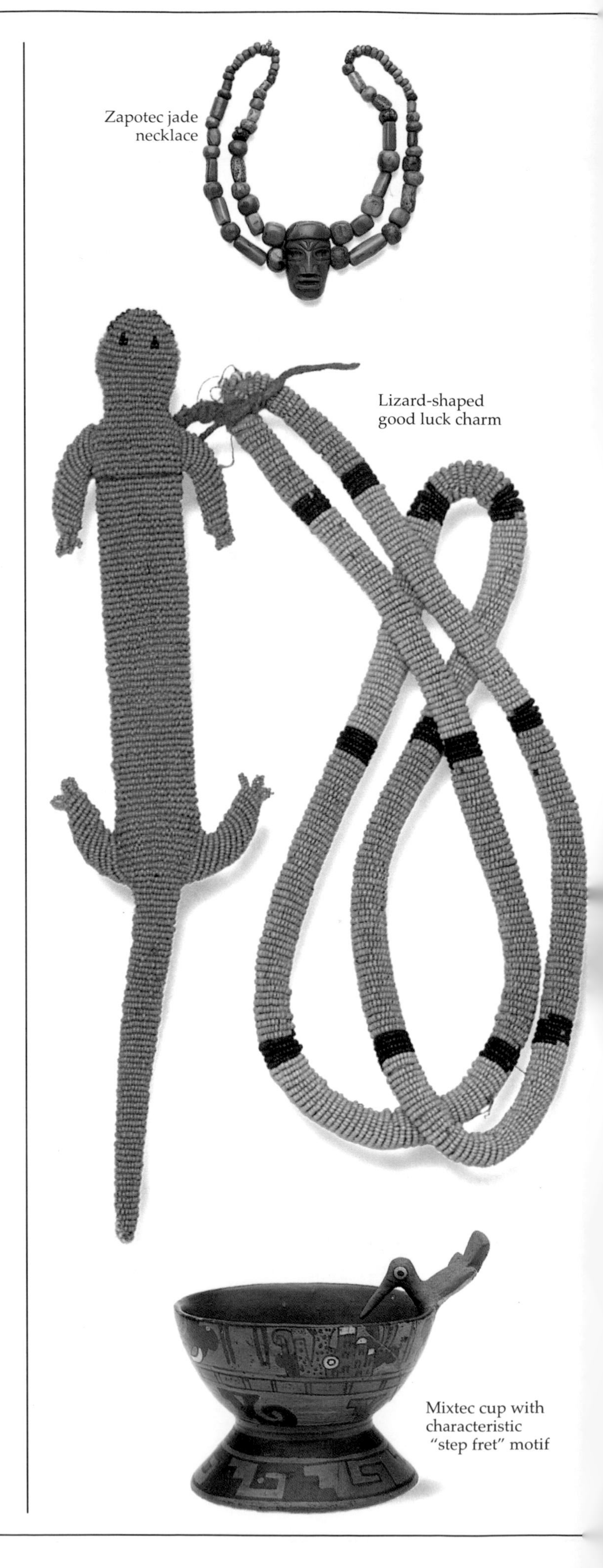

Zapotec jade necklace

Lizard-shaped good luck charm

Mixtec cup with characteristic "step fret" motif

Thompson tribe war club

Moche staff showing figure of a chief

AMERICAN PEOPLES

Mixtec head

NORTH AMERICAN INDIAN

Written by
DAVID MURDOCH

Chief Consultant
STANLEY A. FREED, PhD
Curator, Department of Anthropology, A.M.N.H.

Photographed by
LYNTON GARDINER

In association with
THE AMERICAN MUSEUM OF NATURAL HISTORY

AZTEC, INCA & MAYA

Written by
ELIZABETH BAQUEDANO

Photographed by
MICHEL ZABÉ

Tlingit shaman's wooden rattle

Rare jet ornament found at Pueblo Bonito

Traditional Pueblo pottery

Iroquois harvesting basket

Contents

Dakota medicine box

Ulu knife, used by Inuit women for skinning seals

"Love dolls" used by Menominee shamans

Chapter One

NORTH AMERICAN INDIAN

Written by
DAVID MURDOCH

Chief Consultant
STANLEY A. FREED, PhD
Curator, Department of Anthropology, A.M.N.H.

Photographed by
LYNTON GARDINER

In association with
THE AMERICAN MUSEUM OF NATURAL HISTORY

Shaman's headdress of the Tlingit, a Northwest Coast tribe

Peopling of the Americas

WHO WERE THE FIRST AMERICANS? Archeologists agree that human beings probably trekked across the Ice Age land bridge from Siberia – but they do not agree on when this happened. Once thought to be 12,000 years ago, the date might be 40,000 years ago according to some new scientific theories. Some present-day Native North Americans believe their sacred stories place their beginnings in America, just as some Christians believe human beings were created in the Garden of Eden. Archeology shows that, however they got here, the first Americans, adapting to changing climate and environment, evolved from hunters using stone-tipped weapons to more advanced societies of farmers and artisans.

Glacier (in violet)

Map of North America showing the human migration route from Siberia across the Ice Age land bridge

Exposed land (in green)

MIGRATION THEORY
During the Ice Age huge amounts of water froze into glaciers, Bering Strait became drained, and a wide, low, treeless plain (Beringia) connected Siberia and Alaska. About 12,000 years ago an ice-free corridor opened. Archeologists believe that paleo-Indians crossed Beringia, following the corridor to open country south of the glaciers.

Model of an atlatl – from the Aztec word meaning "spear thrower"

Small Clovis point

Folsom point

Larger Clovis point could measure 5 in (13 cm) in length

Banner stone (a weight of stone) on which spear rested

Wooden bar up to 3 ft (1 m) long

ICE AGE HUNTERS
Definite proof of Ice Age human beings in America came in 1926, with the discovery at Folsom, New Mexico, of carefully shaped stone weapon points dating from 10,000 years ago. In 1932 weapon points from an even older people, up to 12,000 years ago, were unearthed at Clovis, New Mexico.

A STRONGER, LONGER THROW
Hunters of mammoths, mastodons, antique bison, and giant sloths from 10,000 years ago – such as the Folsom people in New Mexico – used an atlatl, a special device for throwing a spear. It was a bar with a flat stone on which the spear rested and a curved tip that engaged the spear's butt. The greater leverage gave a much stronger thrust.

Slate spear point from New England

Copper spear point from the Great Lakes area

Grip of hide with loops for fingers

Chipped-stone spear point from Tennessee

BECOMING EXTINCT
The end of the Ice Age, 10,000 years ago, saw many large animals, like the mammoth, become extinct, perhaps through environmental change or overhunting. From 5000 B.C. to 1000 B.C., the peoples of the Eastern forests learned to hunt woodland game. They lived in permanent settlements and developed complex societies. They were expert toolmakers, making a variety of spear points.

Copper spear point from the Great Lakes region

Polished Anasazi deer-bone spatula

Turquoise and jet inlay

WHY DID THEY DISAPPEAR?
The Anasazi (a Navajo word meaning "ancient enemy") lived on today's Arizona–New Mexico border. By A.D. 1100 they had created the great stone-and-clay buildings later to be called pueblos (pp. 46–47). Their culture faded in the late 1200s, perhaps irreparably damaged by a prolonged drought.

DESERT DWELLERS
The Hohokam people (from the Pima word for "the vanished ones") lived in the desert near the Gila River, Arizona, c. 500 B.C. to A.D. 1500. Expert irrigators, they avoided war, grew corn, built towns, and were superb artisans, making jewelry cleverly cut from shells (left) and fine pottery (below).

Pair of Hohokam shell bracelets

Red-on-buff pottery was traditional Hohokam style

Rare jet ornament found at Pueblo Bonito

Eye made of inlaid turquoise

Frog was symbol of water in Anasazi culture

ANASAZI ARTISANS
Architecture and town design were the noteworthy skills of the Anasazi, their great buildings standing today as reminders of a complex civilization. They also produced interesting pottery and were skilled in working with turquoise (above).

Mimbres pot, a burial offering, was ritually "killed" by puncturing base to let the spirit escape

TRADITIONAL STYLE
The Hohokam, predecessors of the Papago and Pima (pp. 50–51), may have been an offshoot of one of the great Central American civilizations, perhaps the Maya. Their early pottery seems similar to ancient Mexican designs. About A.D. 400, they began making striking two-color red-on-buff pots with simple line patterns. Later, more complex designs included animals, human figures, and their gods. The Hohokam cremated their dead, sometimes placing the ashes in these traditional vessels, which were buried.

Animal head

MOGOLLON–MIMBRES
The Mogollon people (named for their mountain homeland on the Arizona–New Mexico border) lived isolated in mountain valleys c. 300 B.C.– A.D. 1300. The Mimbres, a related group living near New Mexico's Mimbres River, produced remarkable black-on-white pottery from c. A.D. 700. Their artists later created vivid designs of every kind of creature (animal, bird, and human) and geometric patterns – often mixing them.

A vast continent

By 1500, THE AMERICAN LANDS north of Mexico were home to about 1.3 million people. Over 11,500 years, the descendants of the first Siberian migrants had diverged into more than 300 tribes – the densest population lived east of the Mississippi, in California, and in the Northwest. They had evolved ways of life exploiting food resources in different environments and developed high artistic skills. Their world was constantly changing – game animals became extinct; drought and tribal warfare led to migrations. Over the next 400 years, Europeans would bring about such catastrophic changes as loss of territory, population decline, and cultural restrictions for all Native North Americans.

Eagle feather tipped with horsehair

Red cloth, glass beads, and metal disk decorate headdress

Fur tassel

Ceremonial war bonnet of Cheyenne chief White Eagle

THE TERROR OF THE PLAINS
In 1500 the Cheyenne were not yet feared Plains warriors (pp. 28–29). Settled in villages in Minnesota, they farmed and hunted. They migrated westward in the mid-1700s, abandoning farming and becoming nomadic Plains horsemen dependent on the buffalo. An eagle-feather war bonnet (left) became their emblem of an experienced and respected warrior.

Apache buckskin cap decorated with glass beads and metal disk

Eagle-feather plumage

APACHE WARRIOR
The Apache (pp. 48–49) were newcomers in the Southwest in 1500; they seem to have migrated from Canada about 50 years earlier. The Spanish explorer Francisco de Coronado (1510–1554) thought the Chiricahua Apaches he met in 1540 were "a gentle people." Later Spaniards came to disagree with him!

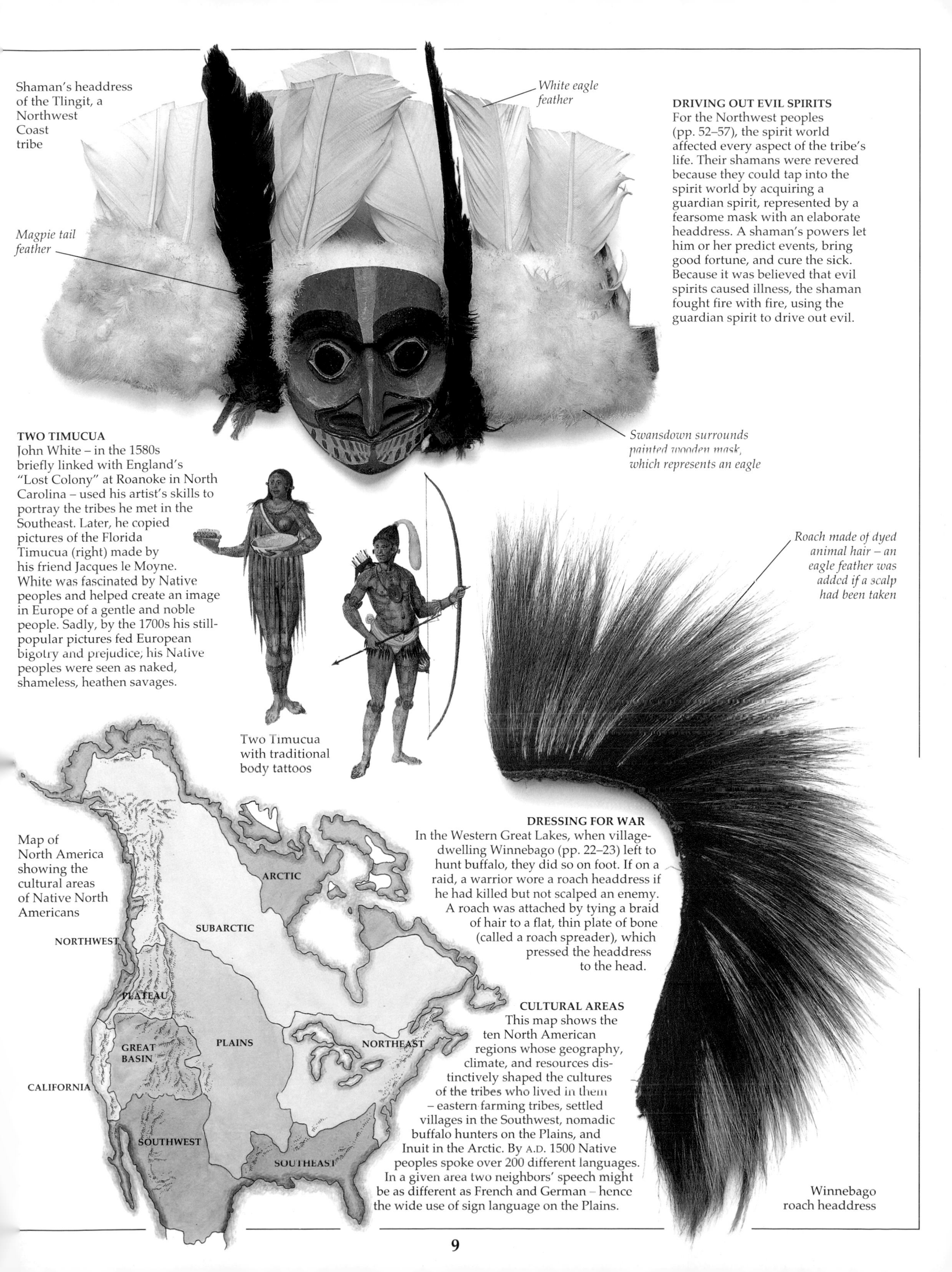

Shaman's headdress of the Tlingit, a Northwest Coast tribe

White eagle feather

Magpie tail feather

Swansdown surrounds painted wooden mask, which represents an eagle

DRIVING OUT EVIL SPIRITS

For the Northwest peoples (pp. 52–57), the spirit world affected every aspect of the tribe's life. Their shamans were revered because they could tap into the spirit world by acquiring a guardian spirit, represented by a fearsome mask with an elaborate headdress. A shaman's powers let him or her predict events, bring good fortune, and cure the sick. Because it was believed that evil spirits caused illness, the shaman fought fire with fire, using the guardian spirit to drive out evil.

TWO TIMUCUA

John White – in the 1580s briefly linked with England's "Lost Colony" at Roanoke in North Carolina – used his artist's skills to portray the tribes he met in the Southeast. Later, he copied pictures of the Florida Timucua (right) made by his friend Jacques le Moyne. White was fascinated by Native peoples and helped create an image in Europe of a gentle and noble people. Sadly, by the 1700s his still-popular pictures fed European bigotry and prejudice; his Native peoples were seen as naked, shameless, heathen savages.

Two Timucua with traditional body tattoos

Roach made of dyed animal hair – an eagle feather was added if a scalp had been taken

Map of North America showing the cultural areas of Native North Americans

DRESSING FOR WAR

In the Western Great Lakes, when village-dwelling Winnebago (pp. 22–23) left to hunt buffalo, they did so on foot. If on a raid, a warrior wore a roach headdress if he had killed but not scalped an enemy. A roach was attached by tying a braid of hair to a flat, thin plate of bone (called a roach spreader), which pressed the headdress to the head.

CULTURAL AREAS

This map shows the ten North American regions whose geography, climate, and resources distinctively shaped the cultures of the tribes who lived in them – eastern farming tribes, settled villages in the Southwest, nomadic buffalo hunters on the Plains, and Inuit in the Arctic. By A.D. 1500 Native peoples spoke over 200 different languages. In a given area two neighbors' speech might be as different as French and German – hence the wide use of sign language on the Plains.

Winnebago roach headdress

Medicine and the spirit world

POWER FILLED THE WORLD of the Native North American. Invisible but everywhere, this supernatural force of the spirit world touched people, animals, and plants. Shamans were special men and women who could heal the sick and capture some of this power to manipulate the ordinary world. Because shamans carried healing herbs, Europeans called them "medicine men," but for a shaman and the tribe all spirit power was "medicine." Shamans used dramatic ceremonies to help a patient's mind reject sickness. They also had drugs. The Five Tribes of the Southeast used the stimulant caffeine and salicylic acid (aspirin). Plains tribes used skunk-cabbage root for asthma and yarrow for minor wounds, both effective remedies. Shamans, like white doctors, were powerless against great European epidemics, especially smallpox which decimated the Native population, falling from 1.3 million people in 1500 to 400,000 before recovering.

Tobacco bowl would be attached here

Sinew string

George Catlin painting of Old Bear, a Mandan shaman

OLD BEAR
The Mandan, like other Plains tribes, believed visions brought spirit-power. To receive a vision, a Mandan would seek solitude, pray, and abstain from food until near delirium. A truly powerful vision made its recipient a shaman. Dress and equipment (above) would be dictated by the shaman's first and later visions and would therefore contain power.

Animal and bird skins decorate this Blackfeet shaman's bearskin robe

A HEALING CEREMONY
American painter George Catlin (1796–1872) was determined to record the way of life of Native Americans before it was destroyed by whites. He made a tour of the American West (1830–36), having gained the confidence of 48 tribes, and produced over 500 vivid paintings and sketches and detailed notes. This portrait shows a Blackfeet shaman of the Plains performing a healing ceremony. Dressed in a bearskin robe, with the head forming a mask, the shaman danced around the patient.

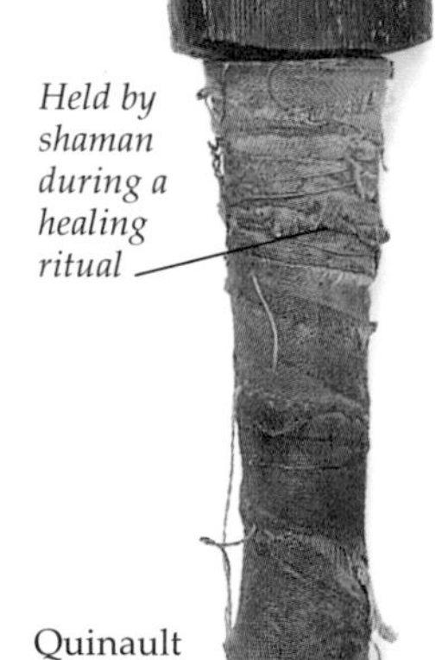

Held by shaman during a healing ritual

Quinault carved wooden wand

HOW TO CURE A STOMACHACHE
The Hidatsa Plains tribe dealt with indigestion or other stomach pains by hand massaging or using a stomach pusher (above). With the patient laid flat, the curved end of this instrument (often made of white cedar) was rubbed against the stomach.

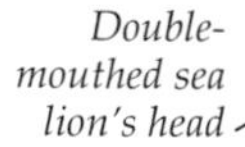

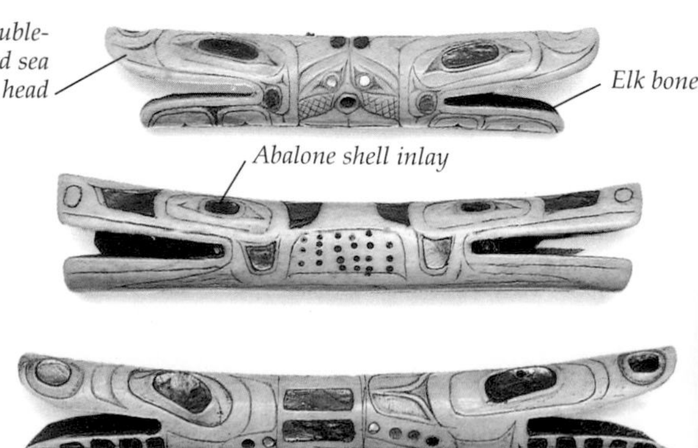

Double-mouthed sea lion's head

Elk bone

Abalone shell inlay

SHAMAN'S SPIRIT HELPER
Like all the tribes of the Northwest, the Quinault believed in a multitude of spirit beings who constantly affected the ordinary world. A shaman's powers came in part from his or her own special guardian spirit. As a doctor casting out an evil spirit, the shaman would carry a carving of the guardian spirit (above).

CATCHING A SOUL
Tsimshian shamans, like those of the other Northwest tribes, believed illness was caused either by an evil spirit or by the loss of the patient's soul – perhaps through a witch's spell. Therefore, one of the shaman's most important instruments was a soul catcher. A carved ivory or bone tube, it captured the soul and returned it to the body. Sometimes blowing through the soul catcher helped to expel the sickness.

FIRST SIGN OF THUNDER
Most revered of the Blackfeet sacred medicine pipes were the thunder pipes. At the first spring thunder, these pipes were removed from their bundles of sacred objects and offered to the thunder spirit. The ceremony asked protection from being struck by lightning (a frequent hazard on the Plains) and also for the power to heal sickness. Possessing a thunder pipe brought great prestige, but it was expected that ownership would be passed on to others.

Blackfeet sacred thunder medicine pipe

Dakota medicine box and herbs

A REMEDY FOR EVERYTHING
In addition to resorting to shamans, with their supernatural powers to cure illness, sick people had available various common medicines obtained from plants. This early 1900s Dakota medicine box contains herbs for headache, earache, stomach pain, bleeding, swelling, and other ailments. The selected herb was reduced to a powder on a tin grater and then steeped in hot water to make a healing tea.

Muslin packet containing herbs, tied with sinew

The far Northeast

Map of North America showing the Northeast Indian lands, including New England, the Mid-Atlantic, Ohio River Valley, and the Western Great Lakes

A LAND OF ABUNDANT CONTRASTS, the wooded Northeast stretched from the St. Lawrence River to present-day North Carolina and west to the Mississippi. Its peoples made the most of an environment rich in game and fish. Except in the very cold far northern areas, they also raised corn, squash, and beans. Northern tribes, like the Penobscot and Malecite, living amid lakes and rivers, developed the birchbark canoe, much envied by their neighbors. From the early 1600s, fur trading with Europeans brought new materials and ideas. However, Northeast peoples (like the powerful Iroquois League) were drawn into the European struggle for North America in the 1700s and were forced to pick sides in the American Revolution (1775–1783) and the War of 1812. Most saw their independence destroyed and some were completely swept away by relentless American settlement.

INGENIOUS DESIGN
Tribes like Nova Scotia's Micmac exploited the fishing resources of their lakes and rivers, using hooks, lines, bows, traps, and spears. They liked to fish at night using birchbark torches. Attracted by the light, the fish came to the surface, where they were speared from birchbark canoes.

Wooden shaft of Micmac spear lashed to three barbs by cord

Central metal barb stabs fish

Wooden side barb prevents fish from struggling free

KING PHILIP
In 1675, angry and fearful at the growth of European power, "King Philip" (or Metacomet), chief of the Wampanoag, attacked the New England settlements. Eventually the rising was crushed, but if King Philip had formed more effective alliances with other tribes, the English colonies might have been destroyed.

Cord ties metal blade to wooden handle, providing a handy grip when drawn toward the woodworker

A CROOKED KNIFE
Birch bark was used to make canoes, wigwams, and paper. Bark sheets were cut with knives (like this Penobscot example). Holes were pierced along the edges with an awl and the sheets sewn together with spruce root to make storage or cooking vessels. Two-tone patterns were created by scraping away a dark coating on the bark's inner surface to reveal a lighter color.

Top (right) and side (below) views of model of a Malecite canoe

Low ends of canoe give it greater stability in calm waters; canoes with high bows and sterns provide protection from waves in choppy waters

Natural grain of bark, running longitudinally, allows sheets of bark to be sewn together more easily

Paddle up to 5 ft (1.5 m) long

Canoe up to 25 ft (7.5 m) long

EUROPEAN INFLUENCES

Before contact with Europeans, clothing in the Northeast was usually made from skins, sometimes decorated with painted symbols or dyed porcupine quills. European settlers brought new materials and decorations, such as woven cloth, glass beads, and tailored coats and trousers. The peoples of the Northeast adopted many of these innovations. Northeastern men traditionally wore a skin coat with painted decorations. This Penobscot buckskin jacket shows European influences – a tailored shape and elaborate glass-bead embroidery.

DEER SLAYER

Though the forest peoples were skilled at hunting, success was uncertain. Aid was sought from the spirit world through sacred charms and by rituals to contact the spirits of the slain animals. The chief hunting weapon was the bow and arrow, but a hit might not be fatal. A stone club (like this Penobscot example) was used for killing a wounded deer.

A DESIGN TRIUMPH

The best canoes were made from bark of the white birch, growing only in Canada and the most northeastern U.S. The framework was made of white cedar, split with hammers and wedges. It was covered with large sheets of bark laced together with roots and waterproofed with resin from the black spruce. Light enough to be carried, the canoe could take a load of 4,000 lb (1,800 kg). It was instantly adopted by European explorers and fur traders of the 1600s.

DECORATED DEERSKIN

Like all the peoples of the northeastern forests, the Penobscot wore moccasins of deerskin, which were usually decorated. The influence of the Europeans shows in the lavish use of colored glass beads for decorations and the adoption of flower designs. Floral motifs were copied from white settlers and became widespread in the clothing of the Northeast. Men and women wore the same style of moccasin.

The League of the Iroquois

OUT OF THE NORTHERN WOODS early in the 1600s, there emerged the strongest political and military force in North America. Five tribes – the Mohawk, Onondaga, Seneca, Oneida, and Cayuga – ended their destructive feuding and formed the Iroquois League. Each tribe remained self-governing, but collective decisions were made by a representative Great Council. Though the members were men, they were chosen by the elder women of the tribes, who also had the power to remove them. The League was conceived to bring peace, but it became a formidable war machine. Because it was able to mobilize its forces effectively, it dominated much of the Northeast. Even as late as the mid-1700s it could hold the balance of power in the colonial wars between the French and the British.

CORNPLANTER
Son of a Dutch trader father and a Seneca mother, Cornplanter (1740?–1836) fought Americans during the Revolution (1775–1783). Later this respected Seneca chief became a tireless spokesman for peace, negotiating many treaties.

Stone celt later replaced by steel blade

TRIBES AT WAR
Iroquois wars were usually short raids with weapons like bows and war clubs. Involvement with Europeans competing with each other for the fur trade changed this. In 1649 the Iroquois League, as ally of the Dutch, virtually destroyed the Erie and Huron tribes, who supported the French.

Rattle made from a whole turtle shell

MOHAWK MUSIC
Music for the Mohawk, as for other eastern peoples, mostly depended on drums and rattles. A turtle-shell rattle was made by drying the animal, then cleaning out the shell, being careful to leave the head, tail, and legs intact. After this, pebbles were inserted and a wooden handle added.

HIAWATHA – A HERO
In the late 1500s, the prophet Dekanawidah, despairing at constant intertribal warfare, saw Iroquois union in a vision. Hiawatha, a Mohawk, then traveled ceaselessly between the tribes, persuading them to unite. *Hiawatha*, the famous poem by Henry Longfellow (1807–1882), gives no indication of the charisma and diplomatic skills of this remarkable leader.

Iroquois belts woven from wampum could be many feet long

Purple beads were twice as costly as white ones

THE COLOR PURPLE
Strings of purple and white tubular shell beads, called wampum, were used as symbolic gifts at marriages, as condolence to the bereaved, or as an invitation to ceremonies such as peace negotiations or a war alliance. White was the color of peace, black of gloomy matters. Purple was the most prized. Realizing the high value placed on it by the tribes, Europeans manufactured wampum from shell, using it in trade as money. Then they began to counterfeit it in glass. As money, wampum became debased and fell out of use.

Iroquois war club made in typical "rabbit's hind-leg" style

Elm-bark covering

Model of a four-fire, eight-family longhouse

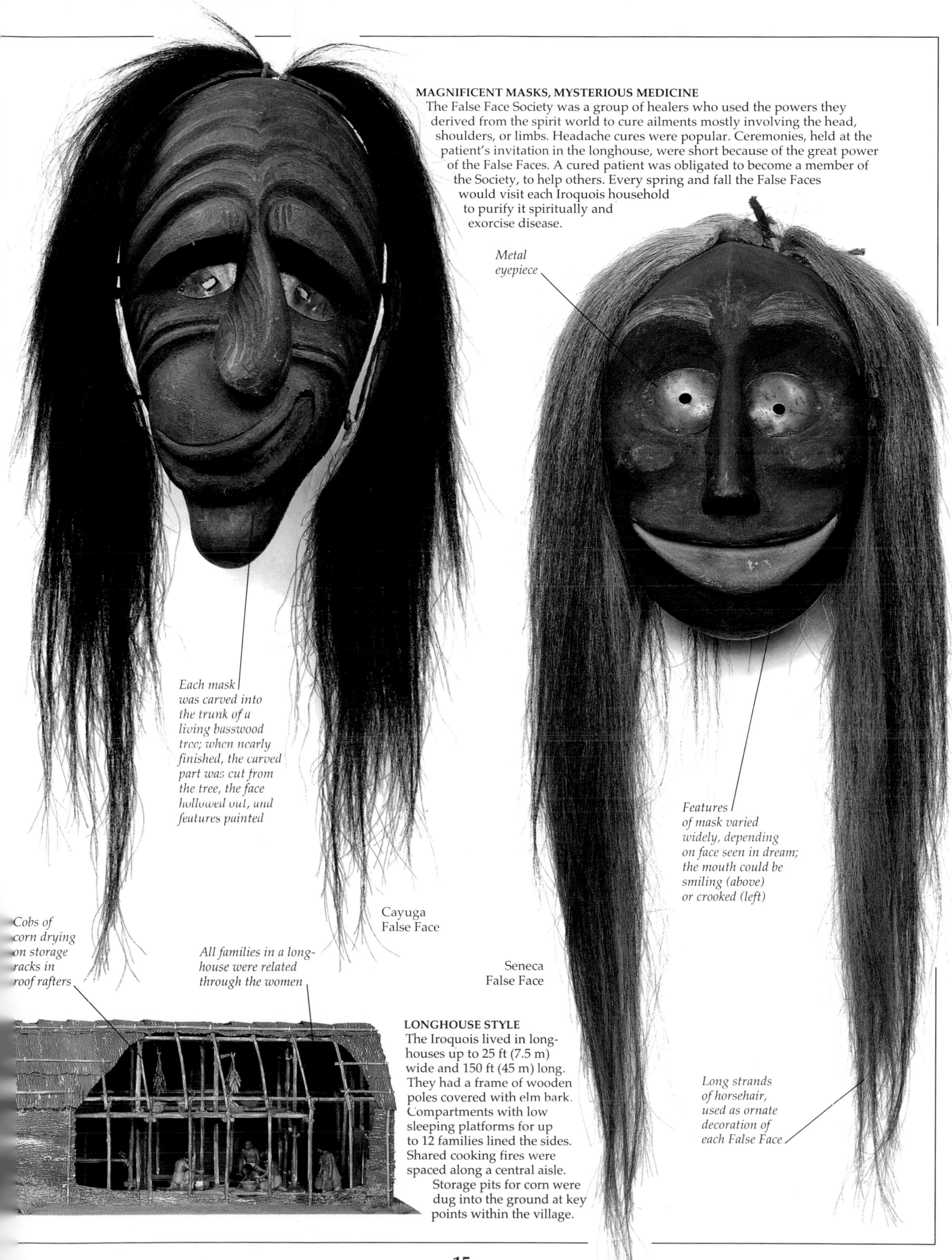

MAGNIFICENT MASKS, MYSTERIOUS MEDICINE

The False Face Society was a group of healers who used the powers they derived from the spirit world to cure ailments mostly involving the head, shoulders, or limbs. Headache cures were popular. Ceremonies, held at the patient's invitation in the longhouse, were short because of the great power of the False Faces. A cured patient was obligated to become a member of the Society, to help others. Every spring and fall the False Faces would visit each Iroquois household to purify it spiritually and exorcise disease.

Metal eyepiece

Each mask was carved into the trunk of a living basswood tree; when nearly finished, the carved part was cut from the tree, the face hollowed out, and features painted

Features of mask varied widely, depending on face seen in dream; the mouth could be smiling (above) or crooked (left)

Cayuga False Face

Seneca False Face

Cobs of corn drying on storage racks in roof rafters

All families in a longhouse were related through the women

Long strands of horsehair, used as ornate decoration of each False Face

LONGHOUSE STYLE

The Iroquois lived in longhouses up to 25 ft (7.5 m) wide and 150 ft (45 m) long. They had a frame of wooden poles covered with elm bark. Compartments with low sleeping platforms for up to 12 families lined the sides. Shared cooking fires were spaced along a central aisle. Storage pits for corn were dug into the ground at key points within the village.

The three sisters

CORN WAS LIFE for tribes throughout the eastern woodlands. Producing starch to make energy, corn can provide 75 percent of the human body's food needs. Many corn varieties were grown (the Iroquois raised 15), and none required much labor. No care was necessary after planting the seed, except for scaring off birds, until the harvest. Beans and squash were often planted in the same field. Beans twined up the cornstalks, and squash choked weeds and kept the ground moist. The Iroquois believed these crops had spirit beings and called them "the three sisters." Dried and stored, corn, beans, and squash guaranteed food supplies, and more time could be devoted to ceremonies, hunting, trading, and war.

AUTUMN TREAT
Ripening in the autumn, pumpkin squash is a valuable vegetable. English colonists learned its use from Native Americans and invented sweet pumpkin pie, traditional at Thanksgiving.

Iroquois wooden bowl containing dried beans

BOWL OF BEANS
Depending on environment and accidents of history, many varieties of bean were grown across the continent. All had the same important qualities. They were a good extra food source because they had high amounts of proteins and essential vitamins (particularly of the Vitamin B group). Equally important, beans can be dried and stored for long periods, even years, without spoiling.

Ojibwa bark basket with dried rings of Sauk and Fox (Western Great Lakes tribes) squash plaited together

Seneca wooden pestle

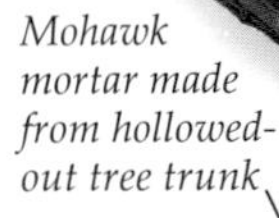

Mohawk mortar made from hollowed-out tree trunk

DRIED SQUASH
Squashes grew thoughout the summer, when they were eaten fresh, providing an important source of Vitamin C, essential for general health. A portion of the crop was cut into strips or rings and sun-dried, or hung up whole inside the dwelling until dry, then stored with the beans and corn.

Iroquois harvesting basket containing cobs of Oneida dried corn

GRINDING CORN
Iroquois women shucked (stripped) the corncob of kernels with deer jawbones, then boiled the kernels in lye (made from boiled ashes) to soften the skins. Next the lye and skins were washed away in a special basket and the kernels were dried. They were turned into meal by laborious pounding with a mortar and pestle (left).

CORN ON THE COB
Some corn had to be saved for the lean winter months. Cobs were dried and hung in the longhouse. Some cobs were shucked and the kernels dried and stored in bins or underground granaries. Ground corn kernels were boiled as a porridge or made into cakes and eaten with maple sugar, honey, or fat.

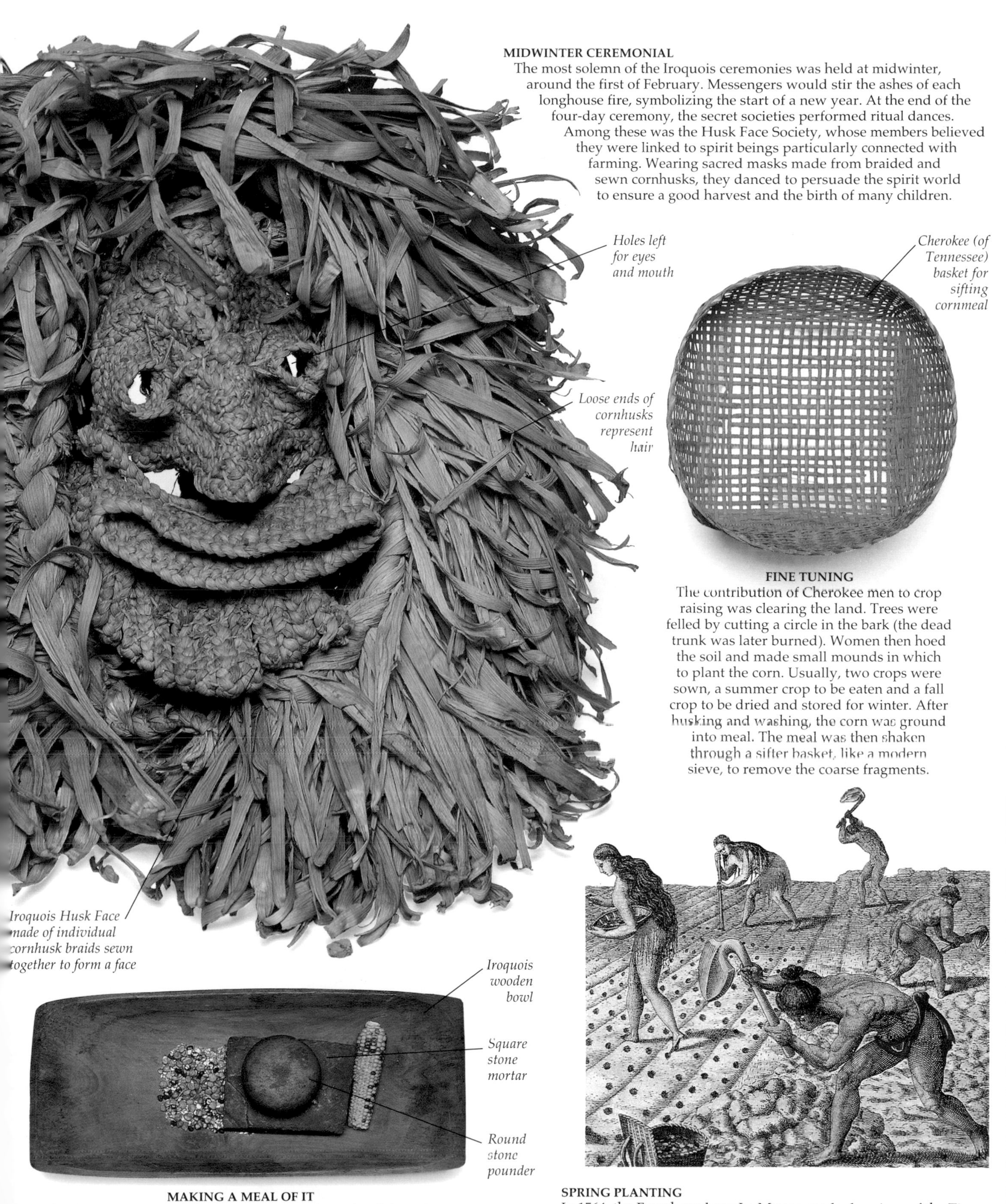

MIDWINTER CEREMONIAL

The most solemn of the Iroquois ceremonies was held at midwinter, around the first of February. Messengers would stir the ashes of each longhouse fire, symbolizing the start of a new year. At the end of the four-day ceremony, the secret societies performed ritual dances. Among these was the Husk Face Society, whose members believed they were linked to spirit beings particularly connected with farming. Wearing sacred masks made from braided and sewn cornhusks, they danced to persuade the spirit world to ensure a good harvest and the birth of many children.

FINE TUNING

The contribution of Cherokee men to crop raising was clearing the land. Trees were felled by cutting a circle in the bark (the dead trunk was later burned). Women then hoed the soil and made small mounds in which to plant the corn. Usually, two crops were sown, a summer crop to be eaten and a fall crop to be dried and stored for winter. After husking and washing, the corn was ground into meal. The meal was then shaken through a sifter basket, like a modern sieve, to remove the coarse fragments.

MAKING A MEAL OF IT

After husking, drying, and shucking (stripping kernels off the cob), Iroquois women had a long, hard job making corn into meal. Dried kernels were pounded in a wooden mortar and pestle (far left), or cracked and ground between two stones. A wooden bowl served to catch the meal.

SPRING PLANTING

In 1564, the French explorer Le Moyne made drawings of the Timucua in Florida. In his picture of them planting spring corn, they look more like French peasants than Native Americans. The Timucua men used hoes with fish-bone heads (not iron-headed mattocks) and the women planted seeds in holes, not loosely scattering them.

The Mid-Atlantic Seaboard

A LAND OF WOODED PLAINS and lush valleys extended along the Mid-Atlantic Seaboard (Delaware, Maryland, Virginia, and North Carolina). Its people lived in villages of bark-covered, domed or arch-roofed dwellings. They raised corn and hunted in the forests. They were led by sachems (chiefs), who ruled by consensus. In 1585 John White, briefly part of the English colony at Roanoke (North Carolina) before it mysteriously disappeared, made paintings of the Secotan. Later published as engravings, they became the European stereotype of "Indians" for the next 200 years. When the English settled the colony of Virginia, they encountered the strong Powhatan alliance, which nearly destroyed them. Even more powerful were the Delaware, a confederation whose influence in the 1600s stretched far to the north and west. Their power was later broken by the Iroquois.

Delaware effigy of a woman, carved simply in wood

Elaborate decorations (silver crosses and buckles) show strong European influence

A SECOTAN VILLAGE
John White (pp. 8–9) painted this scene of a typical Secotan village in 1585. Shown are houses of bent saplings covered with bark and woven mats, surrounded by a defensive palisade (a circle of upright posts). The houses with sleeping platforms resemble those of the Iroquois to the north. The building with the cupola is a temple. Eventually the Secotan disappeared from their territory in North Carolina and were succeeded by other tribes.

A DOLL FOR HEALTH
The Delaware believed in the universal presence of the Great Spirit, and also in a world filled with lesser spirit beings. Spirits shaped their lives, fortunes, and health. Prayers, offerings, and ceremonies were meant to seek the help of these beings. This wooden image is a woman spirit guardian of health. Every fall the Delaware honored her with a feast, presents, and the sacrifice of a deer.

WOODLAND ART
With abundant forests, Eastern tribes used wood for many household utensils, such as bowls, spoons, and ladles. Woodworking was a task for men. To make hollow vessels like this bowl, the wood was first charred and the burned part scraped away with a stone (later iron) knife. Carved from the burled (knotty) parts of elm and maple, these objects were both useful and an expression of woodland art.

Simply carved wooden Delaware serving bowl and spoon

Handy hook topped with a crown

Paddle intricately carved with a star

Handle ornately carved with turtle, horse, and horseshoe

Delaware wooden food stirrer

Bottom filled with stones to sink basket to river bed

Delaware leggings made of woven cloth

Decorated with deer-hoof rattles and silk ribbon appliqué

WEARING APPAREL

Most clothing was made from animal skins, particularly deer hide. Men, taught from boyhood to ignore rain and chilly weather, wore only a breechcloth (front and back flaps held up by a belt) and moccasins in the warmer months, together with buckskin leggings. Women wore a waist-to-knee skirt over knee-high leggings. In winter both men and women added a fur robe. European contact brought woven cloth (left), which was sometimes substituted for skins, and new clothing patterns, such as jackets and trousers.

POCAHONTAS'S WEDDING

In 1607 Captain John Smith (1580–1631), from the English colony of Virginia, was captured by the chief of the Powhatan. Smith's life was dramatically saved by the pleadings of the chief's daughter, Pocahontas (1595–1617). Kidnapped by the English, she met and later married John Rolfe (1585–1622). This marriage kept the peace between the English and the Powhatans until the chief's death in 1618.

TRAPPING FISH

Fish were an important addition to forest game all over the Eastern woodlands, not least because they could be caught all year round. Fish were speared, shot with bows, or taken with hook and line. Where some species migrated upriver to spawn, they could be caught by using nets, weirs, or traps (below).

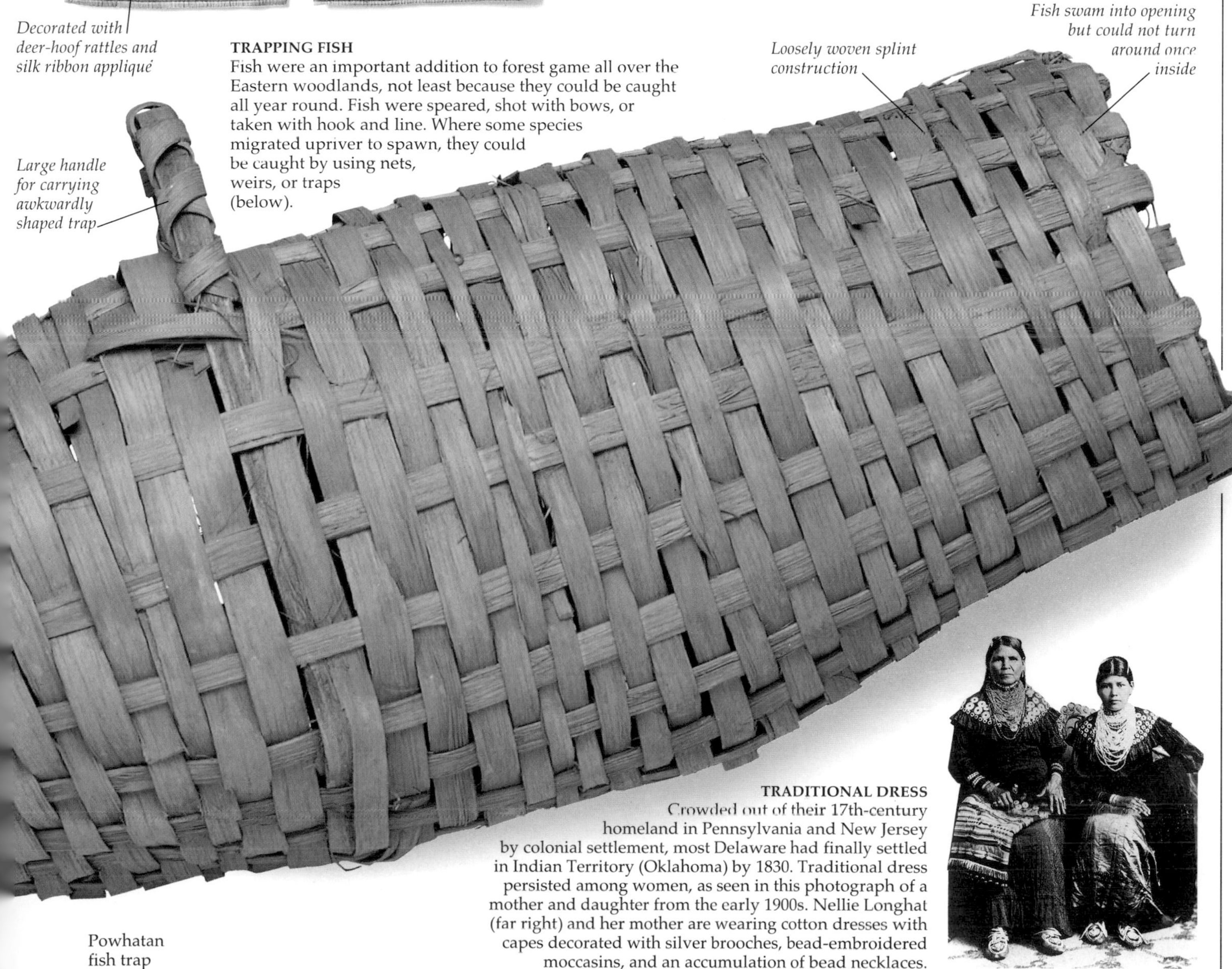

Large handle for carrying awkwardly shaped trap

Loosely woven splint construction

Fish swam into opening but could not turn around once inside

Powhatan fish trap

TRADITIONAL DRESS

Crowded out of their 17th-century homeland in Pennsylvania and New Jersey by colonial settlement, most Delaware had finally settled in Indian Territory (Oklahoma) by 1830. Traditional dress persisted among women, as seen in this photograph of a mother and daughter from the early 1900s. Nellie Longhat (far right) and her mother are wearing cotton dresses with capes decorated with silver brooches, bead-embroidered moccasins, and an accumulation of bead necklaces.

The Ohio River Valley

THE FERTILE LANDS OF THE GREAT VALLEY drained by the Ohio River and its many tributaries (from Illinois east to Pennsylvania and south to Tennessee) offered a rich environment for two great prehistoric cultures, the Adena and later the Hopewell, which together spanned about 1500 years to A.D. 500. The Hopewell culture spread from the Eastern Great Lakes to the Gulf of Mexico and west of the Mississippi. The Hopewell created large burial mounds – almost all we know about them comes from excavating these earthworks. Spectacular artists and artisans, they imported exotic raw materials from a vast trade network. The Hopewell faded as quickly as they had arisen, and simpler hunter-farmer tribes slowly took their place. In the 1700s, France and Britain, with their tribal allies, fought for control of the Ohio Valley as the key to dominating North America. From the 1790s, relentless white American settlement created a short-lived intertribal resistance movement led by the Shawnee statesman Tecumseh.

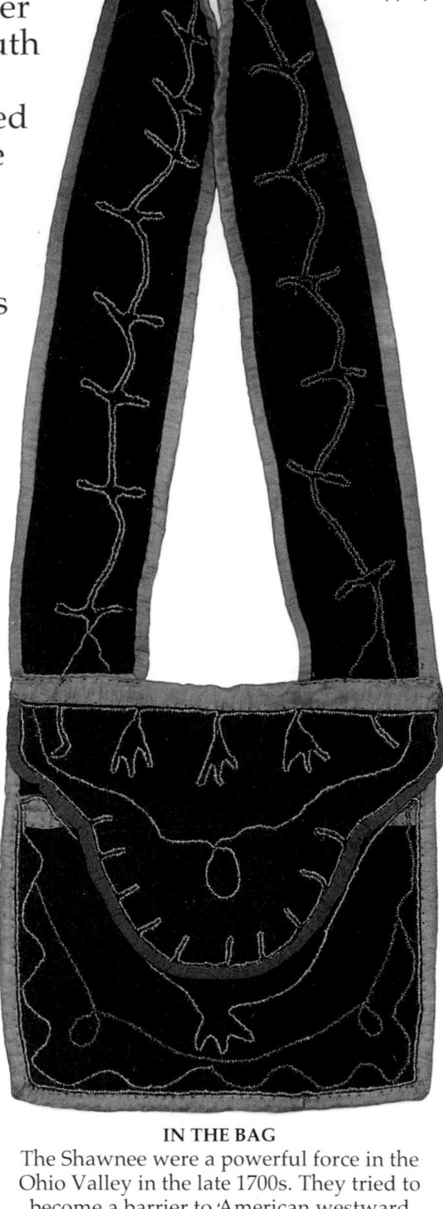

Shawnee cloth storage bag decorated with stitching and appliqué

IN THE BAG
The Shawnee were a powerful force in the Ohio Valley in the late 1700s. They tried to become a barrier to American westward expansion, but they were defeated by General "Mad Anthony" Wayne in 1794. In 1831 they sold what was left of their lands and moved to Oklahoma.

Mother nursing a baby

Distinctive top-knot hairstyle is typically Hopewell

Wrap-round skirt was usual garment of Hopewell women, a style that continued with other area tribes well into the 1800s

GRAVE IMAGES
The Hopewell people buried their dead surrounded by their wealth: ornaments, jewelry, fine stone tools, and pottery. Some of these may have been specially made as grave objects, like these small clay figurines (above). The burial sites give us our only knowledge of the Hopewell people's appearance, clothing, and ornaments, though probably only of those rich enough to afford large burial mounds.

Unusual style in which bird effigy faces away from smoker

Tobacco loaded into bowl in bird's back

Smoke drawn through hole behind bird's body

Massive stone pipe found in western Tennessee

STRIKING BIRD
Hopewell stone-carving shows the same artistry as their other work. Most striking are stone pipes carved in the shape of animals or birds, such as this raven (above). Most, called platform pipes, had a base on which rested the carved figure containing the bowl for tobacco. The smoker drew the smoke through a hole bored through the base.

HURON HUNTERS
The Huron were long-standing enemies of the Iroquois, who dealt them a stunning defeat in 1649. James Fenimore Cooper (1789–1851), who wrote *The Last of the Mohicans,* made the Iroquois the villains of some of his stories. This Huron skinning-knife sheath is decorated with beads, appliqué stitching, and animal hair.

A POTAWATOMI POUCH
For Native Americans, the great issue of the late 1700s was maintaining the Ohio River as the boundary between white settlers and themselves. Like the Miami and Shawnee, the Potawatomi fought to stop the settlers. After several defeats, they and other tribes signed peace treaties in 1815. Despite hostilities, they traded with whites for new clothing materials, so that only bags, tobacco pouches (above), and moccasins continued to be regularly made from deerskin.

MIAMI ALLIANCES
Along with their Ohio Valley allies, the Miami suffered defeats in the 1790s and in the War of 1812. However, trade with whites continued and brought items such as wool, silk ribbon, metal brooches, and glass beads. Miami women used them to add prestige to their clothing and developed techniques to get striking effects, such as the skillful appliqué and nickel-silver decoration on this woolen skirt from the early 1800s.

THE GREAT TECUMSEH
Tecumseh (1768–1813) used his great political skills to forge a tribal alliance opposing white advance into the Midwest. With his shaman twin brother Tenskwatawa (1768–1836), he argued that land could be ceded only with the consent of all the tribes. Despite his belief in peaceful negotiation, in 1811 white forces destroyed the league at the Battle of Tippecanoe (Indiana). Embittered, Tecumseh joined the British (who made him a general) against the U.S. in the War of 1812, in which he was killed.

Western Great Lakes

THE PEOPLES OF THE WESTERN GREAT LAKES (west of Michigan) took full advantage of their access to both woodlands and prairies. In summer the women of tribes such as the Sauk and Fox planted corn and squash while the men hunted buffalo. The Menominee harvested huge quantities of wild rice – their name comes from the Ojibwa name for this plant. In winter the tribes turned to semi-nomadic hunting, living in portable lodges of poles and reed mats as they followed game. The tribes traded with each other, but also were regularly at war. From the early 1600s a powerful force was the Midewiwin, a shaman secret society devoted to healing and encouraging correct behavior as a guarantee of good health.

Male doll given the husband's name, female doll the wife's name

Love medicine is placed in breast of each Menominee doll

Grizzly bear claws separated by triplets of blue beads

SWEET AS MAPLE SUGAR
Maple sugar was greatly valued, used not only on fruit and corn cakes but also as a seasoning on meat and fish. Collection began in late March. Each tree was gashed and a cedarwood spout inserted to allow the sap to drain into a birchbark bucket. Whole Menominee communities moved into the woods, where each family had its own group of trees and a special wigwam.

MEDICINE DOLLS
Shamans used human figures as "medicine" to control others' behavior. The Menominee used "love dolls" (above) tied face-to-face to ensure that a husband and wife would be faithful to each other. The Potawatomi used dolls as charms to make one person fall in love with another.

Ojibwa sap skimmer

Ojibwa wooden trough and Menominee ladle (far left)

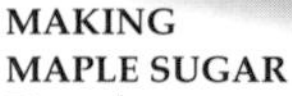

MAKING MAPLE SUGAR
First the sap was boiled to reduce its water content. Boiling was done by dropping heated rocks into birchbark containers. After boiling and skimming, the resulting syrup was strained through fiber matting and poured into a wooden trough. As it cooled, it was worked back and forth with a ladle until it formed granules.

SUGAR CONES
Sugar was stored in birchbark containers for use during the year. Some might be forced into molds, such as these Ojibwa cones (right), much like those Europeans used for making conical sugar loaves from cane sugar.

BEAR-CLAW NECKLACE

Necklaces of grizzly bear claws were greatly prized, not least because of the difficulty of persuading their original fearsome owners to part with the main components! Usually the property of a chief or renowned warrior, bear claws were often passed from one generation to another.

CHIEF KEOKUK

Unlike his rival Black Hawk (1767–1838) who fought a hopeless war against settlers in 1832, Sauk chief Keokuk (1780?–1848) realized that his people had to leave Illinois. His tribe honored him for establishing their claim, and that of the politically affiliated Fox, to territory in present-day Iowa. His realism is shown in his avoiding the fate of Black Hawk's followers, destroyed in their war with the U.S. government.

Bear-claw necklace of the Fox tribe

THE SUPERNATURAL

A person who could gain extra-ordinary power from the spirit world became a shaman. A spirit being, appearing in visions, taught the shaman the uses of many substances (bones, roots, skins), which were stored in a medicine bag (above). Shamans used their power to cure illnesses and to bring success in war and hunting.

WAR OR PEACE PIPE?

Tobacco was thought to have special powers. It was used in offerings to please spirit beings. The Menominee also believed smoking increased their wisdom. At important ceremonies, tribes smoked the sacred calumet, which was passed around clockwise. Because this often marked the end of fighting, the calumet is usually called a peace pipe, but it was also used in the war council.

Sacred Menominee calumet

The settled Southeast

RICH IN FLORA AND FAUNA, with fertile soils and a mild climate, the Southeast was an ideal environment. As skilled builders, artisans, and farmers, with a wide knowledge of medicine, the Southeastern peoples created a flourishing civilization. From A.D. 800 to 1500, the Southeast's Temple Mound Builders developed large towns, traded widely, and held great ceremonies. The rulers lived luxuriously while commoners toiled. The flat-topped mounds seen in the region today are the community sites of this vanished people. The historic Natchez tribe, which also built mounds topped by temples, may have survived the Mound Builders. Contacted by the Europeans in the late 1600s, the Natchez came under pressure from colonists to cede land but fought back. Three wars with the French in the 1700s destroyed their nation, scattering the survivors throughout the Southeast.

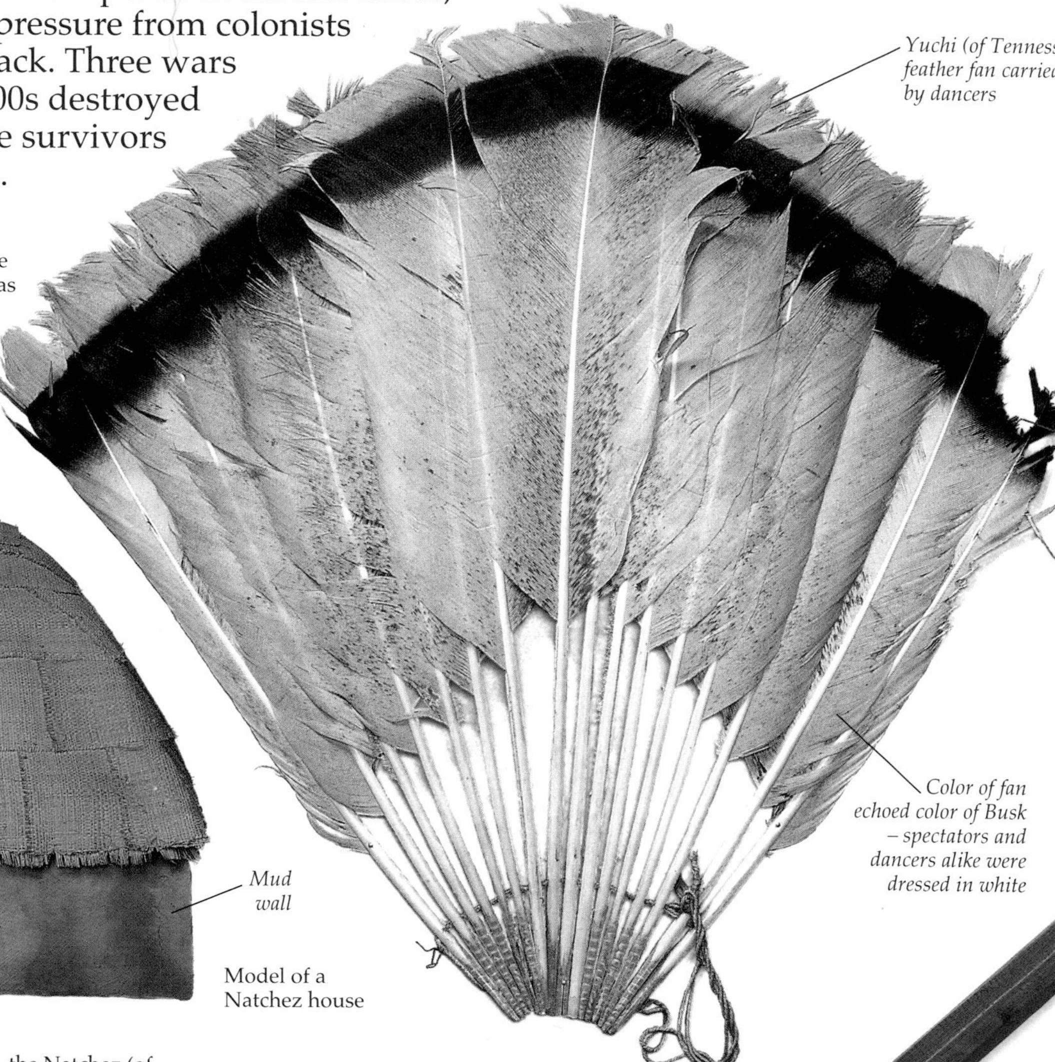

Map of North America showing the Southeast region

Yuchi (of Tennessee) feather fan carried by dancers

Color of fan echoed color of Busk – spectators and dancers alike were dressed in white

THE ANNUAL BUSK

The Green Corn Ceremony (Busk) was the most important rite of the Southeast. It was held when the corn ripened, offering thanks for the harvest and marking the beginning of a new year. It involved ritual purification, dancing around a sacred fire, and a celebratory feast.

Thatched roof

Pole frame

Sleeping platform

Mud wall

Model of a Natchez house

SUNS AND STINKARDS

Successor to the Temple Mound Builders, the Natchez (of Louisiana) amazed French explorers with their complex hierarchical society and elaborate ceremonies. Ruled by an all-powerful monarch, the Great Sun, Natchez society was divided into Suns, nobles, honored men, and commoners (stinkards). The main village had houses such as the one above, and on a mound, a temple that sheltered an eternal flame.

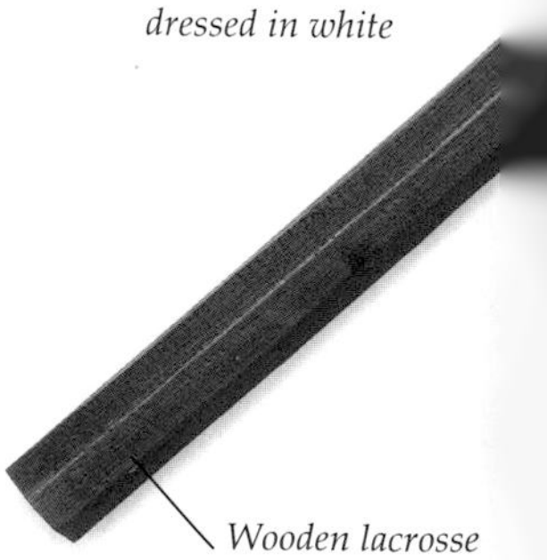

Wooden lacrosse stick measured up to 3 ft (1 m) long

A TWO-HANDLED, THREE-LEGGED POT

Women made the pottery in the Southeast. The clay was cleaned and mixed, and long clay cylinders were layered on top of a small clay disk. A wetted shell was used to smooth the clay, thin the walls, and shape the pot. Before firing, the pot was polished with a smooth pebble and designs cut in with a pointed wooden tool.

Finely etched decoration

Catawba (of South Carolina) pot based on ancient techniques

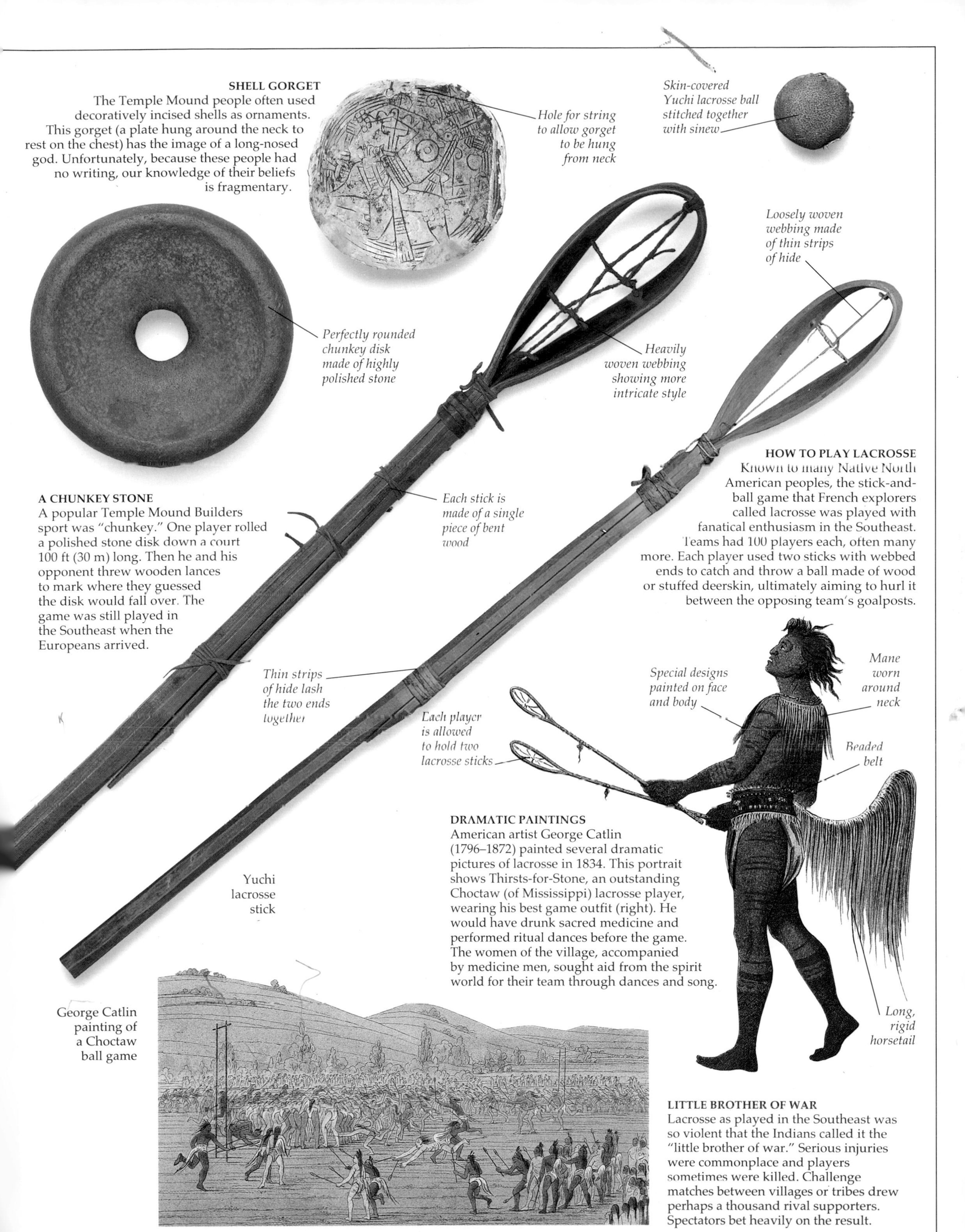

SHELL GORGET
The Temple Mound people often used decoratively incised shells as ornaments. This gorget (a plate hung around the neck to rest on the chest) has the image of a long-nosed god. Unfortunately, because these people had no writing, our knowledge of their beliefs is fragmentary.

A CHUNKEY STONE
A popular Temple Mound Builders sport was "chunkey." One player rolled a polished stone disk down a court 100 ft (30 m) long. Then he and his opponent threw wooden lances to mark where they guessed the disk would fall over. The game was still played in the Southeast when the Europeans arrived.

HOW TO PLAY LACROSSE
Known to many Native North American peoples, the stick-and-ball game that French explorers called lacrosse was played with fanatical enthusiasm in the Southeast. Teams had 100 players each, often many more. Each player used two sticks with webbed ends to catch and throw a ball made of wood or stuffed deerskin, ultimately aiming to hurl it between the opposing team's goalposts.

Yuchi lacrosse stick

DRAMATIC PAINTINGS
American artist George Catlin (1796–1872) painted several dramatic pictures of lacrosse in 1834. This portrait shows Thirsts-for-Stone, an outstanding Choctaw (of Mississippi) lacrosse player, wearing his best game outfit (right). He would have drunk sacred medicine and performed ritual dances before the game. The women of the village, accompanied by medicine men, sought aid from the spirit world for their team through dances and song.

George Catlin painting of a Choctaw ball game

LITTLE BROTHER OF WAR
Lacrosse as played in the Southeast was so violent that the Indians called it the "little brother of war." Serious injuries were commonplace and players sometimes were killed. Challenge matches between villages or tribes drew perhaps a thousand rival supporters. Spectators bet heavily on the result.

The "Five Civilized Tribes"

A REMARKABLE CIVILIZATION had grown up in the lush Southeast by the late 1500s. The tribes lived in planned villages, were skilled farmers as well as hunters, and had advanced medical knowledge. Three hundred years later they had adopted American agricultural methods and had put their laws in written form. Many had become Christians. All this made no difference to the whites, who were determined to seize their tribal lands. In the 1830s, the Choctaw, followed by the Cherokee, Chickasaw, Creek, and finally Seminole (called the "Five Civilized Tribes" by the whites), were forcibly moved to Oklahoma. Many died on the trail.

DRESSING UP
Seminole dolls show how women, up to the early 1900s, combed their hair around a frame and wore skirts and capes of strips of cotton cloth in contrasting colors. A girl was given a string of beads when young and added strings throughout her life, until they almost reached her ears – and weighed several pounds.

Fine beadwork fit for a chief

THE EAGLE DANCE
Before contact with Europeans, a most important Cherokee ceremony was the Eagle Dance, held as part of the rites celebrating both peace and war. Dancers wore eagle feathers on their heads and waved eagle-feather wands to the music of drums and rattles.

Smaller feathers attached with sinew to both ends of wooden handle

CHIEF OF THE CHOCTAW
The Choctaws' home was in Mississippi and Louisiana, until most were removed by the U.S. government to a reservation in Indian Territory, which was later called Oklahoma (the Choctaw name for "red people"). A chief of those Choctaw who managed to stay in Louisiana wore this sash at his wedding in 1871.

Feathers decorate Cherokee Eagle Dance wand

Small entrance leading into windowless house

A LITTLE HUT BY THE WATER
In hot, humid Florida, such as the Everglades swamps, the Seminole lived in open-sided dwellings (chickees). Made from palmetto poles with thatched roofs, these huts were built on platforms to avoid flooding from the heavy rains.

Wall made of dried mud smoothed onto gatelike framework of small poles

MAKING MUSIC
Southeastern ceremonies and games were accompanied by music made by drums and rattles. A water drum had a deerskin stretched over a hollow log containing water so that it resonated. Rattles were made from dried turtle shells, cattle horns, or gourds.

Creek rattle made of hollowed-out gourd filled with corn kernels or small stones to make sounds

THE UNDEFEATED SEMINOLE
Originally mostly Creek from Georgia and Alabama, the Seminole (left) fled to Florida (their name means "runaway") in the 1700s, where they were joined by many runaway slaves. The Seminole fought two wars with the U.S. The second (1835–42) began with the government's efforts to remove them to Oklahoma. Led by the great Osceola (below), the Seminole fought U.S. forces to a standstill. Although many Seminole surrendered in 1841–42 and were sent west, others remained in Florida's Everglades swamps, undefeated. A treaty was signed with them only in 1934, ending possibly the longest war in history.

Conical roof made up of several poles running from the circumference at the bottom of the structure

George Catlin painting of Osceola

A MEETING HOUSE
Creek village dwellings were carefully organized into cool summer houses and warm winter lodges. In summer the Council of Elders met in a square surrounded by sun shelters, and in a round house up to 25 ft (7.5 m) high in bad weather. This council house was also used for ceremonies and festivities.

SEMINOLE HERO
In 1835, enraged by an agreement to move the Seminole to Oklahoma, Osceola (1804–38) killed a rival chief to become leader of those who were determined to stay in their Florida homeland. Small bands of guerrilla forces were led by Osceola against 10,000 U.S. troops until he was captured through a dishonorable false truce.

Roof made of thin tree trunks, covered with bark sheeting to provide extra protection from heavy rains

Central fire

Model of Creek council house in which elders are holding a meeting

The Great Plains

A SEA OF GRASS stretched more than 2,000 miles (3,200 km) north to south between the Rocky Mountains and the Mississippi River. In 1800 this area supported about 150,000 people and 60 million buffalo, all sharing 1 million sq miles (2.5 million sq km) of territory. With sparse rainfall on the western Plains, tribes there were dependent on the huge herds of buffalo, unlike tribes of the better-watered eastern prairie, who combined farming with buffalo hunting. Buffalo migrations dictated the way of living for the 30 Plains tribes. The buffalo meant not just a crucial source of meat – their hides, hair, and horns made dwellings, clothing, tools, and utensils. Before the Spanish brought horses to the Southwest in the 1500s, nomadic Plains tribes traveled and hunted on foot. Of all Native North Americans, Plains peoples were the finest horsemen. Their riding skills dominated the style of their incessant warfare.

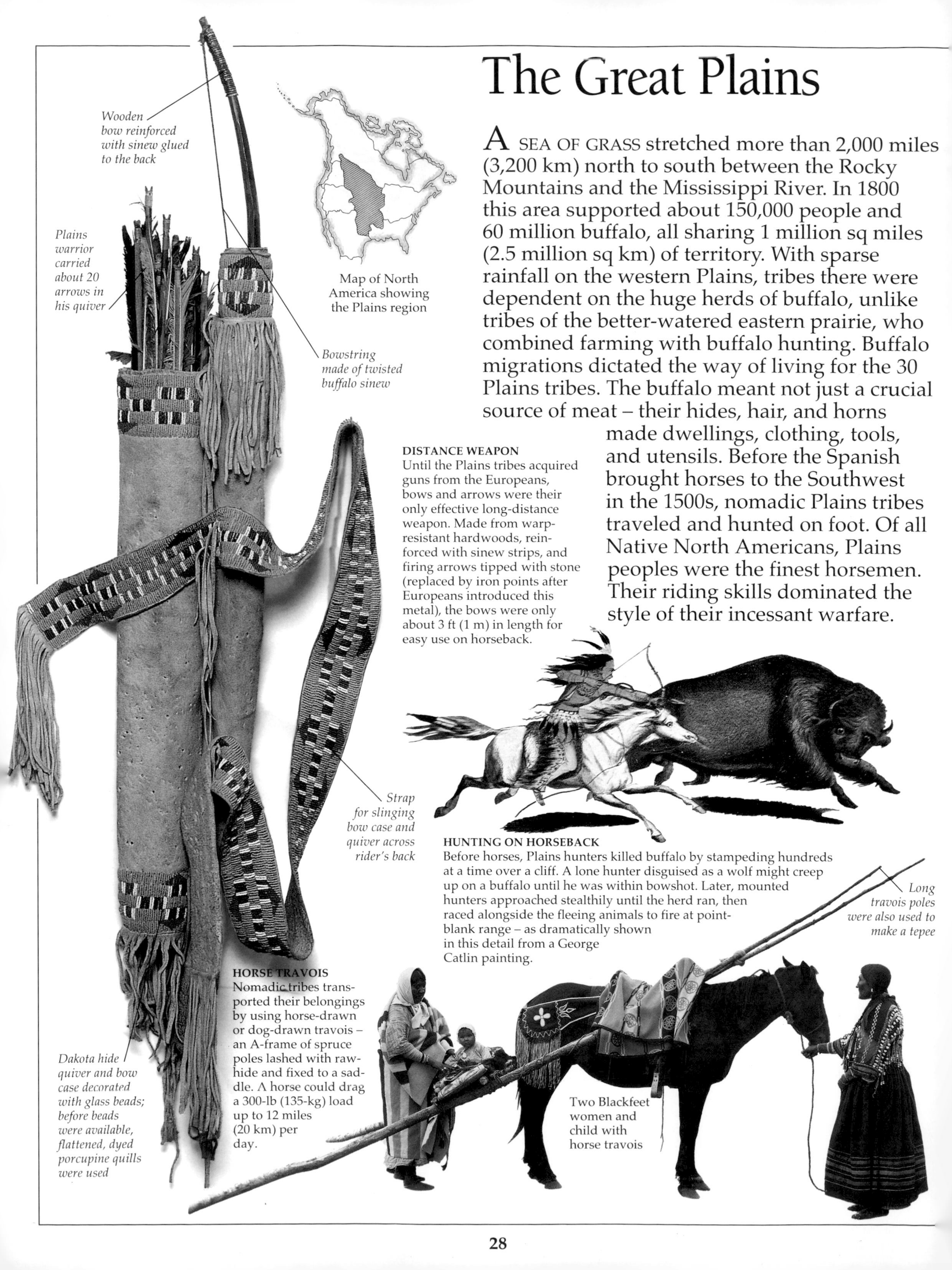

Wooden bow reinforced with sinew glued to the back

Plains warrior carried about 20 arrows in his quiver

Bowstring made of twisted buffalo sinew

Map of North America showing the Plains region

DISTANCE WEAPON
Until the Plains tribes acquired guns from the Europeans, bows and arrows were their only effective long-distance weapon. Made from warp-resistant hardwoods, reinforced with sinew strips, and firing arrows tipped with stone (replaced by iron points after Europeans introduced this metal), the bows were only about 3 ft (1 m) in length for easy use on horseback.

Strap for slinging bow case and quiver across rider's back

HUNTING ON HORSEBACK
Before horses, Plains hunters killed buffalo by stampeding hundreds at a time over a cliff. A lone hunter disguised as a wolf might creep up on a buffalo until he was within bowshot. Later, mounted hunters approached stealthily until the herd ran, then raced alongside the fleeing animals to fire at point-blank range – as dramatically shown in this detail from a George Catlin painting.

Long travois poles were also used to make a tepee

HORSE TRAVOIS
Nomadic tribes transported their belongings by using horse-drawn or dog-drawn travois – an A-frame of spruce poles lashed with rawhide and fixed to a saddle. A horse could drag a 300-lb (135-kg) load up to 12 miles (20 km) per day.

Dakota hide quiver and bow case decorated with glass beads; before beads were available, flattened, dyed porcupine quills were used

Two Blackfeet women and child with horse travois

PLAINS BALL GAME

The Plains peoples played games that tested qualities important to their way of life, such as speed and strength. The most popular game among women was shinny. Two teams armed with curved or straight sticks struggled to get the ball (below) past each other's goalposts. The ball could be batted or kicked but not touched with the hand. Men also played, and sometimes a men's team might challenge a women's.

HAVE TEPEE WILL TRAVEL

For the nomadic hunting tribes, the tepee was a highly practical dwelling, cool in summer and warm in winter. Constructed from a cone of long poles covered with buffalo hides sewn together, it could be erected by two women in an hour. About 15 ft (5 m) in diameter, it comfortably housed a family, their bedding, and their belongings. Tepees were usually decorated with traditional painted designs.

Two sticks used in a Plains Cree throwing game

Model of Arapaho Grass Dancer

GRASS DANCE

In the late 1800s a new ceremony, the Grass Dance, spread throughout the Plains tribes. Originally an Omaha ritual that recalled men's courage and achievements in war, it became a social dance with songs and costumes. To a people threatened with the destruction of their way of life, the Grass Dance became, and remains, a symbol of Native North American solidarity.

The Dakota (Sioux)

THE LORDS OF THE NORTHERN PLAINS by the mid-1800s were the Dakota, called Sioux by Europeans (from an Ojibwa word for "enemy"). In the 1700s they had been forced westward by well-armed Ojibwa from their Western Great Lakes homeland. The Dakota were made up of seven independent groups, ranging from Minnesota west to the Upper Missouri River. The largest of the Plains tribes and outstanding warriors, the Dakota terrorized their Indian enemies and offered fierce resistance to whites. Their lives depended on the buffalo – and the end of the great herds meant the end of their independence. Between 1862 and 1877 they forcefully resisted the U.S. advance into their lands. In 1876, in eastern Montana near the Little Bighorn River, they inflicted on the U.S. Army the most famous defeat by Native North Americans.

USING A BOW AND ARROW
Dakota children were taught proper behavior and encouraged to imitate adults. They were treated with much affection and rarely punished. They were expected, however, to learn skills at a young age. Boys practiced shooting with half-sized bows and arrows (above), first at targets, then at small game, and began hunting seriously in their early teens. Girls were expected to help their mothers in strenuous outside work.

Geometric beadwork style was favored by the Dakota

Unadorned fringed central flap

Flank strap (cinch) of heavy cotton

Hide strap for tying items to saddle

Buffalo rawhide covers wooden stirrup

BETTER THAN BAREBACK
Though Plains tribes long rode bareback, a saddle and stirrups gave better stability and control. The Dakota "pad saddle" was made from two pieces of tanned hide stitched together and stuffed with buffalo or deer hair. It had hardly any cantle to support the rider's back, or pommel at the front. Stirrups, usually wooden, were attached by a rawhide strap.

DEATH ON THE PLAINS
The Dakota did not bury their dead. Instead, the body was wrapped in a buffalo robe and placed beyond the reach of wild animals on a platform supported by poles. Warriors had their weapons and medicine pouch hung beside them, women their important household utensils. Relatives mourned beside the body.

THE BATTLE OF THE LITTLE BIGHORN
Gold seekers invading the sacred Black Hills in South Dakota, guaranteed to the Dakota by treaty, brought about war in 1876. A U.S. Army unit moved against a huge force of Dakota and Cheyenne, not realizing their numbers. General George A. Custer (1839–76) impetuously attacked with an advance guard. On June 25, 1876, he and his 215 men were all killed.

Detail from 1881 pictograph of the Battle of the Little Bighorn, painted on a buffalo hide (below)

THE ART OF QUILLWORK
Before white traders arrived with beads, Plains women took great pride in their quilling skills. Women's saddlebags were made in pairs to hang on each side of a saddle or to store household articles in a tepee.

OLD MAN OF THE PLAINS
Ceremonial dress for a Dakota elder in the mid-1800s marked his status. His headdress of eagle tail feathers (thought to have spirit power) could be worn only by a proven warrior. His costume was completed by bear paws, beaded leggings, and quilled moccasins. A headdress such as this was presented to Sitting Bull when he became a chief of the Teton Dakota.

SITTING BULL
A medicine man who was chosen principal chief of the Teton Dakota in 1868, Sitting Bull (1834?–90) displayed great qualities of leadership. In 1876, with Chief Crazy Horse (1849?–77), he united the Dakota to fight the U.S. army and succeeded in destroying Custer's unit. Later pardoned, he starred in the Wild West Show of Buffalo Bill (William Cody, 1846–1917).

CRADLE WILL ROCK
A Dakota baby spent much of its time in a cradleboard. A lace-up skin bag on a wooden framework, it could be strapped to a mother's back, hung from a saddle, tied to a travois, or just propped upright. A decorated cradleboard like this would usually be made by the sister of the baby's father.

Mandan and Hidatsa

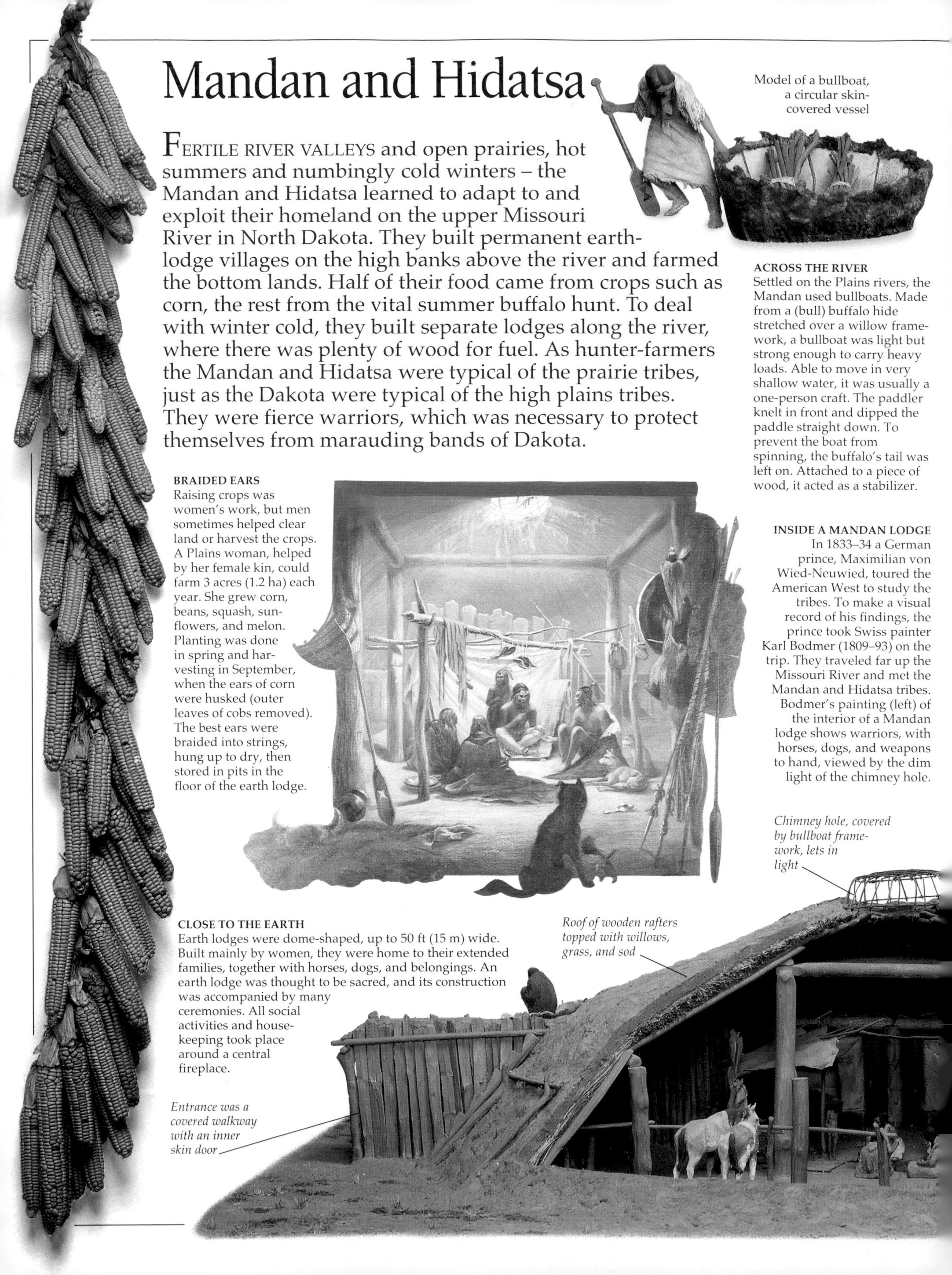

Model of a bullboat, a circular skin-covered vessel

FERTILE RIVER VALLEYS and open prairies, hot summers and numbingly cold winters – the Mandan and Hidatsa learned to adapt to and exploit their homeland on the upper Missouri River in North Dakota. They built permanent earth-lodge villages on the high banks above the river and farmed the bottom lands. Half of their food came from crops such as corn, the rest from the vital summer buffalo hunt. To deal with winter cold, they built separate lodges along the river, where there was plenty of wood for fuel. As hunter-farmers the Mandan and Hidatsa were typical of the prairie tribes, just as the Dakota were typical of the high plains tribes. They were fierce warriors, which was necessary to protect themselves from marauding bands of Dakota.

ACROSS THE RIVER
Settled on the Plains rivers, the Mandan used bullboats. Made from a (bull) buffalo hide stretched over a willow framework, a bullboat was light but strong enough to carry heavy loads. Able to move in very shallow water, it was usually a one-person craft. The paddler knelt in front and dipped the paddle straight down. To prevent the boat from spinning, the buffalo's tail was left on. Attached to a piece of wood, it acted as a stabilizer.

BRAIDED EARS
Raising crops was women's work, but men sometimes helped clear land or harvest the crops. A Plains woman, helped by her female kin, could farm 3 acres (1.2 ha) each year. She grew corn, beans, squash, sunflowers, and melon. Planting was done in spring and harvesting in September, when the ears of corn were husked (outer leaves of cobs removed). The best ears were braided into strings, hung up to dry, then stored in pits in the floor of the earth lodge.

INSIDE A MANDAN LODGE
In 1833–34 a German prince, Maximilian von Wied-Neuwied, toured the American West to study the tribes. To make a visual record of his findings, the prince took Swiss painter Karl Bodmer (1809–93) on the trip. They traveled far up the Missouri River and met the Mandan and Hidatsa tribes. Bodmer's painting (left) of the interior of a Mandan lodge shows warriors, with horses, dogs, and weapons to hand, viewed by the dim light of the chimney hole.

CLOSE TO THE EARTH
Earth lodges were dome-shaped, up to 50 ft (15 m) wide. Built mainly by women, they were home to their extended families, together with horses, dogs, and belongings. An earth lodge was thought to be sacred, and its construction was accompanied by many ceremonies. All social activities and housekeeping took place around a central fireplace.

CHIEF FOUR BEARS
Prince Maximilian believed the Mandan were descendants of the Welsh prince Madoc, who supposedly sailed to America in 1170 – a tale long proved to be false! During the winter of 1833–34, so cold that his paints froze, Karl Bodmer produced several fine pictures, including this portrait of the Mandan chief Mato-Tope (Four Bears). Mato-Tope must have become used to posing for a portrait, since the artist George Catlin (1796–1872) had painted him the previous year.

Karl Bodmer's portrait of Four Bears – the last great Mandan chief

INVALUABLE KNOWLEDGE
The story of the Hidatsa has been strikingly told by Buffalo Bird Woman (1839–1920s?) and her son, Edward Goodbird (1869–1938), who were photographed with Son of a Star (right) in 1906. Much of their story was related to an anthropologist (someone who studies cultures) working in collaboration with the American Museum of Natural History. Besides invaluable knowledge of tribal life and customs, their account detailed the move to a government reservation (1885–88) and the problems this brought.

MAKING PEMMICAN
Pemmican was the all-purpose emergency food of the Plains, with a very long shelf life. It was made by mixing dried buffalo meat, boiled fat, and chokecherries (bitter berries from local shrubs). For pounding the meat until it was nearly powder and for cracking the bones to boil out the fat, a large stone hammer was used. Pemmican was very nutritious and would keep for years.

A SIGN OF THE TINES
For weeding the fields of corn, the Hidatsa preferred rakes with deer antler tines (prongs). This was partly because they believed wooden rakes produced the worms that damaged the corn crop. Tribal stories told of deer weeding the garden of their ancestor, Eternal Grandmother, and of how she made the first rakes from their cast-off antlers.

War and peace

ON THE GREAT PLAINS, warfare was part of life but it rarely involved great battles between tribes. Instead, small bands of warriors made raids to steal horses or to avenge a death – and always to win honor. Audacity and courage were greatly respected and deeds were graded on a system of "coups" (the French word for blows), which included taking a scalp, stealing a horse, or touching an enemy in battle. War was a bloody and deadly business that inflicted serious casualties on each tribe. Tribal warfare was a test of personal courage and spiritual power, rather than a battle for territory and political control conducted by disciplined soldiers. Native North American war customs left them at a great disadvantage when fighting white and black regiments.

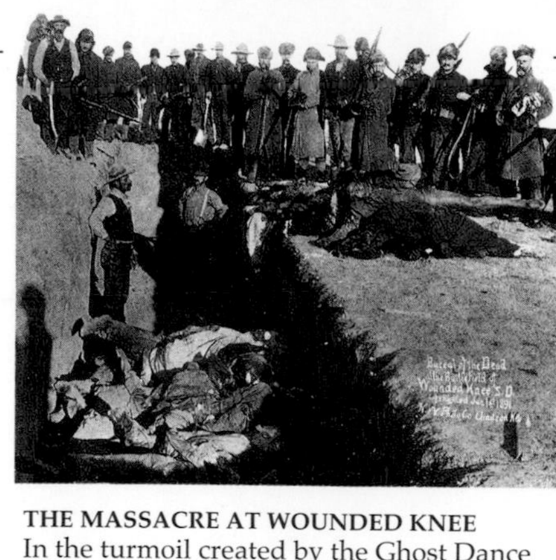

THE MASSACRE AT WOUNDED KNEE
In the turmoil created by the Ghost Dance (below left), on December 29, 1890, 470 7th Cavalry troopers were guarding 340 surrendered Sioux. A tense situation exploded and both sides opened fire. Over 64 soldiers and 200 Sioux (including unarmed women and children) were killed. The Sioux bodies were dumped into a mass grave. Wounded Knee became a symbol to Native North Americans of their mistreatment by whites.

Metal blade fitted around wooden handle

WAR PARTY
A Plains raiding party was armed with bows and arrows, shields, lances, clubs, and scalping knives. A war club might have a blade, spike, or shaped stone at the top. Tomahawk-pipes, like this Dakota example, were used more as prestigious ceremonial objects than as weapons.

Wand made from wooden tube or hollow reed

Carved face is symbol of owner's supernatural helper, who appeared in Ghost Dance vision

Arapaho Ghost Dance wand

Headdress is a circle of magpie and turkey feathers

Wand with white shaft and mottled feathers represents the female calumet

VISION OF HOPE
By the late 1800s, the Plains peoples, in despair on reservations, turned to a new ceremony, the Ghost Dancer. Born in a Paiute prophet's (Wovoka, pp. 40–41) vision, it promised the end of the whites and a return of the buffalo. Soon Ghost Dancers sought visions in which they visited the spirit world and met dead relatives. In later dances, they carried objects seen in the visions (left).

DOG SOCIETIES
Various Plains tribes, such as the Blackfeet, Hidatsa, and Gros Ventre, had a military Dog Society. On a tour of the West in 1833–34, Swiss artist Karl Bodmer painted this striking portrait of a Hidatsa Dog Dancer, Pehriska-Ruhpa (Two Ravens). Hidatsa Dogs were "contraries" and did everything backward – for example, if a warrior was meant to attack in battle, he was told to flee.

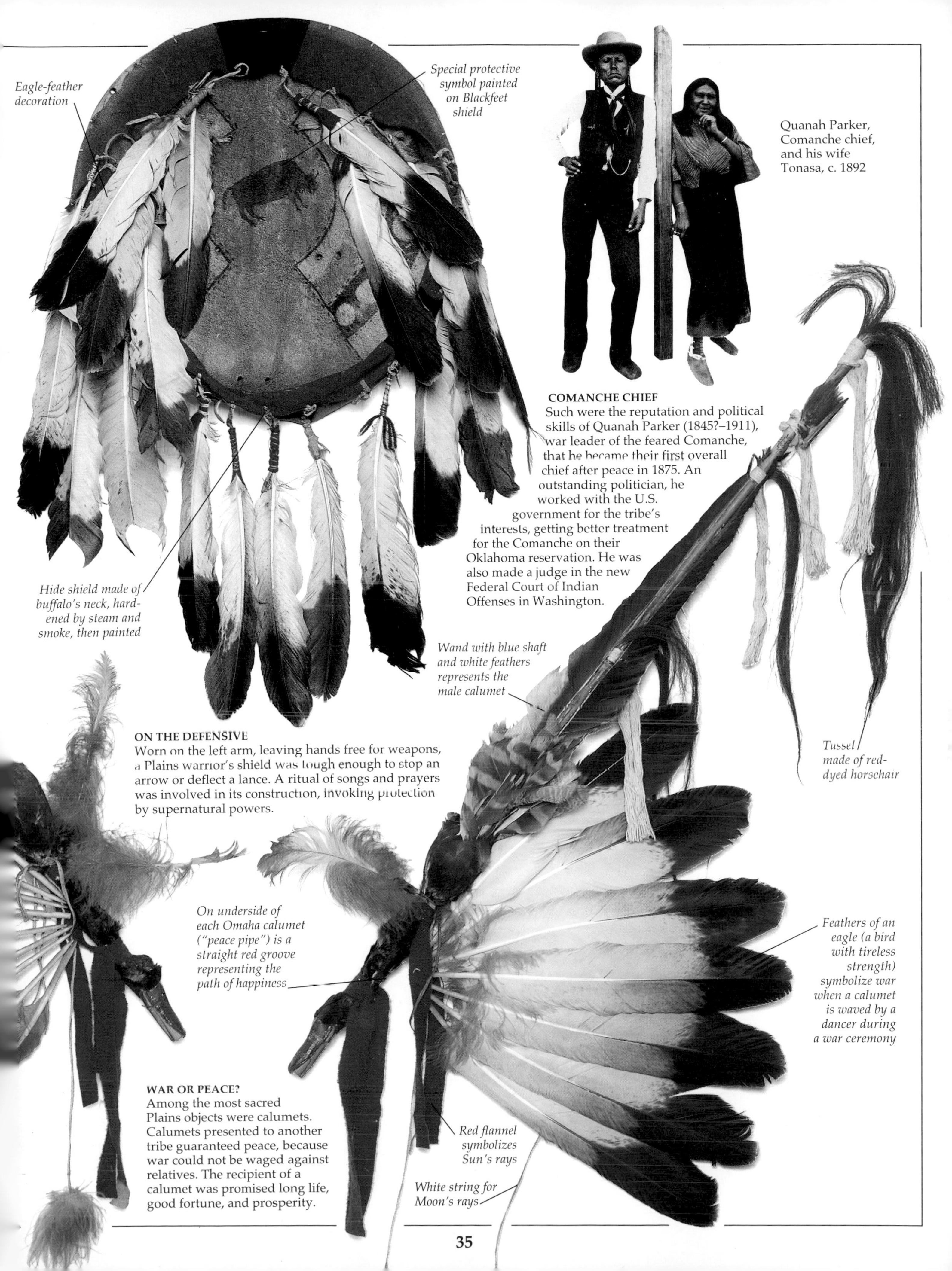

Quanah Parker, Comanche chief, and his wife Tonasa, c. 1892

COMANCHE CHIEF
Such were the reputation and political skills of Quanah Parker (1845?–1911), war leader of the feared Comanche, that he became their first overall chief after peace in 1875. An outstanding politician, he worked with the U.S. government for the tribe's interests, getting better treatment for the Comanche on their Oklahoma reservation. He was also made a judge in the new Federal Court of Indian Offenses in Washington.

ON THE DEFENSIVE
Worn on the left arm, leaving hands free for weapons, a Plains warrior's shield was tough enough to stop an arrow or deflect a lance. A ritual of songs and prayers was involved in its construction, invoking protection by supernatural powers.

WAR OR PEACE?
Among the most sacred Plains objects were calumets. Calumets presented to another tribe guaranteed peace, because war could not be waged against relatives. The recipient of a calumet was promised long life, good fortune, and prosperity.

The Sun Dance

AT THE TIME of the summer buffalo hunt, when each tribe had reunited after scattering widely in the winter, most Plains peoples held the Sun Dance – the greatest of their ceremonies. The rites differed among tribes such as the Dakota, Crow, and Blackfeet, but the purpose was to thank the Great Spirit for past help and pray for future blessings. The ceremony fulfilled a promise by one person (a pledger) to show gratitude for aid from the spirit world, although it was for the benefit of the whole tribe. The ritual lasted several days and nights. Tribes built a sacred Sun Dance Lodge, where a sacred cottonwood tree, forked at the top, was at the center of the ceremony. Found by a warrior, it had been cut down by specially chosen virtuous women. The days of ritual dances ended with several kinds of ordeal. Volunteers chose to accept self-imposed pain in order to have a personal vision. It was also hoped that the Great Spirit would spare the whole tribe from future suffering.

Slow Bull, a Plains medicine man

Buffalo skull specially painted and placed at the altar of the Blackfeet Sun Dance

THE GREAT SPIRIT
The Plains world was filled with spirits who possessed power and inhabited places, persons, animals, even objects. Some tribes believed all power came from the Great Spirit. Individuals might sing to lesser spirits to plead for their aid, or by privation seek a vision that would transmit to them some sacred power. Those who gained great power became "medicine men," tribal leaders and advisers.

MOST POWERFUL MEDICINE
The Crow Sun Dance was held for someone seeking vengeance for the killing of a relative. A ceremonial doll was suspended by a hoop from the sacred cottonwood. Crow sacred stories tell of a warrior grieving for his family, who were killed by enemies. A vision showed him how to make the doll, which would ensure revenge.

Feather headdress decorated with fur and beads

Crow deerskin doll is stuffed with sweetgrass

Feather headdress adorning Dakota effigy

SACRED EFFIGIES
The Dakota attached special objects to the fork of the sacred cottonwood in the Sun Dance Lodge as the focus for a ritual dance. These objects, made of raw-hide, were effigies (symbolic figures). They were simple cut-out figures of a man (symbolizing the enemy) and a buffalo. The ritual ended with dancers firing arrows at the figures.

Simple buffalo effigy cut from a piece of rawhide

RESPECT FOR BUFFALO

As the vital resource at the center of their way of life, the buffalo was featured prominently by most Plains people in their versions of the Sun Dance. Both Blackfeet and Dakota painted buffalo skulls and decorated them with sage and grass.

AN AGONIZING ORDEAL

In the Sun Dance ordeal, all dancers fasted and endured privations. But some chose to have rawhide thongs driven through their chest muscles on wooden skewers and attached to the fork of the sacred cottonwood pole. Swaying to the music and blowing eagle-bone whistles, or even suspended from the fork, they gained release only when the skewers tore out of their flesh. Disturbed by this practice, the U.S. government banned the entire Sun Dance from 1904 to 1935.

Detail from a painting by Frederic Remington (1861–1909)

A SACRED WOMAN

In addition to cutting down the sacred cottonwood tree, women sang during the various dances, brought the dancers presents, and took part in the ordeals. But most important, the Blackfeet ceremony depended on a Sacred Woman for the rituals. Whoever had pledged the Sun Dance had to buy a Natoas bundle, and it was transferred to the Sacred Woman in a special rite. Kept in a rawhide case, the Natoas bundle contained several sacred objects, such as face paints and rattles, but the most important were a headdress and a digging stick.

The high Plateau

THE GREAT PLATEAU, west of the northern Plains, was home to 25 tribes. It stretched from the Rockies westward to the Cascade Mountains of Oregon, and from the Fraser River south to Idaho and western Wyoming. Most tribes lived in tepee-like lodges in summer, and in winter, earth-covered, part-underground houses. Their main food was salmon and edible roots. Some tribes became traders and bartered skins, hemp, and horn bows for buffalo skins, superior robes, and decorated objects from the Plains. The Plateau peoples began using horses only in the 1700s but soon became famous for breeding and trading them. Trade brought prosperity, which ended only with pressure from white expansion after the 1830s.

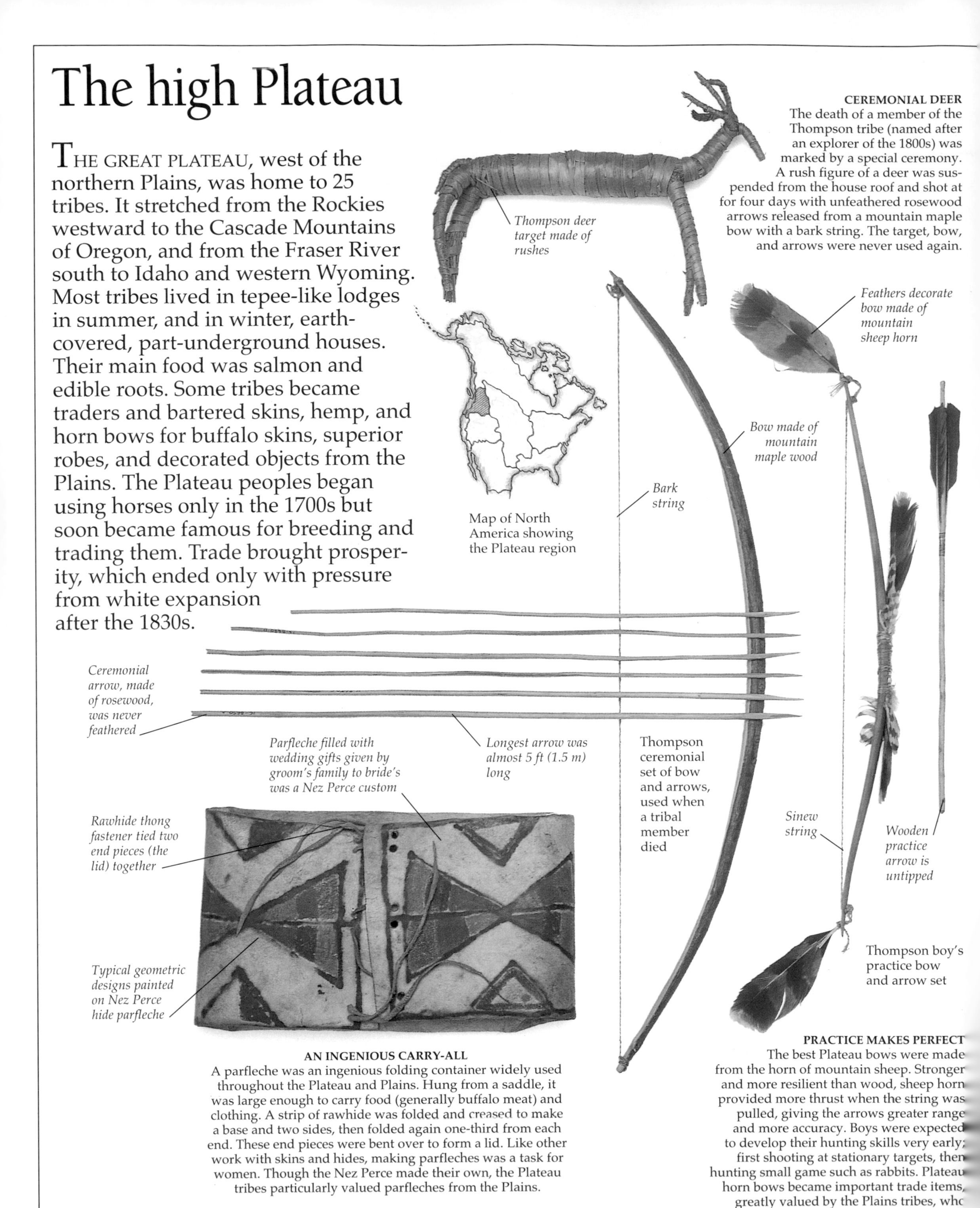

CEREMONIAL DEER
The death of a member of the Thompson tribe (named after an explorer of the 1800s) was marked by a special ceremony. A rush figure of a deer was suspended from the house roof and shot at for four days with unfeathered rosewood arrows released from a mountain maple bow with a bark string. The target, bow, and arrows were never used again.

Thompson deer target made of rushes

Map of North America showing the Plateau region

Feathers decorate bow made of mountain sheep horn

Bow made of mountain maple wood

Bark string

Ceremonial arrow, made of rosewood, was never feathered

Longest arrow was almost 5 ft (1.5 m) long

Thompson ceremonial set of bow and arrows, used when a tribal member died

Sinew string

Wooden practice arrow is untipped

Thompson boy's practice bow and arrow set

Parfleche filled with wedding gifts given by groom's family to bride's was a Nez Perce custom

Rawhide thong fastener tied two end pieces (the lid) together

Typical geometric designs painted on Nez Perce hide parfleche

AN INGENIOUS CARRY-ALL
A parfleche was an ingenious folding container widely used throughout the Plateau and Plains. Hung from a saddle, it was large enough to carry food (generally buffalo meat) and clothing. A strip of rawhide was folded and creased to make a base and two sides, then folded again one-third from each end. These end pieces were bent over to form a lid. Like other work with skins and hides, making parfleches was a task for women. Though the Nez Perce made their own, the Plateau tribes particularly valued parfleches from the Plains.

PRACTICE MAKES PERFECT
The best Plateau bows were made from the horn of mountain sheep. Stronger and more resilient than wood, sheep horn provided more thrust when the string was pulled, giving the arrows greater range and more accuracy. Boys were expected to develop their hunting skills very early; first shooting at stationary targets, then hunting small game such as rabbits. Plateau horn bows became important trade items, greatly valued by the Plains tribes, who thought them much superior to their own

THE GREAT CHASE
Clashes with whites escalated into the Nez Perce War of 1877. The band of Chief Joseph (c. 1840–1904) fought a series of running battles with increasingly larger forces of the U.S. Cavalry and local volunteers. The Nez Perce consistently outfought their enemies in a chase lasting four months and covering over 1,600 miles (2,600 km), until they were forced to surrender only 30 miles (48 km) short of sanctuary in Canada.

Chief Joseph

A REVOLUTION
The horse revolutionized the Plateau peoples' way of life. It extended the range of their summer migrations and spread their trade down into California and deep into the Plains. As a result, they brought back not only bartered goods but many of their neighbors' customs. However, they did not adopt the Plains travois for transport. Instead they used pack saddles and saddlebags, such as this double one from the Thompson tribe, who lived in southern British Columbia.

Red and black geometric design appliquéd to Thompson hide saddlebag

Antler spike

RAIDING PARTY
The Thompson tribe used to raid their neighbors for booty, revenge, and honor, much like most Native North American peoples. This two handed war club is crudely decorated, showing a lake with three warriors nearby. The notches at each end were probably ornamental but may have been for tallying numbers of enemy killed, just as Western gunfighters were alleged to notch their guns.

Thompson birchwood war club, also used for hunting beaver

Hide fringing

Each notch perhaps denoted an enemy or beaver that had been killed with this club

IN THE BAG
The Nez Perce were famous for their cornhusk bags. Made of twisted hemp fiber, twined without using a loom, the bags were decorated with cords made from the inner parts of cornhusks. Cords were dyed with colors made of natural materials to produce typical geometric designs, with a different design appearing on the reverse side of the bag. Flexible, flat containers, cornhusk bags were used to carry foodstuffs, roots, and berries. After horses, they were the Nez Perce's most important trade goods.

The Great Basin

Map of North America showing the Great Basin – Nevada, Utah, Idaho, Oregon, Wyoming, and Colorado

A BAKING DESERT IN SUMMER, lashed by storms and snow in winter, the Great Basin has always had meager resources. Nine tribes, scattered over 400,000 sq miles (1 million sq km), had adapted so well to their environment that their way of life endured for some 10,000 years. Without agriculture, and living on wild foods ranging from insects and seeds to lizards and deer, the ingenuity of these migratory people is easy to miss. They needed no permanent homes, as they migrated with the seasons, gathering in large encampments during pine nut harvests and rabbit drives. After gold was discovered here in 1859, their lives changed drastically.

PAIUTE PROPHET
In 1888 a Nevada Paiute shaman, Wovoka (white name Jack Wilson, 1856?–1932), began to prophesy that by using a new ceremony (the Ghost Dance, which spread rapidly to the Plains), the white man would be swept away, the buffalo returned, and the old ways restored. Though his message stressed nonviolence, the white authorities reacted with brutality.

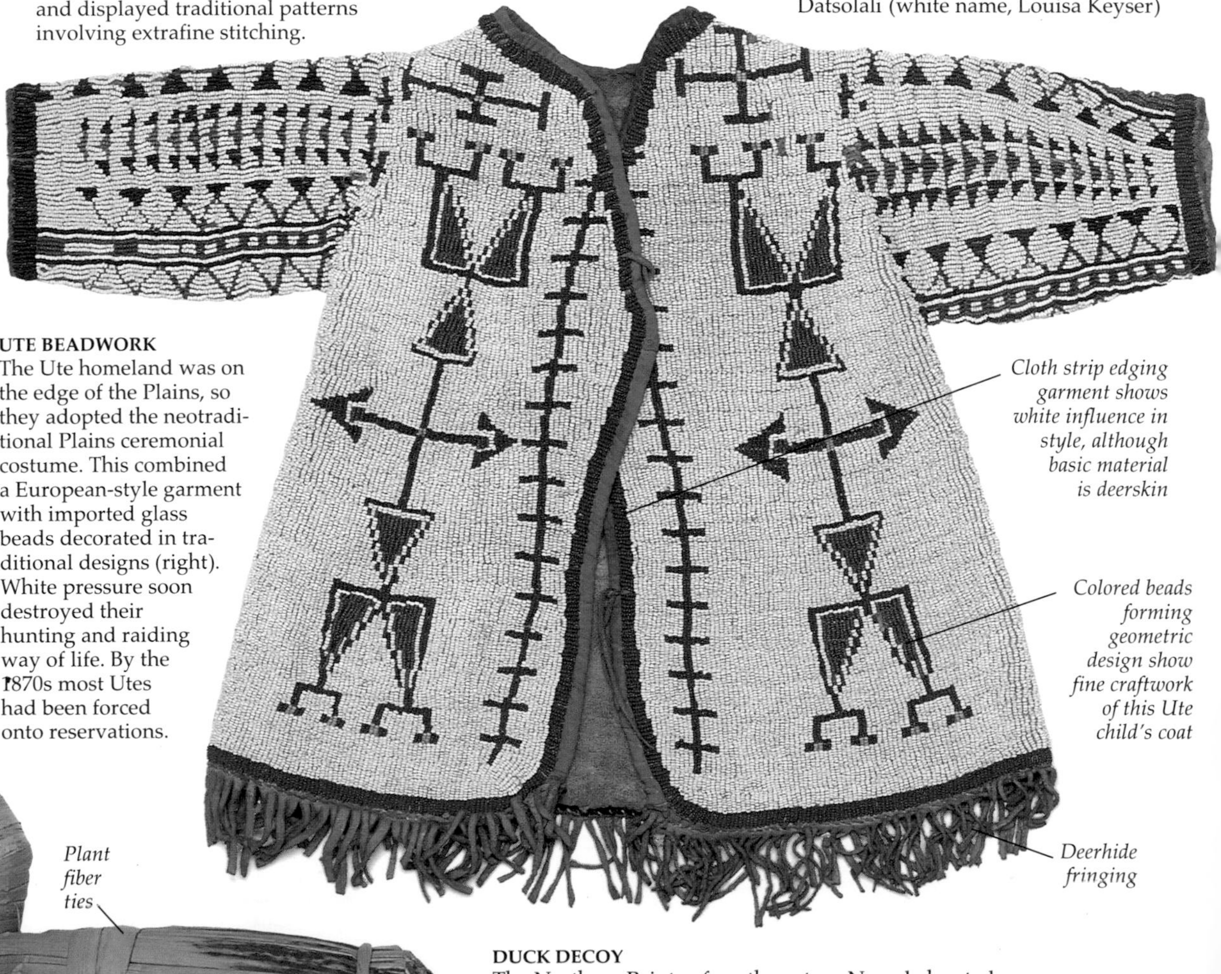

FAMOUS BASKET WEAVER
The Great Basin tribes were expert basket weavers, particularly the Washoe, whose products were greatly valued by white buyers. Datsolali (1835?–1925) was the most famous of all Native American basket weavers. Her baskets showed control of difficult shapes and displayed traditional patterns involving extrafine stitching.

Nevada Washoe basket-maker Datsolali (white name, Louisa Keyser)

UTE BEADWORK
The Ute homeland was on the edge of the Plains, so they adopted the neotraditional Plains ceremonial costume. This combined a European-style garment with imported glass beads decorated in traditional designs (right). White pressure soon destroyed their hunting and raiding way of life. By the 1870s most Utes had been forced onto reservations.

Cloth strip edging garment shows white influence in style, although basic material is deerskin

Colored beads forming geometric design show fine craftwork of this Ute child's coat

Deerhide fringing

Northern Paiute duck decoy made from bundles of tule reed

Plant fiber ties

DUCK DECOY
The Northern Paiute of northwestern Nevada hunted any game available, including rabbits and marmots. In the spring, migrating birds, such as ducks, were hunted with the help of duck-shaped decoys made from bulrush (tule) bundles tied together with rush fiber. Floating realistically on reed marshes within range of the hidden hunters' bows, they convinced the ducks it was safe to land.

HOLDING A BABY
A cradleboard left the mother's hands free. If some accident caused a board to fall or tip over, the projecting top protected the baby's head.

ENDURING COURAGE
Paiute interests were vigorously defended by Sarah Winnemucca (1844–91). With some white schooling, she became official translator between the Paiute and unsympathetic government-appointed Indian agents. Later she campaigned for white support in the East. Her 1883 autobiography is an indictment of white brutality as well as a tribute to her people's enduring courage.

GOOD-LUCK CHARM
Sometimes personal ornaments had a purpose. The umbilical cord of a newborn child was often put in a beaded bag, which was hung on the cradleboard or worn like a locket to ward off bad luck. The bags were shaped like a lizard or turtle because these creatures represented a long life.

BABY CARRIER
Like the Plains tribes, the Paiute used cradleboards to carry their babies. The frame was made of thick twigs and a covering of soft animal skin. Laced into it, the baby was in a secure but comfortable carrier that could ride on the mother's back or be tied to a saddle. Even if just propped upright, it meant that the baby was always able to see its surroundings.

SUMMER SANDALS
In summer, most Basin peoples went barefoot, but some tribes made sandals from coarsely woven tree bark. Sometimes the Southern Paiute made buckskin moccasins, or wove sandals from yucca fiber. These were made according to a traditional design of the Kaibab band of the Southern Paiute.

Californian hunter-gatherers

Map of North America showing the California region

NATIVE AMERICANS found California as attractive in the 1760s as their American successors did in the 1960s. The reasons were simple. Except for the southeastern desert, the climate and resources made life easy. Warfare was rare and farming almost unknown, the people preferring to be hunter-gatherers. Isolated by deserts and mountains from the warlike tribes to the east, the 50 tribes lived on fish and game, but seeds (especially acorns) played a major role in their diet. Their ceremonies petitioned the spirit world to ensure food and health. The arrival in 1769 of the Spanish, establishing missions in the south, began the erosion of this way of life, and the Gold Rush of 1849 in the north destroyed it.

THE MODOC WAR
In 1864, Kintpuash (Captain Jack) led a group of Modoc who refused to accept their new reservation, resulting in the Modoc War of 1872. The U.S. Army besieged Kintpuash and 80 men for six months near Tule Lake. After violating a peace parley, Kintpuash surrendered and was hanged.

FEATHER BUNCH
The Maidu, nicknamed "Digger Indians" by the Europeans (because they searched for edible roots to supplement their acorn diet), lived in partly underground dwellings, up to 40 ft (12 m) across. At some of their ceremonies, both men and women wore feather bunches (right).

Maidu dance plume, or bunch (worn on crown of head), made of quills, feathers, wood, and string

Single piece of curved wood forms basic frame of Pomo flail

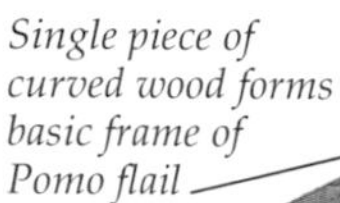

Elaborate design on ceramic doll echoes tattoo designs on a Mohave warrior

DESERT PEOPLE
The Mohave, typical of the Yuman tribes along the lower Colorado River, farmed the bottom land, relying on the annual flooding of the river for raising crops. By the late 1800s, confined to a reservation, they were selling souvenirs, like these ceramic dolls (above), at a nearby railroad station.

Closely woven netting made of willow

GATHERING SEEDS
The Pomo lived between the ocean and the Coast Range. Their dwellings, each home to several families, were 30-ft (9-m) -long pole frameworks covered with thatch. They were expert hunters and fishermen, but the most important part of their diet was acorns, ground into meal. They also ate seeds, roots, and berries. Women used flails (right) to knock seeds into a collecting, or burden, basket.

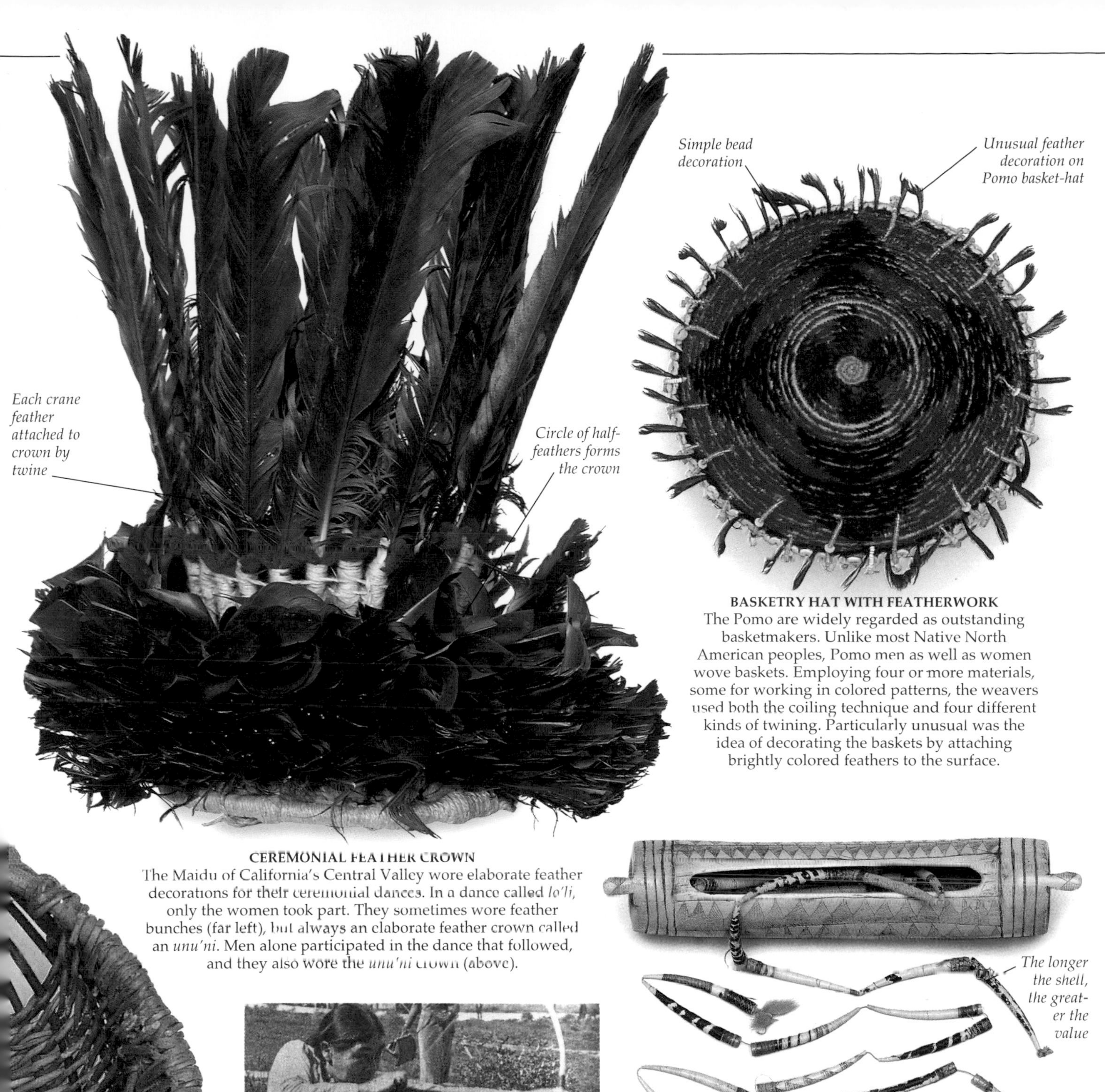

BASKETRY HAT WITH FEATHERWORK
The Pomo are widely regarded as outstanding basketmakers. Unlike most Native North American peoples, Pomo men as well as women wove baskets. Employing four or more materials, some for working in colored patterns, the weavers used both the coiling technique and four different kinds of twining. Particularly unusual was the idea of decorating the baskets by attaching brightly colored feathers to the surface.

CEREMONIAL FEATHER CROWN
The Maidu of California's Central Valley wore elaborate feather decorations for their ceremonial dances. In a dance called *lo'li*, only the women took part. They sometimes wore feather bunches (far left), but always an elaborate feather crown called an *unu'ni*. Men alone participated in the dance that followed, and they also wore the *unu'ni* crown (above).

THE LAST OF THE YAHI
In 1911 the last survivor of the isolated Yahi tribe, long believed to have died out, appeared in a northern California town. He was "adopted" by anthropologists at the University of California, who wished to learn about his way of life. They named him Ishi (Yahi for "man"). Ishi died of tuberculosis in 1916.

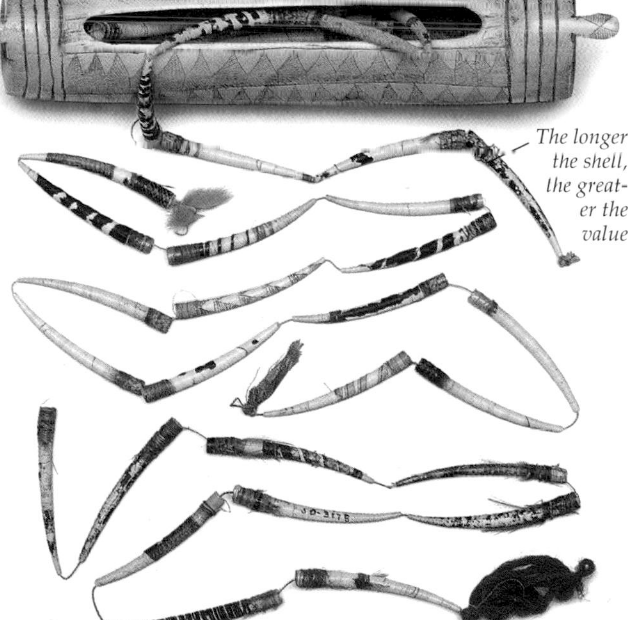

SPENDING MONEY
Far to the north, on Vancouver Island, strings of dentalium shells (above) were highly valued ornaments. Brought south by traders of the Tolowa tribe, they were used as a form of money by many of the California peoples. But the Pomo preferred to make a rival currency from the white mineral magnesite, or from clamshells. Most Northern tribes made purses from elk antlers (top), which were strikingly decorated.

The stunning Southwest

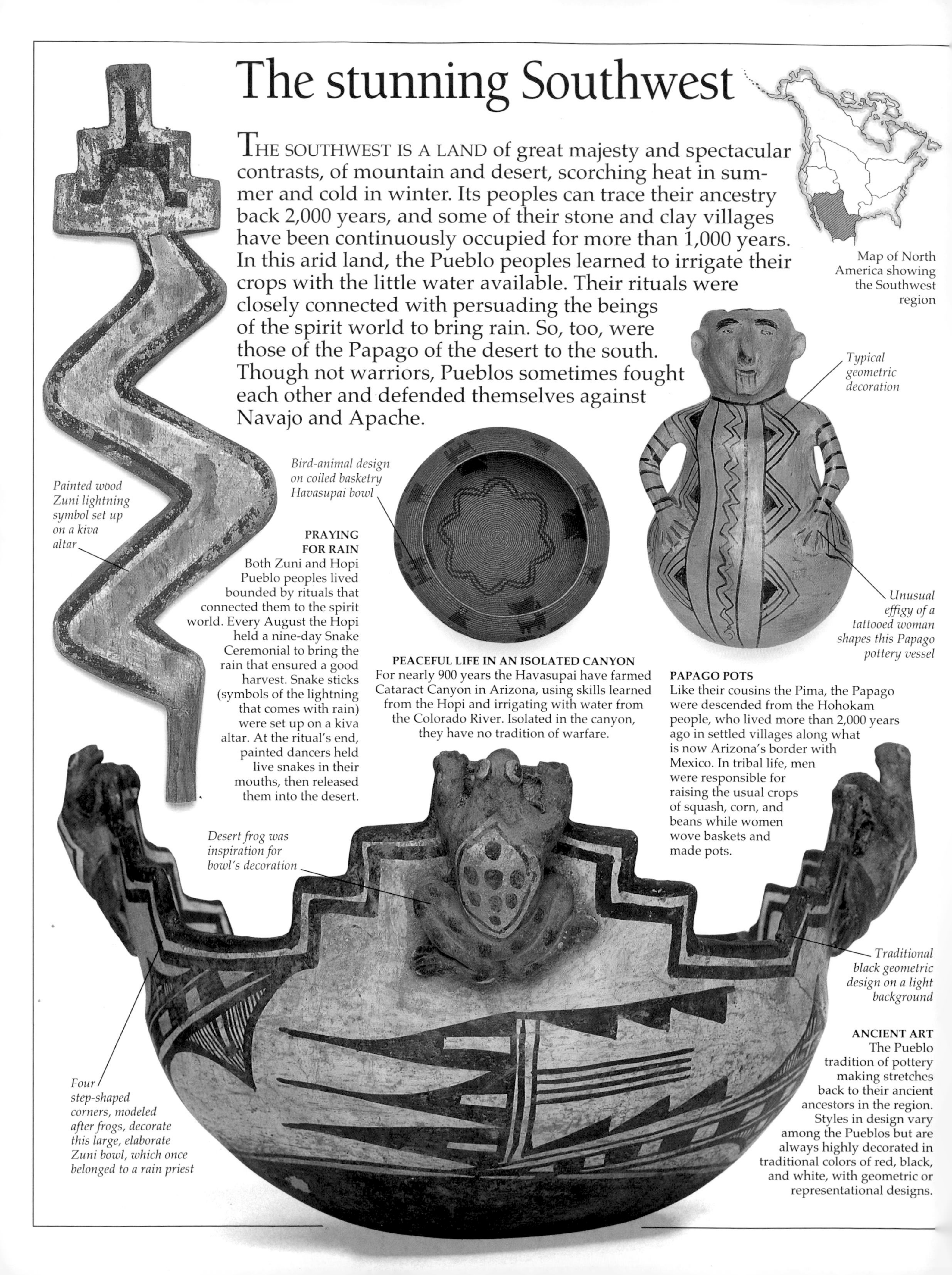

THE SOUTHWEST IS A LAND of great majesty and spectacular contrasts, of mountain and desert, scorching heat in summer and cold in winter. Its peoples can trace their ancestry back 2,000 years, and some of their stone and clay villages have been continuously occupied for more than 1,000 years. In this arid land, the Pueblo peoples learned to irrigate their crops with the little water available. Their rituals were closely connected with persuading the beings of the spirit world to bring rain. So, too, were those of the Papago of the desert to the south. Though not warriors, Pueblos sometimes fought each other and defended themselves against Navajo and Apache.

Map of North America showing the Southwest region

Painted wood Zuni lightning symbol set up on a kiva altar

Bird-animal design on coiled basketry Havasupai bowl

Typical geometric decoration

Unusual effigy of a tattooed woman shapes this Papago pottery vessel

PRAYING FOR RAIN

Both Zuni and Hopi Pueblo peoples lived bounded by rituals that connected them to the spirit world. Every August the Hopi held a nine-day Snake Ceremonial to bring the rain that ensured a good harvest. Snake sticks (symbols of the lightning that comes with rain) were set up on a kiva altar. At the ritual's end, painted dancers held live snakes in their mouths, then released them into the desert.

PEACEFUL LIFE IN AN ISOLATED CANYON

For nearly 900 years the Havasupai have farmed Cataract Canyon in Arizona, using skills learned from the Hopi and irrigating with water from the Colorado River. Isolated in the canyon, they have no tradition of warfare.

PAPAGO POTS

Like their cousins the Pima, the Papago were descended from the Hohokam people, who lived more than 2,000 years ago in settled villages along what is now Arizona's border with Mexico. In tribal life, men were responsible for raising the usual crops of squash, corn, and beans while women wove baskets and made pots.

Desert frog was inspiration for bowl's decoration

Traditional black geometric design on a light background

Four step-shaped corners, modeled after frogs, decorate this large, elaborate Zuni bowl, which once belonged to a rain priest

ANCIENT ART

The Pueblo tradition of pottery making stretches back to their ancient ancestors in the region. Styles in design vary among the Pueblos but are always highly decorated in traditional colors of red, black, and white, with geometric or representational designs.

AMERICA'S FIRST APARTMENT HOUSE
About A.D. 750, the ancient Anasazi abandoned their pit dwellings to build pueblos. In New Mexico's Chaco Canyon lie the ruins of one of the greatest – Pueblo Bonito. Once a giant semicircular building of 700 apartments rising in terraces and housing 1,200 people, it overlooked a plaza containing two underground ceremonial chambers (kivas).

PUEBLO REVOLT
In 1528, nearly a century before other Europeans attempted to settle on the continent's eastern shore, Spanish invaders looking for gold penetrated the Southwest. Missionaries, soldiers, and brutality followed. In 1680, Popé (a Taos Pueblo medicine man) united all the Pueblos and drove the Spaniards out for 12 years. Though defeated in the end, the Pueblos preserved their religion and many traditions to this day.

The Pueblo peoples

ON THE WINDSWEPT TABLETOP ROCKS towering above the desert and along the Southwest's few rivers stand stone and adobe settlements. Today Native Americans inhabit some 30 villages from the Rio Grande to northern Arizona. The first Spanish explorers called the inhabitants Pueblo (village) people, but they were not a single tribe. The villages were independent and the people (including Hopi and Zuni) spoke different languages. From early times they have raised crops of squash, beans, and corn. Their lives are guided by kachinas, spirit beings who enter the bodies of selected men wearing masks and performing sacred dances. Men also govern the community, but women own all property which is inherited by their daughters.

PASSING THE TEST
Hopi girls were judged fit for marriage after passing tests of women's skills. Then they were allowed to style their hair in complicated squash blossom coils.

AMAZING BIRD
From about A.D. 500 the Anasazi, people of the Southwest, created small pottery figures of birds and animals. Remarkably similar figures were produced by Zuni potters 1300 years later (above).

CEREMONIAL BOWS AND ARROWS
On June 26 (five days after the summer solstice) the Hopi begin an elaborate ceremony called Niman. It is held to ensure a successful harvest. For 16 days, solemn rituals and prayers for rain mark the return of the kachinas to the spirit world. The departing kachinas offer the villagers symbolic gifts, including ears of corn and bows and arrows (far left).

Natural pigment decorates wooden rabbit stick

BOOMERANG THAT ISN'T
In the fall and winter, rabbit hunting is both a sport and a ritual ceremony for the Hopi community. A mile-round circle of hunters contracts until rabbits can be hit with throwing sticks (left). The sticks are curved and often decorated. They strike like boomerangs but don't return when they miss.

Narrow strips of sinew glued to back of wooden bow for extra strength

Wooden kachina doll represents Aholi, who accompanies the Chief Hopi Kachina

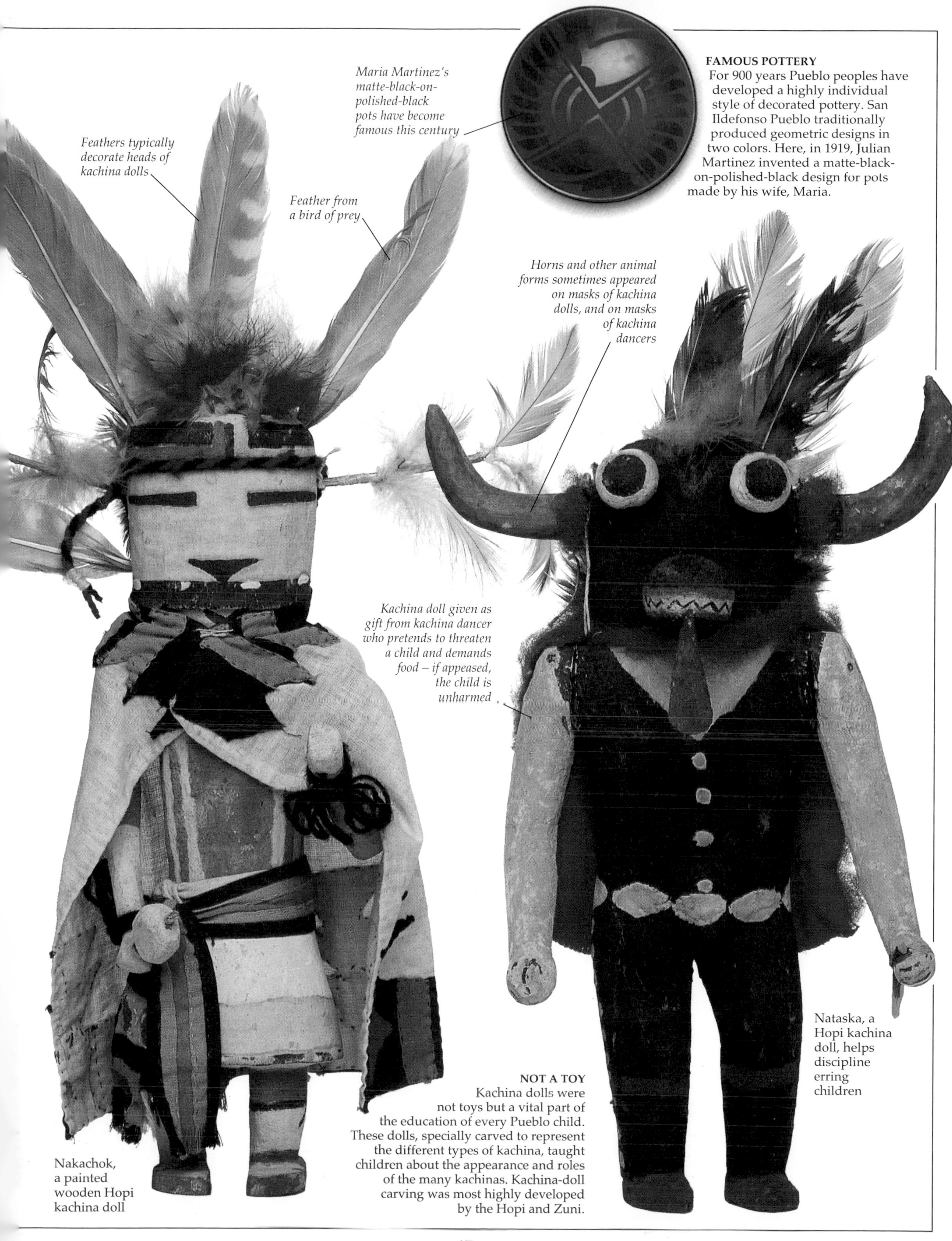

Maria Martinez's matte-black-on-polished-black pots have become famous this century

FAMOUS POTTERY
For 900 years Pueblo peoples have developed a highly individual style of decorated pottery. San Ildefonso Pueblo traditionally produced geometric designs in two colors. Here, in 1919, Julian Martinez invented a matte-black-on-polished-black design for pots made by his wife, Maria.

Feathers typically decorate heads of kachina dolls

Feather from a bird of prey

Horns and other animal forms sometimes appeared on masks of kachina dolls, and on masks of kachina dancers

Kachina doll given as gift from kachina dancer who pretends to threaten a child and demands food – if appeased, the child is unharmed

Nakachok, a painted wooden Hopi kachina doll

NOT A TOY
Kachina dolls were not toys but a vital part of the education of every Pueblo child. These dolls, specially carved to represent the different types of kachina, taught children about the appearance and roles of the many kachinas. Kachina-doll carving was most highly developed by the Hopi and Zuni.

Nataska, a Hopi kachina doll, helps discipline erring children

Apache and Navajo

BEJEWELED
Famous for their beautiful jewelry, the Navajo decorated this leather wrist guard in their typical style, with silver and turquoise.

THE ARID MOUNTAINS and deserts of the Southwest became home to the Apache and Navajo, who may have migrated south from the far Northwest in the 1400s. Hunters and warriors, they raided first their Pueblo neighbors and later the colonizing Spanish pushing north from Mexico. From both they learned important agricultural skills. The Navajo combined sheep raising, farming, and raiding until local American forces under Kit Carson (1809–68) forced their surrender in 1864. Rebuilding their way of life, they added silverwork to their arts. Some Apache, learning from the Pueblo villagers, took up farming, but most remained hunter-raiders. Feared by other tribes and by Europeans as the fiercest warriors in the Southwest, they faced their final defeat in the mid-1880s.

BRAVE WARRIOR
Geronimo (1829–1909) was his Mexican name; his Apache name (Goyanthlay) meant "the Yawner." He became the most famous Apache warrior and fought the American invasion of Apache lands in the 1860s and 1870s. He was caught in 1877 and confined on the San Carlos reservation in Arizona. On his escape in 1881, he resumed raiding – to the terror of both Mexican and American settlers. He was photographed (above, far right) just before he finally surrendered in 1886.

BEST FOOT FORWARD
As an alternative to wearing moccasins with separate hide leggings to protect their legs from thornbrush, Apaches wore a one-piece soft boot, or "long moccasin," made from antelope skin or deerskin. Usually, men's long moccasins reached to just below the knee, while those of women extended above it.

Metal stud decoration

Hide tie for fastening child's long moccasin below the knee

Fine beadwork decoration

Head of stone on Apache war club

Delicately colored beadwork decoration

Wooden shaft covered in rawhide for a firm grip

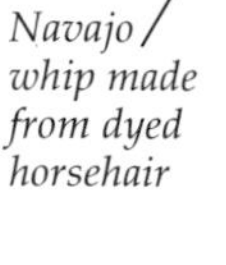

Navajo whip made from dyed horsehair

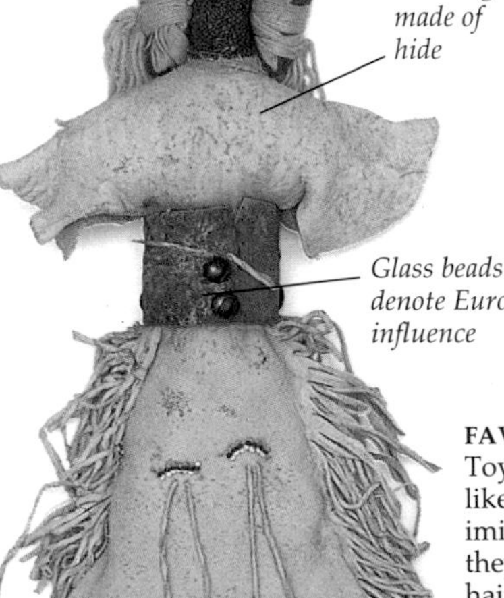

Clothing made of hide

Glass beads denote European influence

FAVORITE DOLL
Toys of Apache children, like those of children everywhere, imitated the adult world into which they would grow. This rag doll has its hair arranged in the Hopi style worn by an unmarried girl. When an Apache girl entered puberty, a four-day ceremony was held. Ritual singing alternated with feasting. Like the Hopi girls, an Apache girl was taught her future responsibilities by an older woman and ran a ritual race to prove her strength and courage. After this, she was ready for marriage.

INTO BATTLE!
Like all Native Americans, the Navajo and Apache knew nothing of horses until they met Spanish colonists with their mounts in the 1500s. However, they quickly learned to use and breed them, especially for warfare. The Navajo whip (far right) is very similar to the quirt (from the Spanish *cuerta*) used by American cowboys and Mexican *vaqueros*. The Apache war club was a good close-quarter weapon – the decoration on this example (near right) is particularly handsome.

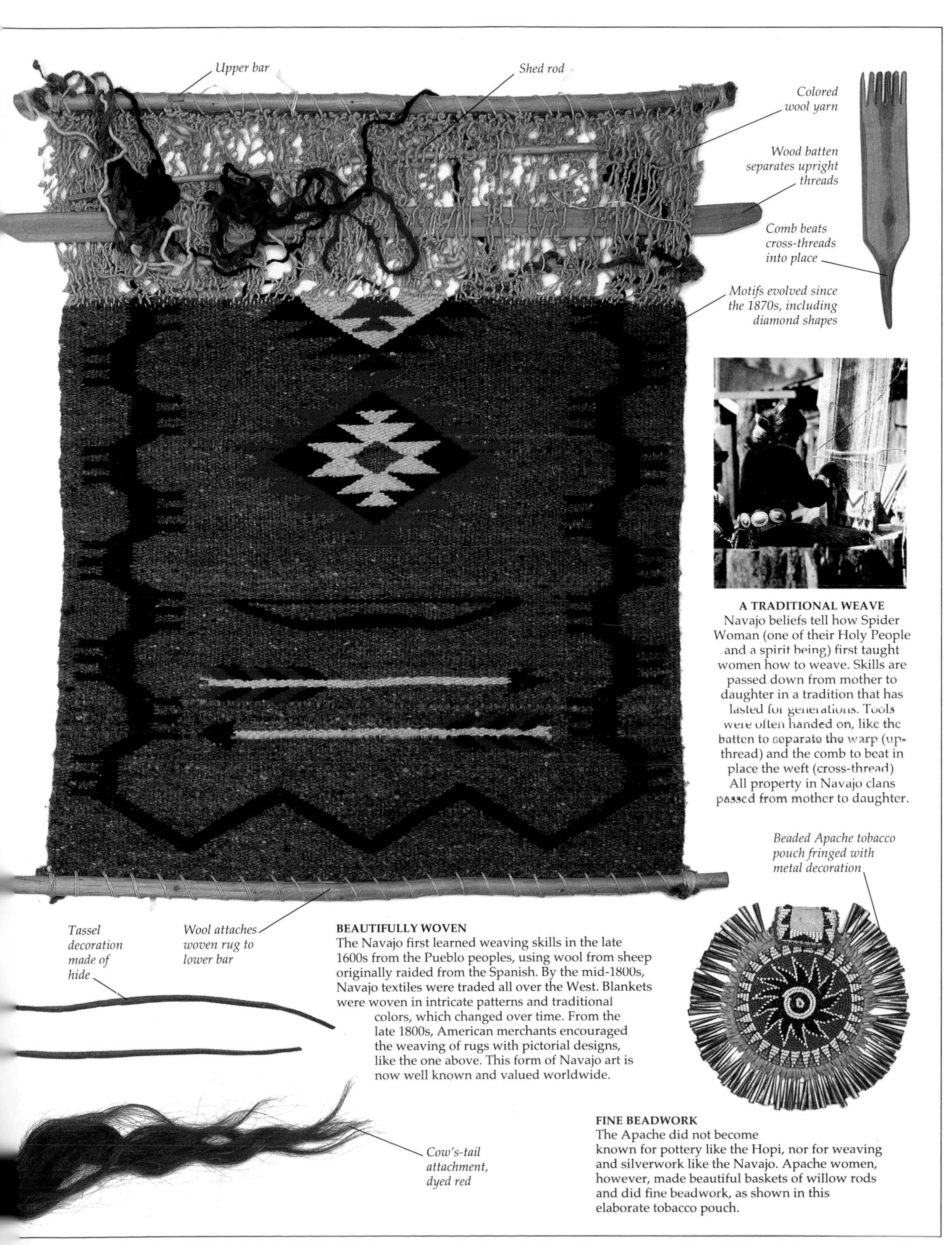

A TRADITIONAL WEAVE
Navajo beliefs tell how Spider Woman (one of their Holy People and a spirit being) first taught women how to weave. Skills are passed down from mother to daughter in a tradition that has lasted for generations. Tools were often handed on, like the batten to separate the warp (up-thread) and the comb to beat in place the weft (cross-thread). All property in Navajo clans passed from mother to daughter.

BEAUTIFULLY WOVEN
The Navajo first learned weaving skills in the late 1600s from the Pueblo peoples, using wool from sheep originally raided from the Spanish. By the mid-1800s, Navajo textiles were traded all over the West. Blankets were woven in intricate patterns and traditional colors, which changed over time. From the late 1800s, American merchants encouraged the weaving of rugs with pictorial designs, like the one above. This form of Navajo art is now well known and valued worldwide.

FINE BEADWORK
The Apache did not become known for pottery like the Hopi, nor for weaving and silverwork like the Navajo. Apache women, however, made beautiful baskets of willow rods and did fine beadwork, as shown in this elaborate tobacco pouch.

Papago and Pima

In the parched deserts of what is now Arizona and northern Mexico, over 2,000 years ago the Hohokam people built irrigation systems to raise crops. Their descendants are the Pima and Papago (the Papagos' name for themselves, O'Odham, means "the People"). Using this inherited knowledge of river irrigation, the Pima settled in villages by the Salt and Gila rivers, raising corn, squash, and beans, and adding wheat around 1700. Their surplus of food became so large, they supplied California miners and, during the Civil War, the Union Army. The desert-dwelling Papago had to rely on seasonal flood water for farming and so stayed seminomadic. From the fermented fruit of the saguaro cactus they made wine to be used in rituals. Both tribes had similar ceremonies and both worshiped two main divine beings – Elder Brother and Earthmaker.

Traditional horned toad on Pima basket

ENDLESS USES

As nearly unbreakable containers, baskets had endless uses. Bowl-shaped ones were used for storing corn and shallow ones for carrying fruit collected from the top of the saguaro cactus. Designs picturing animals began to emerge in the 1800s.

THE ART OF BASKETMAKING

Basketmaking became an art among the Pima. Traditional techniques involved close coils of willow wound around bulrushes. Patterns were produced by adding pieces of the black devil's claw plant to make a striking contrast. Papago basketry also borrowed from Spanish designs. A basket was sometimes so large that the maker had to climb inside to finish it!

BRIDLE WEAR

The Papago were seminomadic, with few water resources. Horses were useful for traveling between their summer field villages in the desert and their winter well villages near mountain springs.

Natural and dyed horsehair used to make this Papago bridle rein

Feather-decorated hide covers this Papago wooden shield

MOCK BATTLES

Papago and Pima ceremonies included mock battles in which shields like this one were used. Though not fierce raiders like the Apache, they found war with other tribes was often unavoidable and were effective and successful warriors. In the Civil War, the Pima defended Arizona on behalf of the Union, defeating Confederate forces. After 1865 they served as valued scouts for the army in its campaigns against the Apache.

SIMPLE BUT EXQUISITE

Like the other peoples of the Southwest, the Pima and Papago were potters. Compared with the Hopi and Zuni, however, their designs were much simpler.

Rounded bottom of this Papago pottery water jar fits into a basketry ring worn on top of the head, so the jar could be easily carried

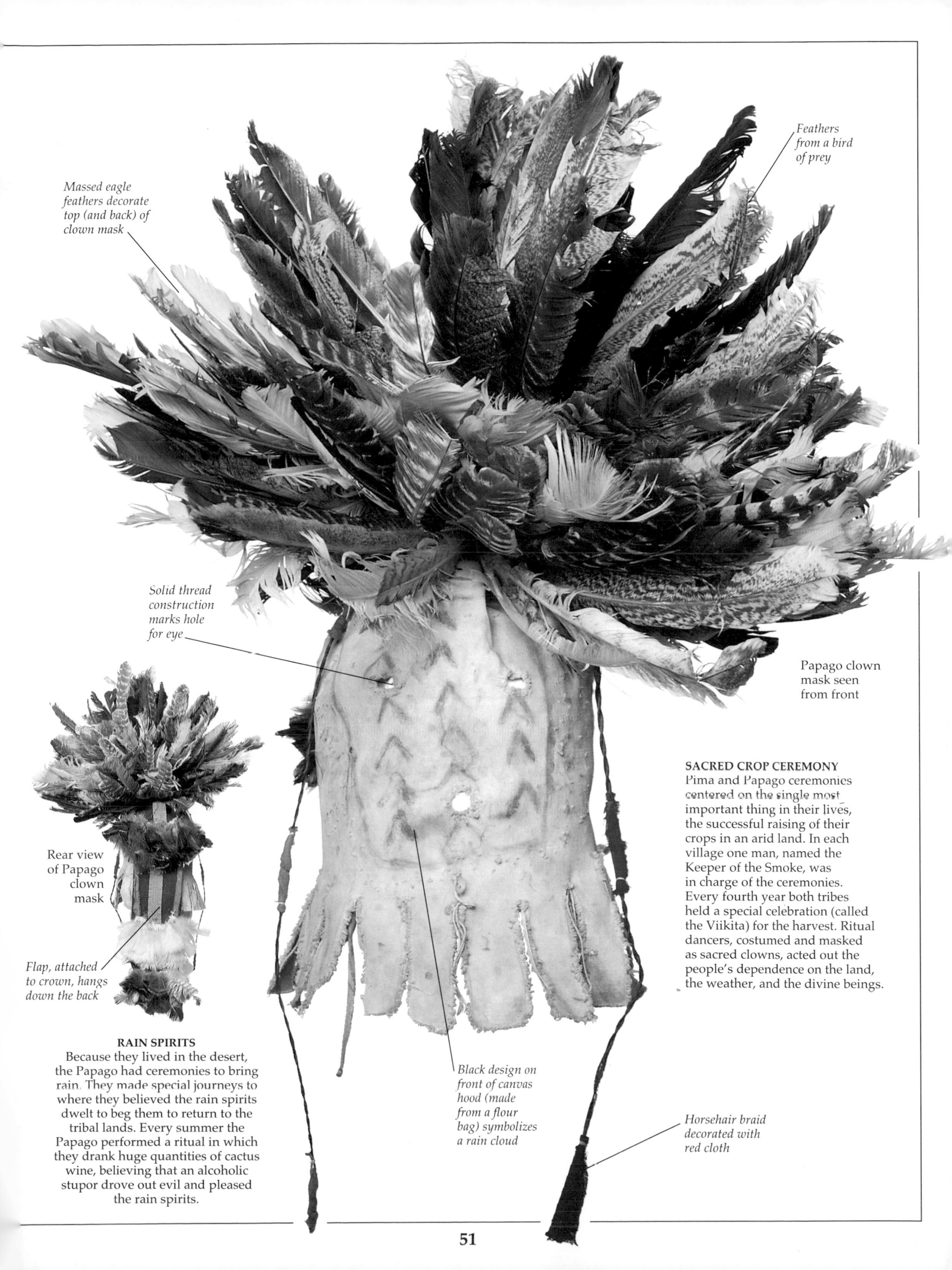

Papago clown mask seen from front

SACRED CROP CEREMONY

Pima and Papago ceremonies centered on the single most important thing in their lives, the successful raising of their crops in an arid land. In each village one man, named the Keeper of the Smoke, was in charge of the ceremonies. Every fourth year both tribes held a special celebration (called the Viikita) for the harvest. Ritual dancers, costumed and masked as sacred clowns, acted out the people's dependence on the land, the weather, and the divine beings.

RAIN SPIRITS

Because they lived in the desert, the Papago had ceremonies to bring rain. They made special journeys to where they believed the rain spirits dwelt to beg them to return to the tribal lands. Every summer the Papago performed a ritual in which they drank huge quantities of cactus wine, believing that an alcoholic stupor drove out evil and pleased the rain spirits.

Land of the totem poles

Raven above a bear

Abalone-inlaid ivory handle

Between the dark forests and the ocean's edge in the rainy Northwest, there grew an extraordinary culture almost untouched by Europeans until the late 1700s. The people of this area, divided into about 30 tribes, never developed agriculture, but were able to live comfortably from the teeming riches of the sea, the forest, and the rivers that filled with salmon during their annual runs. The bountiful environment allowed development of a splendid art and a complex society of nobles, commoners, and slaves. Wealthy families, proud of their status, expressed it in sumptuous ceremonies and monumental artworks, especially the towering wood totem poles.

Map of North America showing the Northwest region

Hide strap used to lash knife to wrist

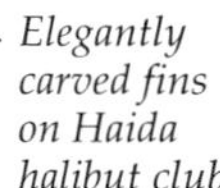

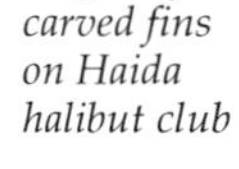

Elegantly carved fins on Haida halibut club

Iron blade of Tlingit fighting knife

HOOKED ON HALIBUT
The island-dwelling Haida relied on fishing. Halibut were caught by setting hooks close to the ocean bed. Once hauled to the surface, such fish had to be stunned with clubs immediately – at up to 400 lb (180 kg), their struggles might upset the canoe. The canoe was dug out of the trunk of a giant cedar and its prow decorated with an elaborate abstract carving.

Carving on the upper part of this Haida totem pole represents a raven

WAR PARTIES
Northwest Coast warfare was typically a quick raid, either for revenge or to acquire plunder and slaves. The northernmost tribes also waged wars to drive away neighboring enemy tribes and control their land. Warriors wore wooden helmets and body armor made from strips of wood joined with rawhide. Weapons were bows, clubs, and knives (above). War knives originally had blades of stone or bone, later of traded iron. Knives were lashed to the wrist during battle.

Intricate carving adorns this model of a Haida tomb

TOTEM POLE VILLAGE
Architecture was one of the great achievements of the Northwest Coast peoples. The huge wooden houses had walls of cedar planks fitted over a massive cedar framework. They were designed by architects who supervised skilled artisans and gangs of laborers, often slaves from other tribes. Several related families lived in a house. Living space reflected rank, the highest place of honor being the back wall. A forest of totem poles dotted the village. Some were built into the fronts of houses, with holes at their bases for door openings. Free-standing poles were often memorials.

PERIOD OF MOURNING
A dead Haida was mourned ceremonially at home for a period of four to six days. The body was then placed in a grave box and taken out of the house through a specially made exit. The remains were put in a grave house, perhaps as large as an ordinary home, and commemorated with a memorial post.

A FAMILY'S STATUS
Totem poles were not idols, as Christian missionaries believed, but monuments proclaiming a family's status by recording its family tree. Every household claimed through its legends a relationship with a spirit being in the form of a noble animal such as a raven, wolf, bear, or eagle. Carvings representing these beings were family crests, much like coats of arms in medieval Europe.

SMOKING PIPES
Tlingit men never smoked until they obtained tobacco from white traders, c. 1800. Then they began to produce an astonishing variety of intricately carved wooden pipes with metal bowls, used only by men – women did not smoke. Designs depicted crests. This Tlingit pipe has two carved and painted wooden wolves and is inlaid with abalone shells.

Small Haida totem pole or grave post

SECRETS BEHIND TOTEM POLES
Wealthy families commissioned sculptors to carve totem poles for various purposes, mostly related to burial rites and memorials to the dead. The heir of a deceased chief might erect a pole in the chief's honor as part of the process of taking over his role and titles. Sometimes a dead chief's remains were interred in a box on top of the pole. Raising a totem pole was always accompanied by a great ceremony: the potlatch (pp. 56–57).

Art second to none

IN THE FLICKERING FIRELIGHT of a Northwest house during the winter ceremonies, two great arts were dramatically displayed together – ritual dances and intricately carved masks. The dances, held by secret societies to initiate a new member, enacted the links between ancestors and spirit beings. Masked dancers represented the power and continuing presence of the spirit world. The ceremony was both ritual and theater, for the dancers used spectacular special effects to enhance the story they were telling. Membership in a society, the right to dance, and the possession of masks helped define privileges in this status-conscious culture. Both male and female shamans also wore ritual masks in their role as doctors.

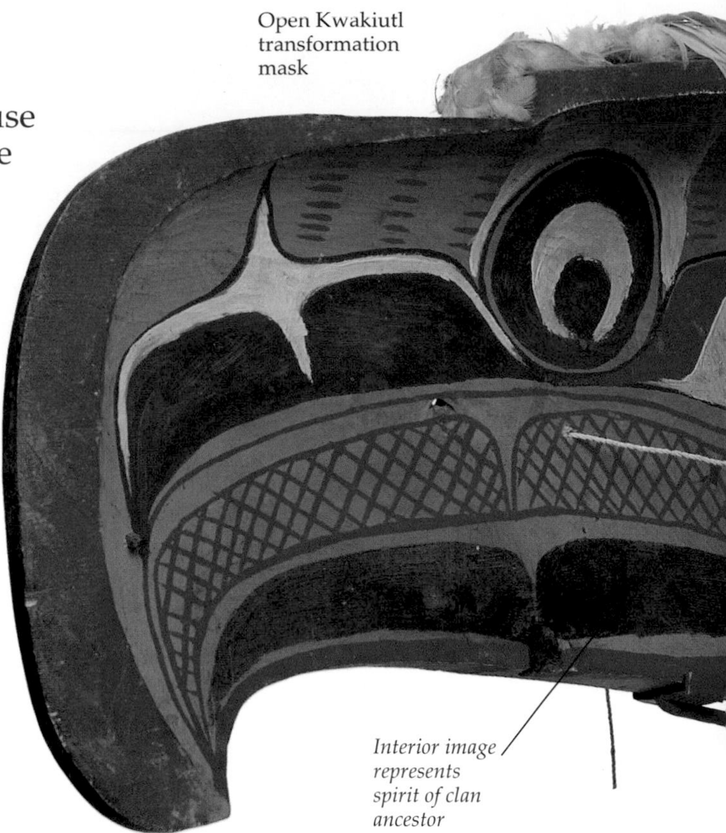

Open Kwakiutl transformation mask

Interior image represents spirit of clan ancestor

Cord, looping through eye and cheekbones, is pulled to open up the mask

Bar supplies leverage to pull open the beak

When closed, this Kwakiutl transformation mask looks like an eagle's head

Haida wooden rattle in form of a hawk

SHAMAN'S RATTLES

Shamans were revered by the tribe for their awesome powers. These derived from special access to the spirit world through a personal guardian spirit, summoned by singing and the shaking of a sacred rattle. Illness was thought to be caused by the intrusion of a small object into the body or by the loss or theft of the soul by spirits, often manipulated by witches. In a dramatic ceremony performed for a fee, a shaman cured the sick person by removing the object or by restoring the lost soul. The witch was then identified and punished.

Abalone shell forms the bird's eye

Three witches planning evil activities are guarded by an octopus (near handle)

Tlingit shaman's wooden oyster catcher rattle

Dead man with protruding tongue in bill of kingfisher

Red ball is the Sun, once stolen; raven is now releasing it to light up the world

Tlingit wooden raven rattle

SECRET SOCIETIES

The Kwakiutl, who probably began the secret societies that eventually spread across the Northwest, had three: the Shaman Society, representing violent and threatening spirits; the Dluwulaxa, linked to the sky spirits; and the Nutlam, whose ancestor was the wolf spirit. Most important to the Shaman Society was a cannibal spirit – the dancers in this ceremony, called Hamatsa, had great prestige and wore particularly elaborate masks. Starting in mid-November the Kwakiutls held Winter Rituals for four months to establish a connection between uninitiated youths and a particular supernatural being, after which the youths became members of the appropriate secret society.

BEHIND THE MASK

Separate from the winter ceremonies were dances that displayed the household's privileges. This spectacular Kwakiutl transformation mask (changing from a bird's face to a human one) was probably part of such a dance. It was fixed to the dancer's head by a frame of wickerwork and animal sinews. The two bars at the back were linked by draw cords to the sides of the beak, and a third cord led to the lower part of the beak. Manipulating the cords instantly transformed an eagle spirit into one with a fierce human face.

RED AS THE SUN

The Bella Coola lived in northern British Columbia, Canada, between two groups of the Kwakiutl. Membership in their Dance Society, usually hereditary, was a coveted privilege because it brought great status. At their four-night winter ceremony, members performed dances taught to them by the spirit beings of the sky. Wearing spherical masks, such as the Spirit of the Sun (at right), the dancers acted out with great drama the central stories of the tribe's beliefs. Masks were designed for a striking effect rather than a readily identifiable spirit.

The power of potlatch

In the Northwest, gaining wealth brought the possibility of status, but in the great potlatch ceremonies, giving wealth away guaranteed it. Potlatches were lavish distributions of gifts from host to guests, who might number in the hundreds. They took place in order to gain acceptance for a change in status or the acquisition of privileges. Potlatches did not bankrupt the giver. Being host at one potlatch guaranteed being a guest – and therefore a receiver of gifts – at others. In a society of often intense rivalries, potlatches siphoned off the tensions that otherwise might have led to war. Potlatches are still held today. A Canadian government ban, from 1884 to 1951, was defied by the Kwakiutl, and there has been a general revival of the ceremony since the 1960s.

Decoration made from sea lion whiskers

Inlaid abalone shell

Carved wooden beaver with dragonfly on its belly

Flicker feather

Luxurious Haida headdress displays wealth of its owner

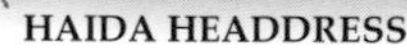

HAIDA HEADDRESS
Much of the artistic activity among Northwest Coast tribes went into creating their magnificent potlatch costumes. In the 1800s the Haida copied headdresses for ceremonial dances from more northern tribes. Such a headdress (above) would have been worn in association with a Chilkat blanket (below).

Ermine pelt

Image of family crest engraved on this 3-ft-high (1-m) Haida copper

MOST PRECIOUS POSSESSION
Shield-shaped plaques of engraved metal, called coppers, were immensely valuable and highly prized as potlatch gifts. Although coppers as symbols of wealth were invented by the Northwest Coast tribes before the arrival of the Europeans, they became even more popular during the 19th-century fur trade period because of the tribes' easy access to copper.

Chief Tutlidi and son at Fort Rupert in 1894

BESTOWING A COPPER
The gift of a copper demonstrated great wealth and thus earned prestige, honoring both giver and receiver. Alternatively, in a flamboyant gesture a chief might deliberately break a copper; shown at left is a chief giving away a copper in honor of his son and heir. Rivalry between chiefs was often intense, so one might break a copper and give the pieces to his rival. To avoid shame the recipient was instantly expected to break a copper of equal or greater value.

DRESSED FOR A POTLATCH

Chilkat blankets and dancing dresses (right) were highly valued. They were woven from mountain goat's wool and cedar bark by Tlingit women. The weavers were paid a high fee, so possession of such objects showed the owner's wealth. The dresses were passed on to relatives and were ostentatiously displayed at potlatches, where a host honored his guests by giving them pieces cut from his dress.

A CEREMONIAL HAT

Potlatches were held to celebrate the marriage of a chief, to inaugurate a new clan house, or to mark the death of an old chief. The chief of a household was responsible for managing its harvest from sea and forest (from which he took a share) and for managing relations with other households. At potlatches a host, wearing ceremonial hat (left) and costume, had help from a speaker, who made the formal announcements, and from a master of ceremonies, who also invited the many guests.

WHAT A FEAST!

Potlatches were accompanied by a spectacular feast that might last up to 12 days. The host tried to provide more food than could be eaten by his guests. They paid respect by eating until they were sick. Food included seal meat, fish, berries, and vegetables served with fish oil in feast dishes like this large bear-shaped vessel.

A WORK OF ART

Feast dishes were elaborately carved works of art, part of the visible symbols of a household's rank and wealth. The largest, which could be the size (and shape) of a small canoe, were placed in front of the guest chiefs, who ate from them using spoons of mountain goat horn or wood. Ordinary guests had their food ladled into smaller dishes (above).

Northern hunters

Map of North America showing the Subarctic region

LIFE IN THE SUBARCTIC demanded extraordinary ingenuity, courage, and self-reliance. Summers were short and winters ferocious in the far northern forests and on the tundra. In this hard land, the search for food dominated life. All 30 Subarctic tribes survived by hunting and fishing, adapting to a nomadic life. The Chipewyan depended on caribou and followed the great herds on their seasonal migrations. The Ojibwa were forest hunters, moving between summer and winter camps. The Naskapi of the taiga (coniferous forests) relied on caribou and all kinds of game, like moose and beaver. Meat and fish were preserved by sun-drying or smoking. Hallmarks of the region were wigwams, snowshoes, the birchbark canoe, and skin clothing.

Hood on Ojibwa child's winter coat protects face from severe cold and wind

Hide fastening

Strips of rabbit skin woven together

WARM WINTER WRAP

Winter clothing, generally made of tanned caribou skins with hair side inward, consisted of coats, mittens, leggings or trousers, moccasins, and hoods. Children sometimes wore winter coats woven from strips of rabbit skin. There were big differences between Eastern and Western tribes in styles of decoration. For example, Easterners painted unique red designs on their coats, while Far Westerners used porcupine quills, shells, and beads.

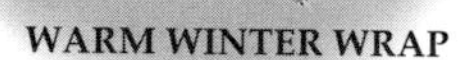

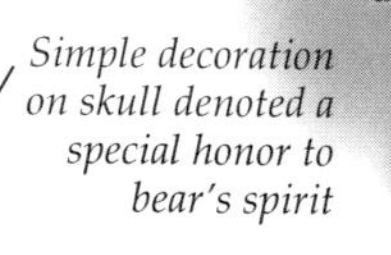

Simple decoration on skull denoted a special honor to bear's spirit

A CHARMED HEAD

Though hunted, bears were regarded with awe by the Subarctic peoples, who believed they possessed powerful spirits. Skulls were thought to retain the bear's spirit and were kept as charms. A hunter would always pray to apologize to a bear's spirit, explaining his need for food and to ask for future successful hunts.

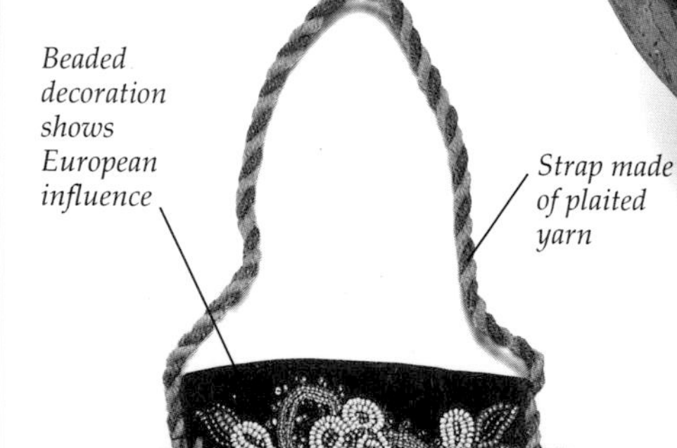

Beaded decoration shows European influence

Strap made of plaited yarn

Slavey tobacco pouch

A BEAR-FUR BAG

Spirits (both good and evil) were soothed through prayers and offerings of tobacco, the smoke rising to comfort the spirits. Tobacco was important in religious and ceremonial life. It was often presented as an invitation to a ceremony or feast, and a gift of tobacco was accepted by the recipient as a great honor.

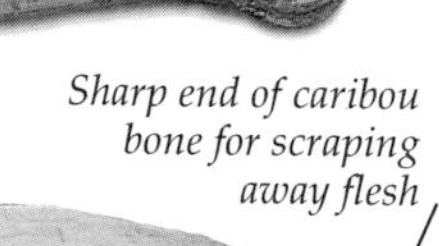

Sharp end of caribou bone for scraping away flesh

SKIN DRESSING

Preparing caribou skins was a woman's job, and a long and messy one. Split caribou bones, like this Chipewyan set, were used to remove the hair, if not needed, and to scrape away bits of flesh. Next a soup of rotting caribou brains was rubbed into the skin for a smelly but effective tanning process. After a washing, the skin was stretched on a frame and dried, then pulled and worked by hand until pliable. Last, it was smoked over a fire for a final curing.

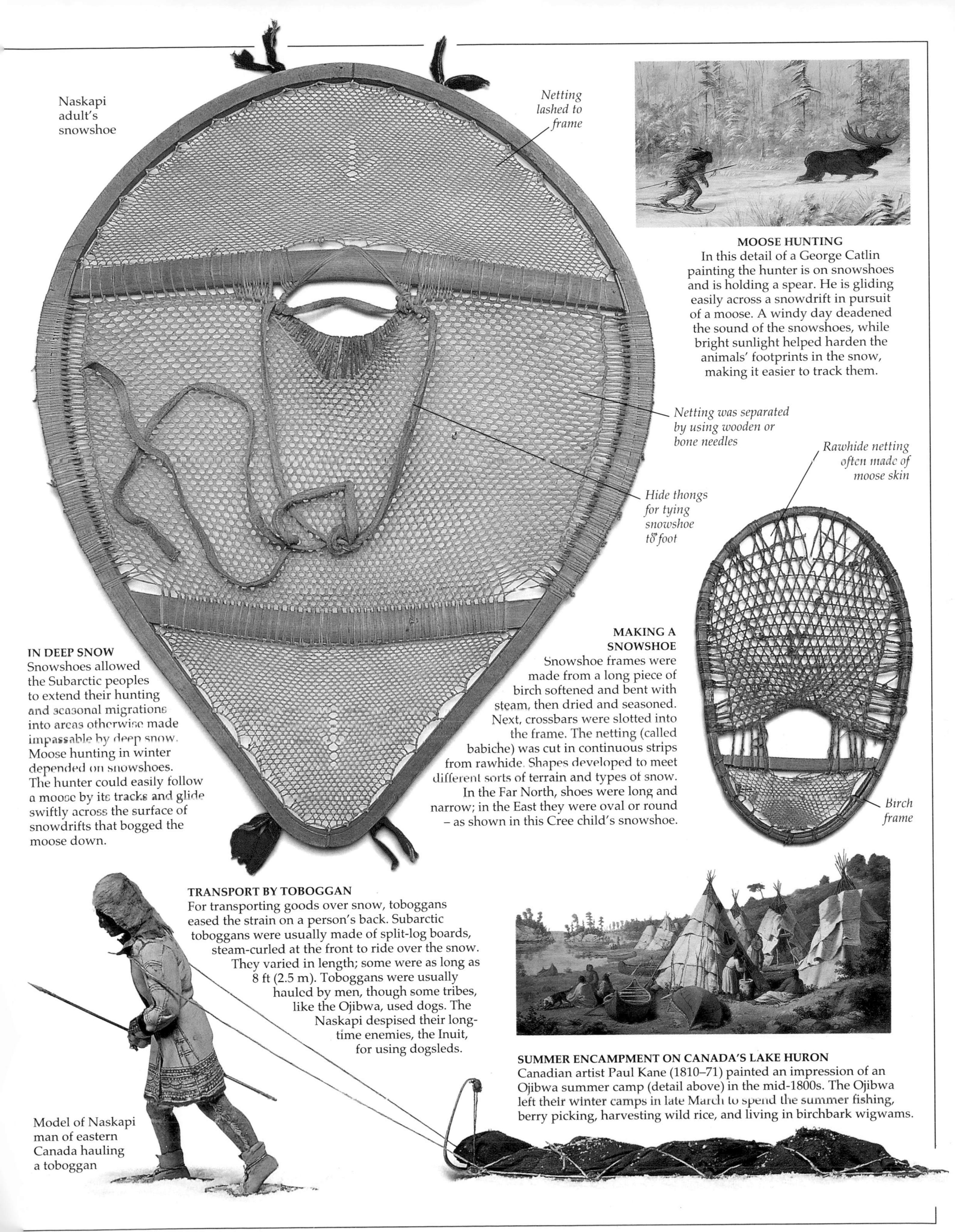

MOOSE HUNTING
In this detail of a George Catlin painting the hunter is on snowshoes and is holding a spear. He is gliding easily across a snowdrift in pursuit of a moose. A windy day deadened the sound of the snowshoes, while bright sunlight helped harden the animals' footprints in the snow, making it easier to track them.

MAKING A SNOWSHOE
Snowshoe frames were made from a long piece of birch softened and bent with steam, then dried and seasoned. Next, crossbars were slotted into the frame. The netting (called babiche) was cut in continuous strips from rawhide. Shapes developed to meet different sorts of terrain and types of snow. In the Far North, shoes were long and narrow; in the East they were oval or round – as shown in this Cree child's snowshoe.

IN DEEP SNOW
Snowshoes allowed the Subarctic peoples to extend their hunting and seasonal migrations into areas otherwise made impassable by deep snow. Moose hunting in winter depended on snowshoes. The hunter could easily follow a moose by its tracks and glide swiftly across the surface of snowdrifts that bogged the moose down.

TRANSPORT BY TOBOGGAN
For transporting goods over snow, toboggans eased the strain on a person's back. Subarctic toboggans were usually made of split-log boards, steam-curled at the front to ride over the snow. They varied in length; some were as long as 8 ft (2.5 m). Toboggans were usually hauled by men, though some tribes, like the Ojibwa, used dogs. The Naskapi despised their long-time enemies, the Inuit, for using dogsleds.

SUMMER ENCAMPMENT ON CANADA'S LAKE HURON
Canadian artist Paul Kane (1810–71) painted an impression of an Ojibwa summer camp (detail above) in the mid-1800s. The Ojibwa left their winter camps in late March to spend the summer fishing, berry picking, harvesting wild rice, and living in birchbark wigwams.

The frozen Arctic

OUTSIDERS THOUGHT of the Arctic as a terrifying trackless ice-desert, but the Inuit made it their home from Siberia east to Greenland. They lived from the treeless tundra, with its winter temperatures of -50°F (-45°C), to the shores of the Arctic Ocean, which freezes to a depth of 6 ft (2 m). The Inuit thus proved that human beings are the most adaptable of Earth's creatures. They built a way of life on hunting seal, walrus, whale, and caribou. On land they traveled with fast dogsleds. At sea they used skin boats – either one-person kayaks or umiaks, used for killing the largest sea mammals. They developed the world's most efficient cold-weather clothing and housing, fashioning the sturdy igloo from blocks of snow.

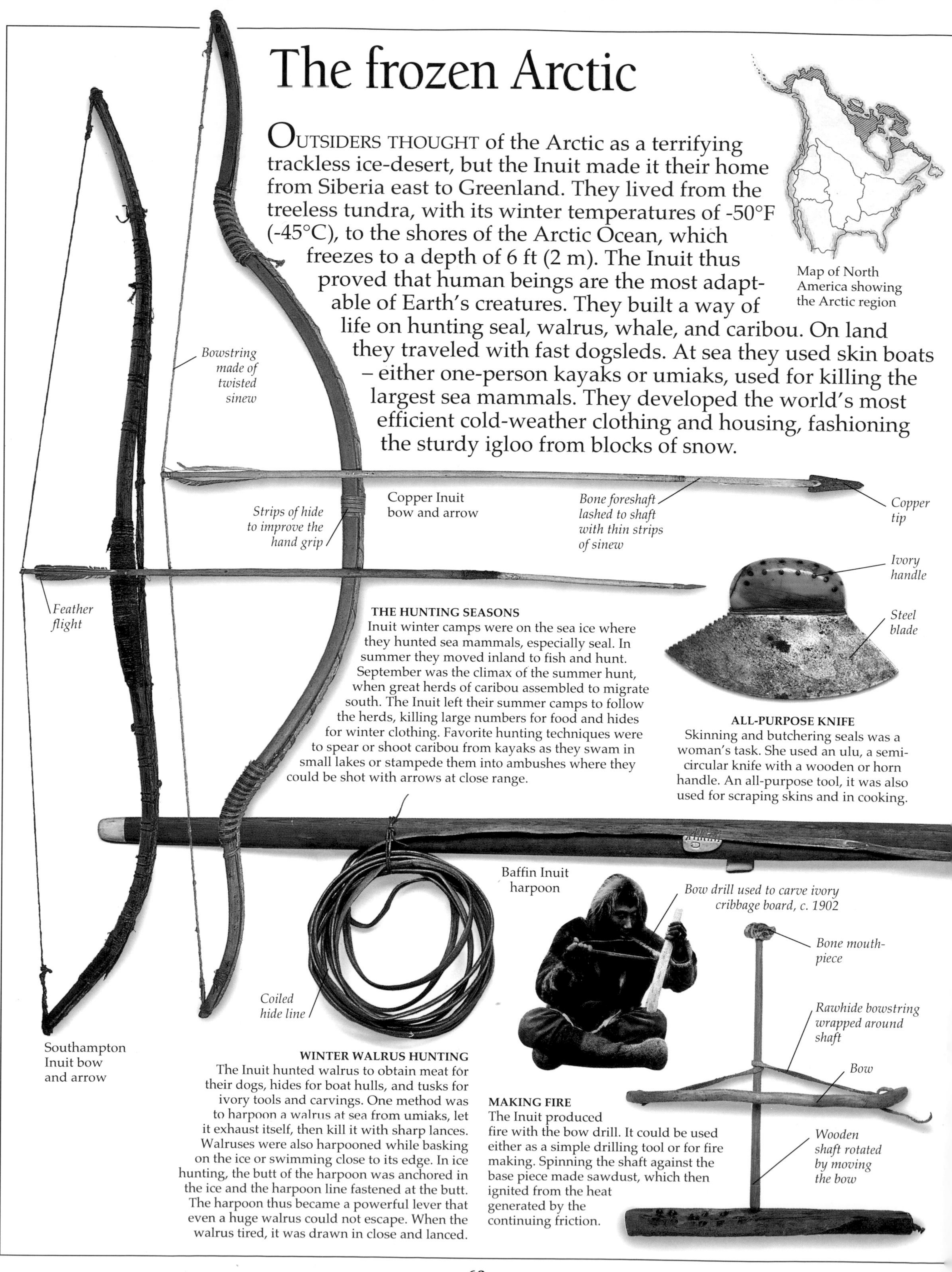

Map of North America showing the Arctic region

Copper Inuit bow and arrow

Southampton Inuit bow and arrow

Baffin Inuit harpoon

THE HUNTING SEASONS
Inuit winter camps were on the sea ice where they hunted sea mammals, especially seal. In summer they moved inland to fish and hunt. September was the climax of the summer hunt, when great herds of caribou assembled to migrate south. The Inuit left their summer camps to follow the herds, killing large numbers for food and hides for winter clothing. Favorite hunting techniques were to spear or shoot caribou from kayaks as they swam in small lakes or stampede them into ambushes where they could be shot with arrows at close range.

ALL-PURPOSE KNIFE
Skinning and butchering seals was a woman's task. She used an ulu, a semicircular knife with a wooden or horn handle. An all-purpose tool, it was also used for scraping skins and in cooking.

WINTER WALRUS HUNTING
The Inuit hunted walrus to obtain meat for their dogs, hides for boat hulls, and tusks for ivory tools and carvings. One method was to harpoon a walrus at sea from umiaks, let it exhaust itself, then kill it with sharp lances. Walruses were also harpooned while basking on the ice or swimming close to its edge. In ice hunting, the butt of the harpoon was anchored in the ice and the harpoon line fastened at the butt. The harpoon thus became a powerful lever that even a huge walrus could not escape. When the walrus tired, it was drawn in close and lanced.

MAKING FIRE
The Inuit produced fire with the bow drill. It could be used either as a simple drilling tool or for fire making. Spinning the shaft against the base piece made sawdust, which then ignited from the heat generated by the continuing friction.

PERFECT INSULATION

Inuit clothing is light but provides excellent insulation. The hooded anorak is made of animal skins. It is airtight, but it traps a layer of insulating air against the body. Loose at the bottom, it can be ventilated periodically if the wearer starts to perspire by pulling it forward at the neck – hot air escapes upward and cold air enters at the bottom. In kayaks the anoraks were tied around the rim of the manhole to keep water out. Some Inuit wore waterproof anoraks made from seal intestines (right).

ARCTIC SUNGLASSES

Arctic peoples invented sunglasses long before Europeans. Snow and ice glare can cause temporary blindness. Wood or bone goggles, blackened on the inside, blocked most sunlight. Vision was through a horizontal slit.

KEEPING THE SUN OFF

In the summer seal hunts, the Inuit used kayaks – fast, lightweight canoes easily maneuvered by one person. With little or no access to timber, they made the frame of driftwood and covered it with dressed seal skin, which was waterproofed with seal oil. To protect their eyes from the sun's glare off the water and drifting ice floes, hunters wore wooden helmets, often beautifully decorated (right).

CEREMONIAL MASKS

At Inuit rituals male dancers wore wooden face masks representing the spirits of creatures or natural forces, as seen in visions by the shamans. The women wore finger masks (tiny replicas of the men's masks), which focused attention on their flowing hand gestures.

Modern times

THE "VANISHING INDIAN" was how Native North Americans were regarded a century ago. They were expected eventually to join white society or simply die out, but they have refused to do either. Now numbering 2.5 million in the U.S. and Canada, more than half living outside reservations, Native North Americans are reviving tribal traditions and seeking their own role in a multicultural nation. U.S. and Canadian government policy, even when well-meant, tended to make reservations dependent on government support, while tribal resources were plundered by business interests. Despair accompanied unemployment, disease, and lack of education – all far higher than the national average. From the 1970s, militant protests have dramatized key issues but have been less effective than using the law to force compensation for lost rights. Today, many Native peoples hope to bring back traditional forms of decision making and leadership.

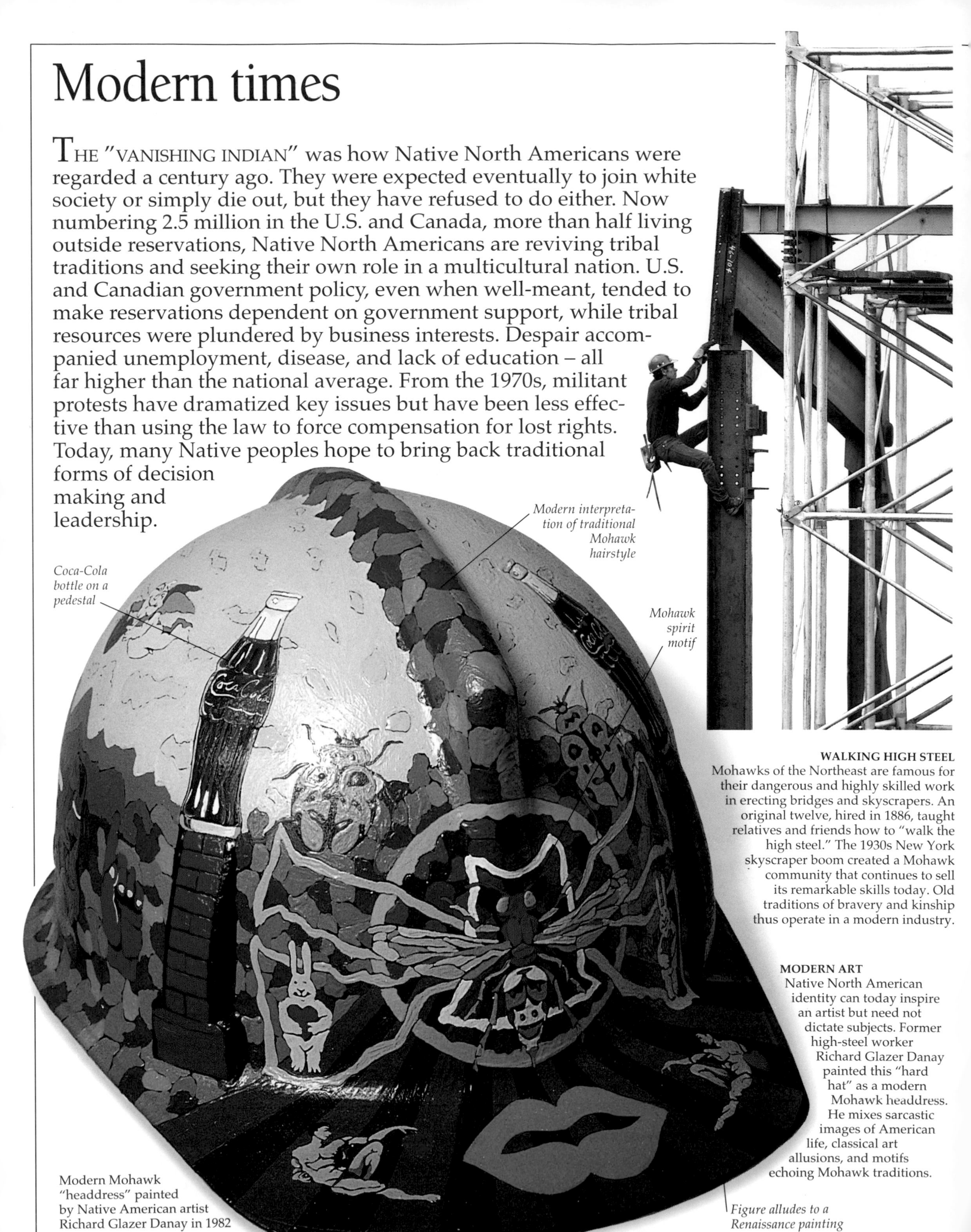

Modern interpretation of traditional Mohawk hairstyle

Coca-Cola bottle on a pedestal

Mohawk spirit motif

Figure alludes to a Renaissance painting

Modern Mohawk "headdress" painted by Native American artist Richard Glazer Danay in 1982

WALKING HIGH STEEL
Mohawks of the Northeast are famous for their dangerous and highly skilled work in erecting bridges and skyscrapers. An original twelve, hired in 1886, taught relatives and friends how to "walk the high steel." The 1930s New York skyscraper boom created a Mohawk community that continues to sell its remarkable skills today. Old traditions of bravery and kinship thus operate in a modern industry.

MODERN ART
Native North American identity can today inspire an artist but need not dictate subjects. Former high-steel worker Richard Glazer Danay painted this "hard hat" as a modern Mohawk headdress. He mixes sarcastic images of American life, classical art allusions, and motifs echoing Mohawk traditions.

ANCIENT CEREMONIES
Traditional ceremonies retain force and meaning for the Apache. Dancers (left) wearing symbolic masks, headdresses, and body paint represent Gans (mountain spirit beings). Directed by a shaman, the Gans impersonators perform rituals to gain protection against hostile spirits or to heal the sick. Gans dancers may also provide entertainment at the four-day celebrations marking a girl's coming of age.

Navajo woman baking bread, using traditional oven and equipment

CARRYING ON TRADITIONS
Over 200,000 Navajo live on their 15-million-acre (6-million-ha) reservation, chiefly in Arizona – the largest in the U.S. The Navajo have long been divided over how far to accept white American ways. The tribal council still holds meetings in Navajo, and ceremonies (particularly those for curing illness) remain central to tribal life. Traditional Navajo art, such as weaving and silverwork, is an important source of income.

SOCIAL BENEFITS
Using their rights over their own lands, confirmed by a 1988 Act of Congress, Native Americans have opened gambling casinos in 33 states across the U.S. Casinos provide jobs, and profits pay for housing, schools, and health care. However, arguments over how to spend the money have already divided tribes, and some leaders fear gambling will have bad social effects.

Group of Ojibwa children at a powwow

THE POWER OF POWWOW
Though never abandoned, powwows have again become hugely popular. Nearly a thousand were held in 1993, attended by 90 percent of Native North Americans. They are a way of asserting Native peoples' identity. Many tribes participate in these weekend celebrations focused on dancing. Social dances ("intertribals") are mixed with traditional competition dances.

GETTING AN EDUCATION
Since the 1960s Canadian and U.S. governments have provided funds for new education programs run by the tribes themselves. New schools (teaching in both the tribal language and English) mean that nearly all reservation children now attend school.

NORTHWEST TERRITORIES TRIBAL MEETING
In the 1970s new legal help groups, such as the Native American Rights Fund, won cases before the U.S. Indian Claims Commission. Set up in 1946, it settles land claims arising from broken treaties. The Lakota have received $105 million, and tribes in Maine were awarded $40 million. The Canadian government and the Inuit agreed on a new self-governing Inuit territory (Nunavut) in 1991.

Peruvian mummy cloth

Aztec sacrificial knife

Mesoamerican farming tools

Ceremonial urn showing Chaac, Maya god of rain

Aztec ceramic flute

Marigolds, given as offerings to goddesses by the Aztecs

Moche vessel showing fisherman in boat

Peruvian silver portrait beaker

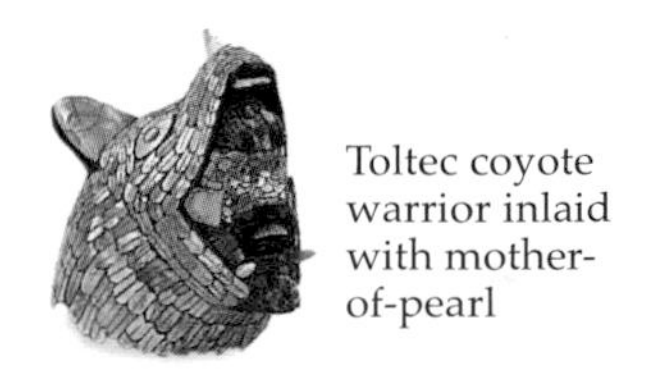
Toltec coyote warrior inlaid with mother-of-pearl

Gold Mixtec lip ornament

Peruvian feather fan

Chapter Two

AZTEC
INCA & MAYA

Written by
ELIZABETH BAQUEDANO

Photographed by
MICHEL ZABE

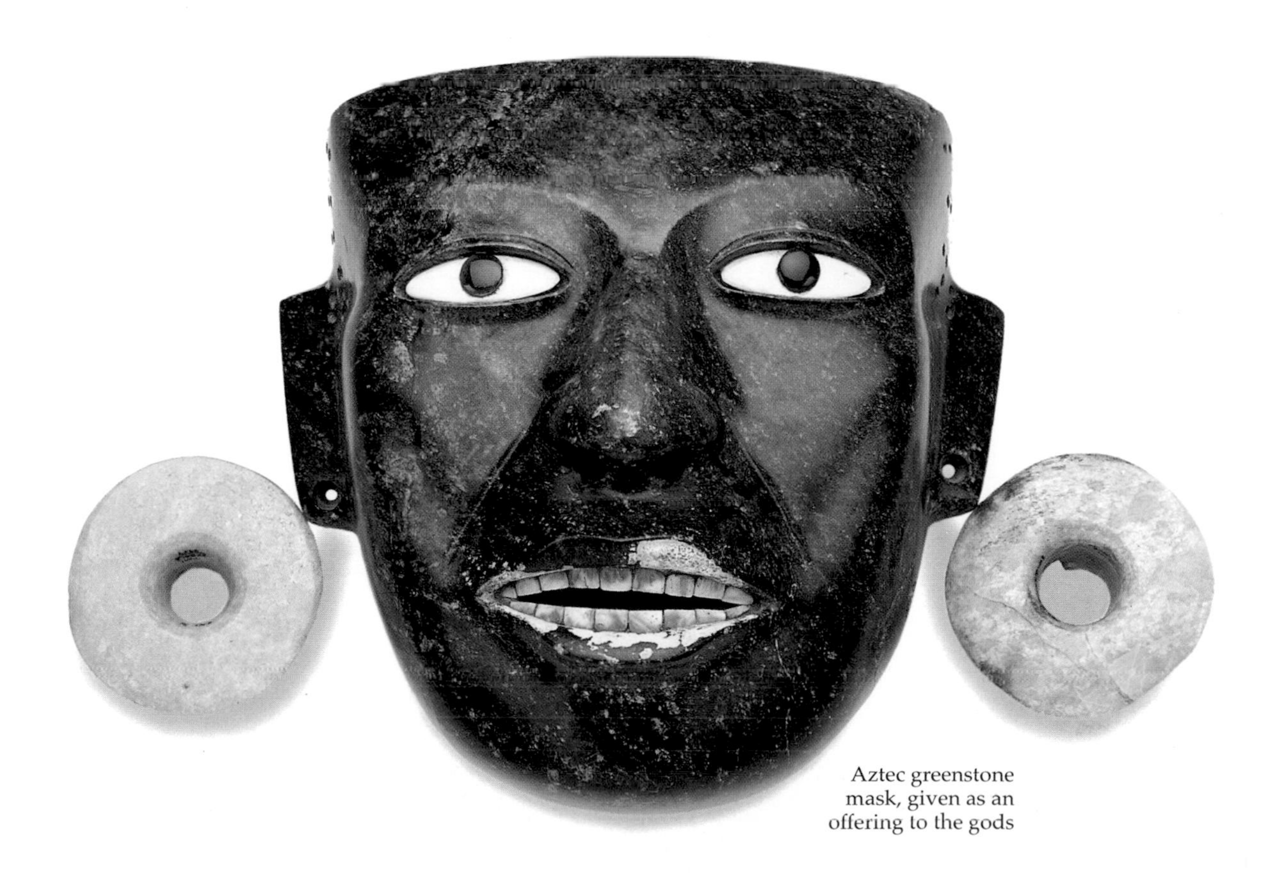
Aztec greenstone mask, given as an offering to the gods

Ancient empires

IN THE 16TH CENTURY, Spanish explorers in the Americas encountered two great civilizations – one in Mesoamerica (the territory controlled by the Aztecs and the Mayas at the time of the conquest) and the other in South America (the territory in the central Andean region under Inca rule). The people of these regions were a mosaic of tribes and nations, whose great achievements included masterpieces of art, spectacular cities, and a unique approach to life. The strong foundations of economic, political, and social organization typical of each of these empires had already been laid by earlier American cultures.

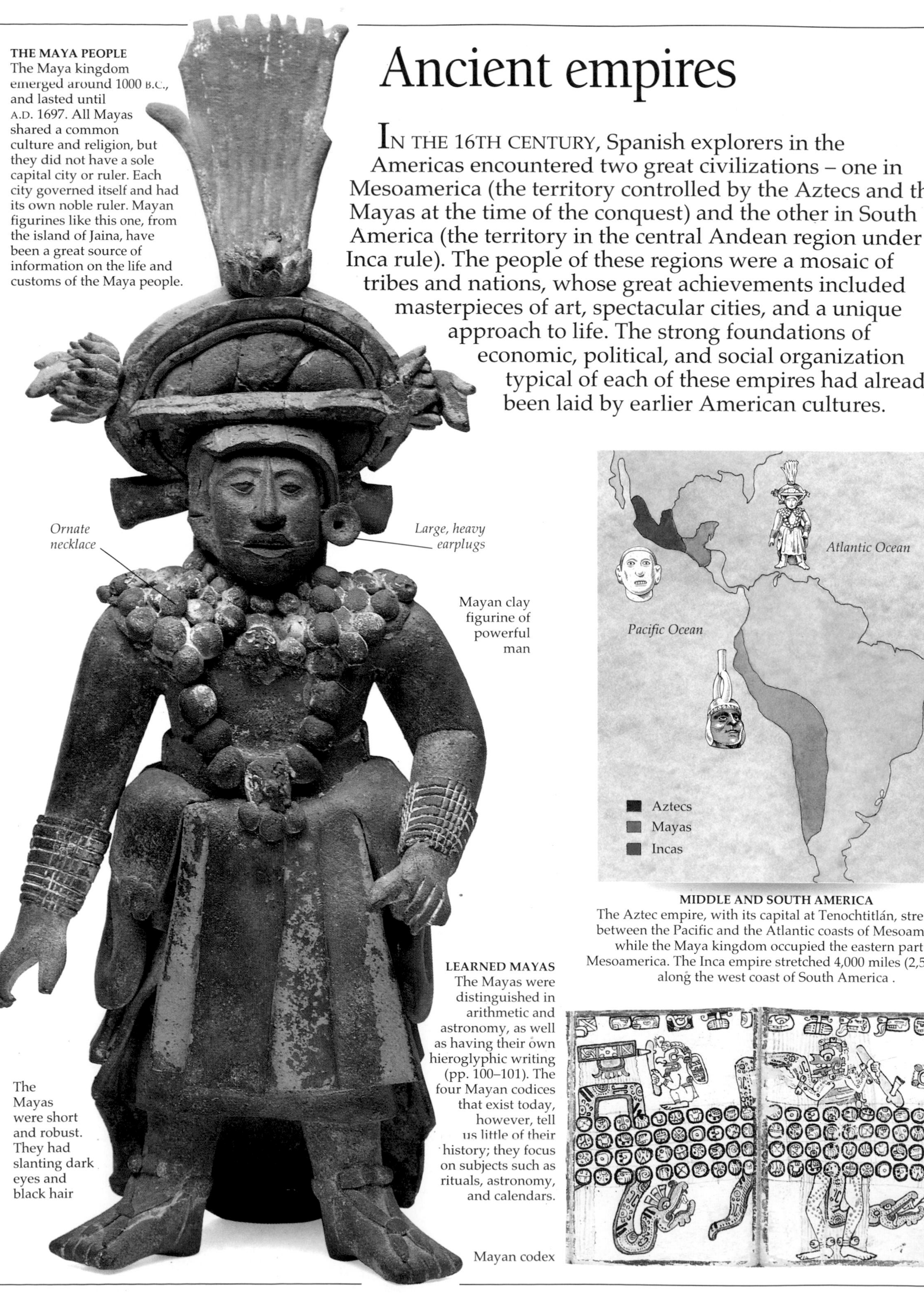

THE MAYA PEOPLE
The Maya kingdom emerged around 1000 B.C., and lasted until A.D. 1697. All Mayas shared a common culture and religion, but they did not have a sole capital city or ruler. Each city governed itself and had its own noble ruler. Mayan figurines like this one, from the island of Jaina, have been a great source of information on the life and customs of the Maya people.

Mayan clay figurine of powerful man

The Mayas were short and robust. They had slanting dark eyes and black hair

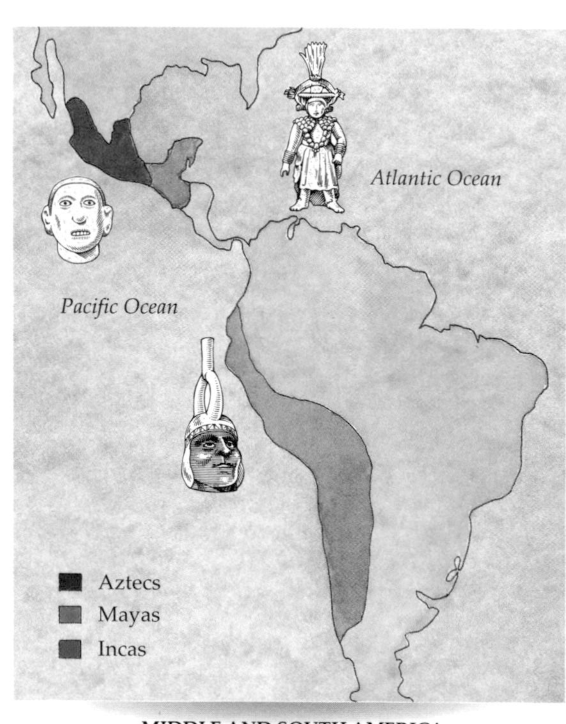

MIDDLE AND SOUTH AMERICA
The Aztec empire, with its capital at Tenochtitlán, stretched between the Pacific and the Atlantic coasts of Mesoamerica while the Maya kingdom occupied the eastern part of Mesoamerica. The Inca empire stretched 4,000 miles (2,500 k along the west coast of South America .

LEARNED MAYAS
The Mayas were distinguished in arithmetic and astronomy, as well as having their own hieroglyphic writing (pp. 100–101). The four Mayan codices that exist today, however, tell us little of their history; they focus on subjects such as rituals, astronomy, and calendars.

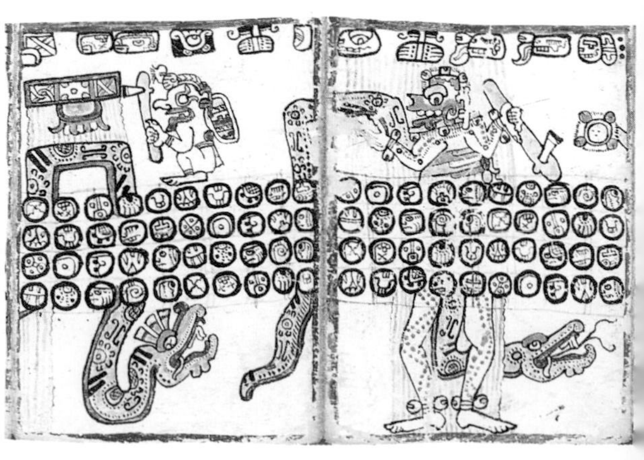

Mayan codex

THE AZTECS

The Aztecs were a wandering tribe before they settled in the Valley of Mexico on swampy land in Lake Texcoco and founded Tenochtitlán. It grew in size and importance until it became the capital of the mighty Aztec empire. The Aztecs conquered many people, demanding tribute from them (pp. 86–87). The Aztecs were short and stocky, with brown skin and broad faces.

THE FOUNDING OF TENOCHTITLAN

According to Aztec mythology, Huitzilopochtli, their tribal god, promised to show his people the place where they were to settle and build their great capital, Tenochtitlán. He told them to look for an eagle perched upon a cactus with a serpent in its beak. This would be a sign that they had found their promised land. The first page of the Codex Mendoza (a book telling the history of the Aztecs) illustrates the foundation of Tenochtitlán in either 1325 or 1345. Mexico City is built on the same site.

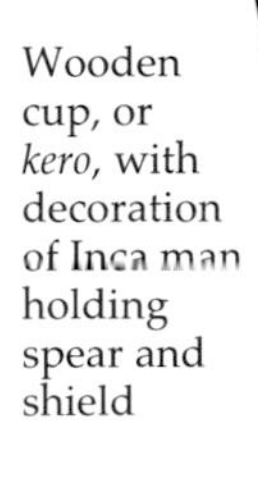

Wooden cup, or *kero*, with decoration of Inca man holding spear and shield

INCA GOLD

The Incas excelled at working metals such as silver, copper, and gold (pp. 110–111). Female figures like this one have been found with Inca offerings to the gods.

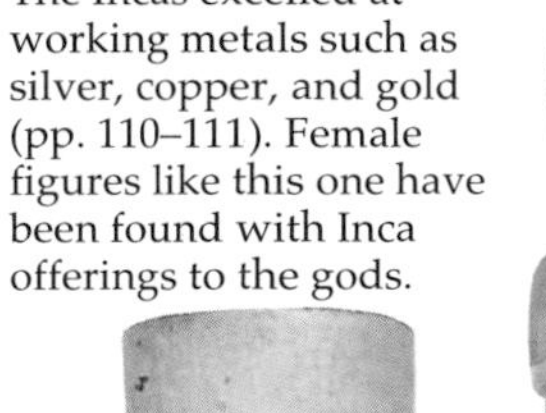

THE ANDEAN PEOPLE

The Inca empire developed the most important state in the Andean highlands in 1438, when they conquered the area around the city Cuzco and made it their capital. The Incas conquered provinces and incorporated them into their empire. Due to their efficient administration system, they kept control over all their empire. The people of the Andean area were typically small, with straight black hair and brown skin.

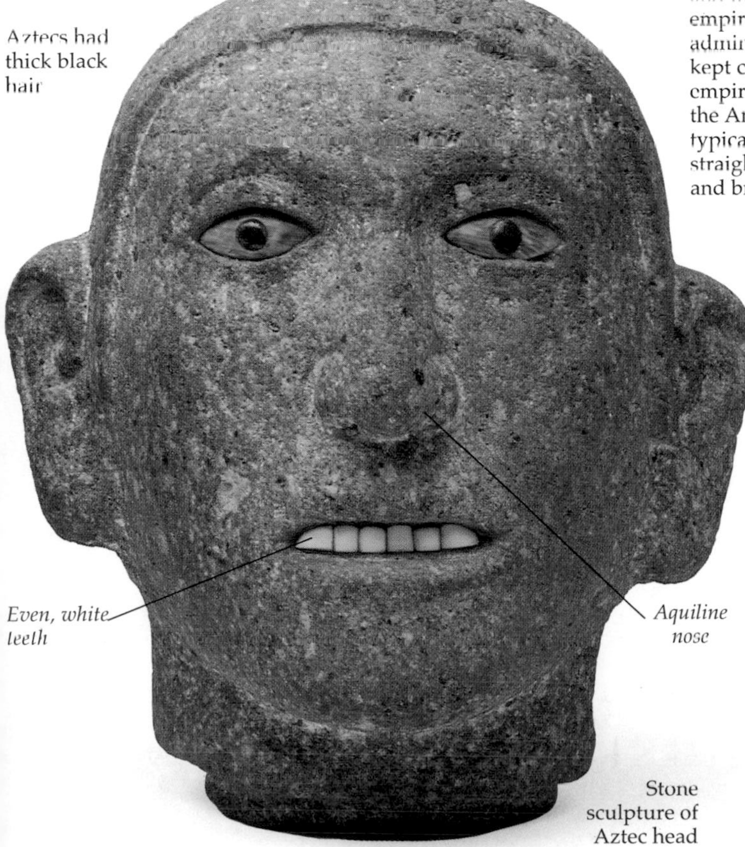

Stone sculpture of Aztec head

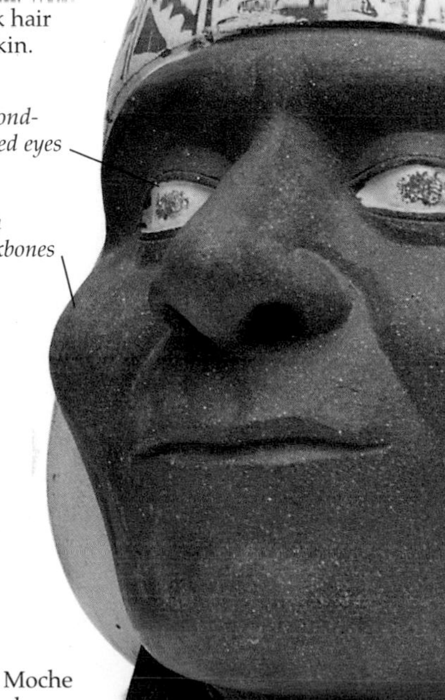

Moche clay portrait vessel

People of Mesoamerica

MESOAMERICA is one of two areas in the Americas (the other being the central Andes) that had urban civilizations, or "high cultures," at the time of the Spanish conquest in 1519. The fact that Mesoamericans built spectacular pyramids and temples (pp. 90–91), had large markets (pp. 86–87), the ball-game (pp. 118–119), a sacred calendar, hieroglyphic writing (pp. 100-101), and a group of gods (pp. 92–93); and practiced human sacrifice (pp. 96–97) sets Mesoamerica apart from its neighbors. Mesoamerican cultural history is divided into three main periods: the Preclassic, the Classic, and the Postclassic, stretching from about 2000 B.C. until the Spanish conquest (pp. 122–123). During these periods Mesoamerica saw the rise and fall of many civilizations. The Olmecs were the dominant culture in the Preclassic period. The Classic period saw the rise of the mighty Teotihuacán culture and the Mayas. The Postclassic period was one of militarism, and warring empires, such as the Toltecs and Aztecs.

WARRING AZTECS
At its height, the Aztec empire was strong and prosperous. Conquered areas were controlled by the powerful Aztec army. This illustration shows an army commander.

MAYAN RITUAL
Religion was the center of every Mayan person's life. One of the major achievements of the Mayas was the construction of superb temples and other buildings to honor their gods. These were decorated with carvings such as this lintel showing a woman drawing blood from her tongue. Self-sacrifice was common throughout Mesoamerica.

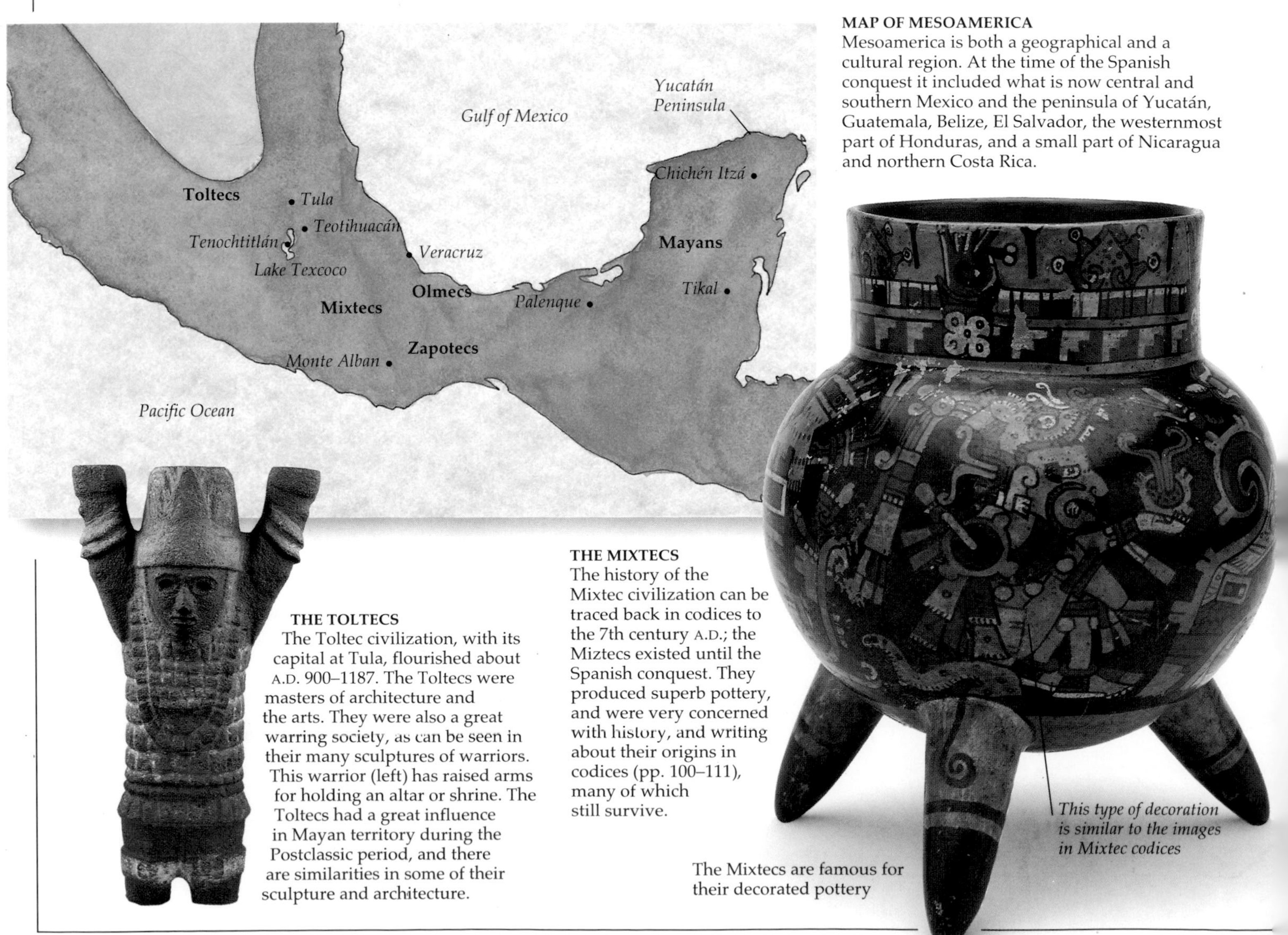

MAP OF MESOAMERICA
Mesoamerica is both a geographical and a cultural region. At the time of the Spanish conquest it included what is now central and southern Mexico and the peninsula of Yucatán, Guatemala, Belize, El Salvador, the westernmost part of Honduras, and a small part of Nicaragua and northern Costa Rica.

THE TOLTECS
The Toltec civilization, with its capital at Tula, flourished about A.D. 900–1187. The Toltecs were masters of architecture and the arts. They were also a great warring society, as can be seen in their many sculptures of warriors. This warrior (left) has raised arms for holding an altar or shrine. The Toltecs had a great influence in Mayan territory during the Postclassic period, and there are similarities in some of their sculpture and architecture.

THE MIXTECS
The history of the Mixtec civilization can be traced back in codices to the 7th century A.D.; the Miztecs existed until the Spanish conquest. They produced superb pottery, and were very concerned with history, and writing about their origins in codices (pp. 100–111), many of which still survive.

This type of decoration is similar to the images in Mixtec codices

The Mixtecs are famous for their decorated pottery

TEOTIHUACAN
The Teotihuacán culture flourished between A.D. 1 and 750. The city Teotihuacán is the most impressive city to be seen in the Americas.

The Teotihuacán culture was the most influential culture in Mesoamerica. We know little about the physical appearance of the people, but the masks found at Teotihuacán give us a good idea of what they looked like.

Hole in earlobe for earring

Masks may have been portraits of the dead

Greenstone mask from Teotihuacán

Head made of basalt is 5 ft (1.5 m) tall and weighs more than 20 tons

COLOSSAL HEAD
Several heads such as this one have been found in the Olmec heartland in the Gulf Coast region. They may be the heads of ball-game players, or "portraits" of rulers or chiefs.

THE OLMECS
The Olmec civilization flourished between about 1200 and 200 B.C. Its legacy to other cultures in Mesoamerica included platform mounds, plazas, ball-courts, and hieroglyphic writing. Olmec artifacts have been found in many parts of Mesoamerica. Olmec art is naturalistic and symbolic. This figurine seems to represent a bald-headed baby.

Facial features similar to peoples of Southeast Asia

Zapotec nobleman trying on jeweled headdress in a detail from a painting by Diego Rivera, called "Cultivation of Maize".

ZAPOTEC CIVILIZATION
The Zapotecs, with their capital at Monte Alban, were established about 600 B.C.; they declined about A.D. 800. The Zapotec state was one of the largest at the time in Mesoamerica. The Zapotecs excelled in the art of featherwork and manufacturing gold jewelry.

Olmec figurine of a bald-headed baby

The Incas and their ancestors

BEFORE THE INCA empire reached its peak in South America, many Andean cultures had already laid the framework for its success. These cultures left no written records of their history, and all that is known of them comes from the study of their architecture, pottery, and the remains found in their graves. Archaeologists have identified separate periods of cultural growth, culminating with the Incas. The first complex societies were formed in around 1800 B.C. Between this time and the rise of the Incas in the mid-15th century, various cultures emerged, gradually becoming highly organized civilizations with social structures, political and economic systems, specialized artisans, and a religion where many gods were worshipped. Along the desert coast of Peru there were civilized states such as the Nazca, the Moche, and the Chimu. In the highlands, the Huari and the Tiahuanaco were highly organized cultures. Between A.D. 1438 and 1534, all of these elements were brought together and improved on under the Inca empire.

NAZCA
The Nazca inhabited the southern coastal valleys of Peru from 300 B.C. to A.D. 600 and were well-known for their arts which included textiles and metalwork. However, the hallmark of the Nazca civilization is its painted pottery, decorated with realistic and mythological scenes.

INCA NOBLES
The scenes painted on vessels and other objects help us learn more about Andean life and culture. For example, Inca nobles usually carried a lance, as this painting on a *kero* or wooden cup, shows.

Moche person of high status wearing headband with jaguar decoration and earplugs

MOCHE
The Moche people flourished on the northern desert coast of Peru between about the time of Christ and A.D. 600. They were skilled goldsmiths and weavers, and remarkable potters. Their representations of people, plants, animals, and gods in a wide range of activities, give us an insight into their lives.

TIAHUANACO
The Tiahuanaco empire from the Peruvian highlands flourished between about A.D. 500 and 650. It was a strong state with an impressive ceremonial center.

Tiahuanaco pottery jaguar

The Tiahuanaco and the Huari art styles shared many symbols, especially of the cat family

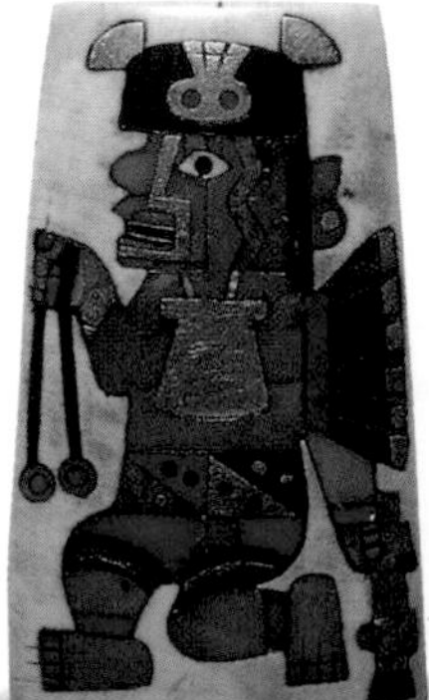

HUARI
The Huari (A.D. 500 to 900) were neighbors of the Tiahuanaco. Theirs was a highly organized state, with an advanced irrigation system and a distinctive architectural style. It expanded by conquering neighboring areas. Many Huari ideas, such as pottery techniques, were adopted by other Andean cultures. The Huari had their own art style. A common theme is an "angel" figure with wings

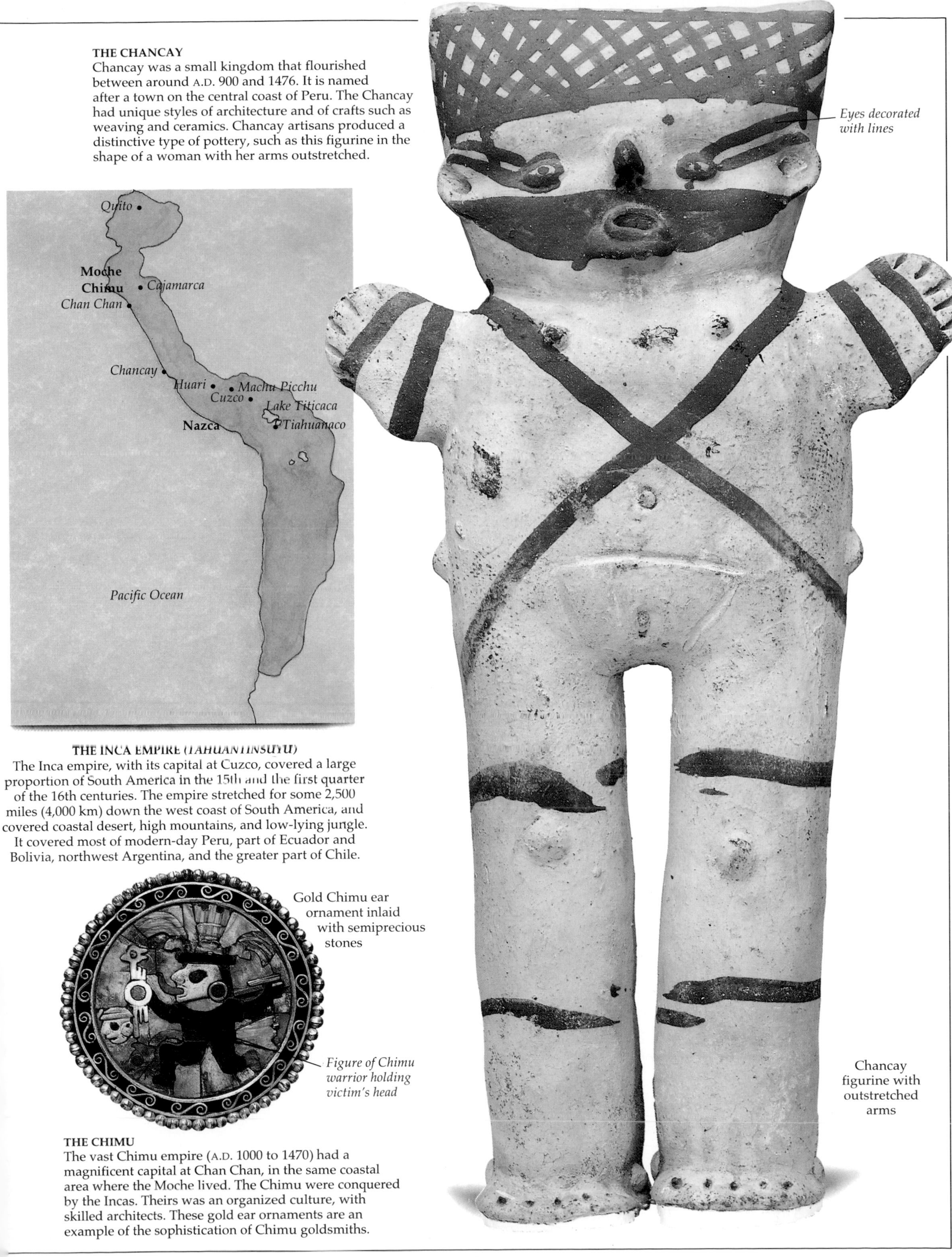

THE CHANCAY

Chancay was a small kingdom that flourished between around A.D. 900 and 1476. It is named after a town on the central coast of Peru. The Chancay had unique styles of architecture and of crafts such as weaving and ceramics. Chancay artisans produced a distinctive type of pottery, such as this figurine in the shape of a woman with her arms outstretched.

Eyes decorated with lines

THE INCA EMPIRE (TAHUANTINSUYU)

The Inca empire, with its capital at Cuzco, covered a large proportion of South America in the 15th and the first quarter of the 16th centuries. The empire stretched for some 2,500 miles (4,000 km) down the west coast of South America, and covered coastal desert, high mountains, and low-lying jungle. It covered most of modern-day Peru, part of Ecuador and Bolivia, northwest Argentina, and the greater part of Chile.

Gold Chimu ear ornament inlaid with semiprecious stones

Figure of Chimu warrior holding victim's head

Chancay figurine with outstretched arms

THE CHIMU

The vast Chimu empire (A.D. 1000 to 1470) had a magnificent capital at Chan Chan, in the same coastal area where the Moche lived. The Chimu were conquered by the Incas. Theirs was an organized culture, with skilled architects. These gold ear ornaments are an example of the sophistication of Chimu goldsmiths.

Farming

AGRICULTURE WAS A VITAL PART of life in pre-Columbian times. Farmers used sophisticated methods of cultivation, and by the time of the Spanish conquest (p. 122) the ancient Americans were the greatest plant cultivators in the world. Maize from Mesoamerica and potatoes from the Andes (pp. 84–85) were some of their contributions to the European diet. Human labor was the vital ingredient in both regions, as there were no animals for carrying loads or plows in Mesoamerica. The Andean people had only the llama, which could carry very small loads. Farming methods varied depending on the climate and geography of the area. For the Aztecs, the most productive crops were grown on the *chinampas*, plots of land built in swampy lakes.

GODDESS OF AGRICULTURE
This incense burner (used to burn a resin called *copal*) represents an agricultural goddess. Agricultural goddesses were often adorned with a pleated paper fan, like this one.

FERTILE PLOTS
Crops of vegetables and flowers were grown on the fertile *chinampas*, as well as medicinal plants and herbs.

BUILDING *CHINAMPAS* below
Chinampas were made by staking out narrow, rectangular strips in marshy lakes. Narrow canals were built between them for canoes to pass along. Each *chinampa* was built up with layers of thick water vegetation cut from the surface of the lake and mud from the bottom of the lake. They were piled up like mats to make the plots. Willow trees were planted around the edge of each *chinampa* to make it more secure.

FARMER'S TOOL
The digging stick, or *uictli,* was the essential farmer's tool. Digging sticks were used for various jobs, such as hoeing and planting.

DIGGING STICK
Digging sticks were made with the strongest and longest-lasting woods.

HARVEST TIME
Life in Mesoamerica and in the Andes revolved around the cycles of planting, cultivating, and harvesing crops such as maize.

PLANTING THE SEED
This illustration from the Codex Florentino shows an Aztec farmer planting maize using a digging stick.

MAIZE CROP
Maize was the staple food of the Mayans as well as the Aztecs. It is still an important crop today.

AXE
Axes were used for chopping or as hammers.

CORNCOB VESSEL
Andean pottery was often made in the shape of the fruit and vegetables that were grown. Maize originated in Mesoamerica, but was widely grown in the Americas.

HOE
This tool was used as a spade to turn the soil of the plots.

TERRACES AT MACHU PICCHU
To get the highest yield from their crops, the Incas used sophisticated terracing and irrigation methods on hillsides in the highlands. Building terraces meant that they could use more land for cultivation, and also help to resist erosion of the land by wind and rain.

TENDING CROPS
In the Andean region cultivating the soil was the basis of life. Farmers tended their crops using simple tools such as a digging stick, a clod breaker, and a hoe.

Hunting and fishing

HUNTING AND FISHING were important activities in Mesoamerica and in the Andean regions. Meat and fish were part of the diet, especially in the Andean region, depending on what was available in the area. Animal life in the Andes was most abundant in the high mountains of the north, where large mammals such as vicuñas (wild relatives of the llama) and deer roamed. In Mesoamerica, the largest creatures were the peccary (a relative of the pig) and the deer. These were hunted with bows and arrows. Smaller animals such as rabbits and dogs were caught in nets. Mesoamericans and South Americans fished for anything from shellfish to large fish and sea mammals with nets, harpoons, and by angling. They made hooks from sturdy cactus thorns, shell, and bone. Hooks were also made of copper in South America.

JADE FISH
People from coastal regions drew inspiration from fish and marine life to decorate pottery and jade objects.

IN THE NET
Catching waterfowl in nets was widespread in Mesoamerica around the lake areas.

GONE FISHING
This stirrup-spouted Moche vessel depicts a fisherman rowing on a balsawood raft. This was a typical scene on the Peruvian coast.

FAMILY TRADITION
Many trades, such as fishing, were passed from father to son. Boys were taught to fish at an early age; at the age of 14 they went out fishing alone.

FISHING NET
The lake system in and around Tenochtitlán provided people with fish and waterfowl, fresh water for drinking, and irrigation for crops. Sometimes fish were transported in canoes to markets and sold. Many nets in present-day Mexico are similar to those produced by the Aztecs and other Mesoamerican peoples. The most common net used by the Aztecs was bag-shaped like this one, made of fiber from the agave plant.

The Aztecs and the Mayas made their canoes from hollowed-out tree trunks

REED RAFT
Watercraft were fashioned from reeds because of the shortage of wood in areas where few or no trees grew. This type of raft was – and still is – used high in the Andes around Lake Titicaca and on the coast. Large rafts between 14.5 and 20 ft (4.5 and 6.1 m) long had a wooden mast made of reeds for raising and lowering the sail.

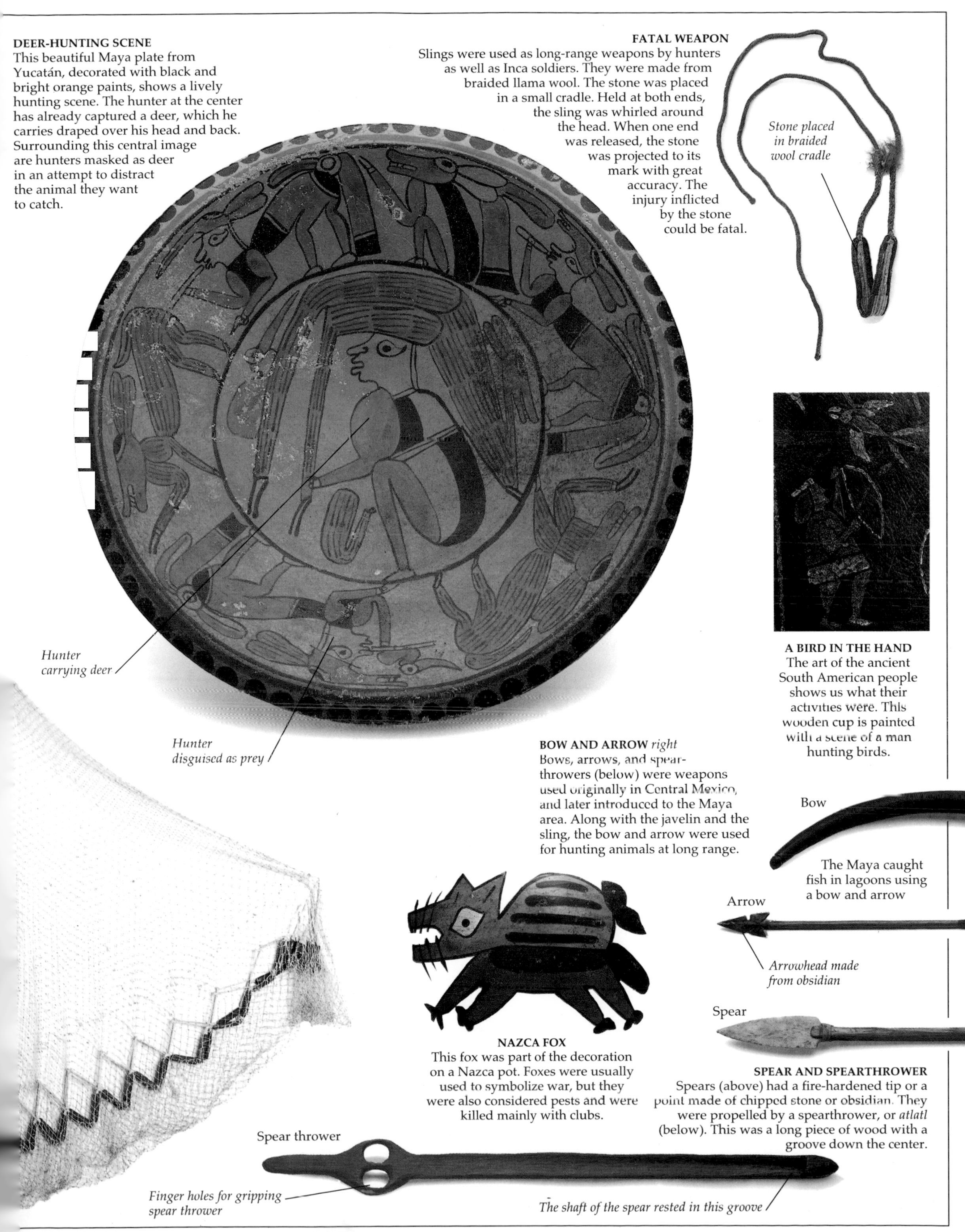

DEER-HUNTING SCENE
This beautiful Maya plate from Yucatán, decorated with black and bright orange paints, shows a lively hunting scene. The hunter at the center has already captured a deer, which he carries draped over his head and back. Surrounding this central image are hunters masked as deer in an attempt to distract the animal they want to catch.

FATAL WEAPON
Slings were used as long-range weapons by hunters as well as Inca soldiers. They were made from braided llama wool. The stone was placed in a small cradle. Held at both ends, the sling was whirled around the head. When one end was released, the stone was projected to its mark with great accuracy. The injury inflicted by the stone could be fatal.

A BIRD IN THE HAND
The art of the ancient South American people shows us what their activities were. This wooden cup is painted with a scene of a man hunting birds.

BOW AND ARROW *right*
Bows, arrows, and spear-throwers (below) were weapons used originally in Central Mexico, and later introduced to the Maya area. Along with the javelin and the sling, the bow and arrow were used for hunting animals at long range.

The Maya caught fish in lagoons using a bow and arrow

NAZCA FOX
This fox was part of the decoration on a Nazca pot. Foxes were usually used to symbolize war, but they were also considered pests and were killed mainly with clubs.

SPEAR AND SPEARTHROWER
Spears (above) had a fire-hardened tip or a point made of chipped stone or obsidian. They were propelled by a spearthrower, or *atlatl* (below). This was a long piece of wood with a groove down the center.

Mesoamerican cities

THE PEOPLES OF MESOAMERICA built their cities in a variety of geographic and climatic areas. Some were built in the highlands, and others in jungles or coastal regions. The Olmecs built their cities in tropical regions, and the people of Teotihuacán, the Toltecs, and the Aztecs, in the highlands. The Mayas built their cities in both highland and lowland regions. These geographical differences influenced the architecture of the cities. As time passed, the cities grew in size. The Olmecs (1200 B.C.) lived in small cities, while Teotihuacán (A.D. 200) had an estimated 150,000 inhabitants or more. The central areas of Mesoamerican cities were reserved for religious and public buildings, and the houses of rulers and of the elite. The houses for the common people were built outside these areas.

CHICHEN ITZA
The Mayan city of Chichén Itzá was built in a strategic place in the center of the Yucatán Peninsula. It became an important commercial center which kept contact with many areas. It is thought that Toltec invaders established themselves there.

Temple-pyramid El Castillo at Chichén Itzá

TRIBUTE TOWNS
The Codex Mendoza (p. 67) gives the names of towns that paid tribute to Tenochtitlán, as well as the goods required. Each of these hieroglyphs (left) represents a subject town.

PALENQUE
This Mayan temple is situated in Palenque, in the midst of tropical jungle. Hidden in the pyramid was the funeral chamber of lord Pacal (p. 113), who ruled for 68 years and was buried in his magnificent resting place in A.D. 683. His sarcophagus contained some of the most beautiful jade objects ever found in Mesoamerica.

Temple of the Inscriptions at Palenque

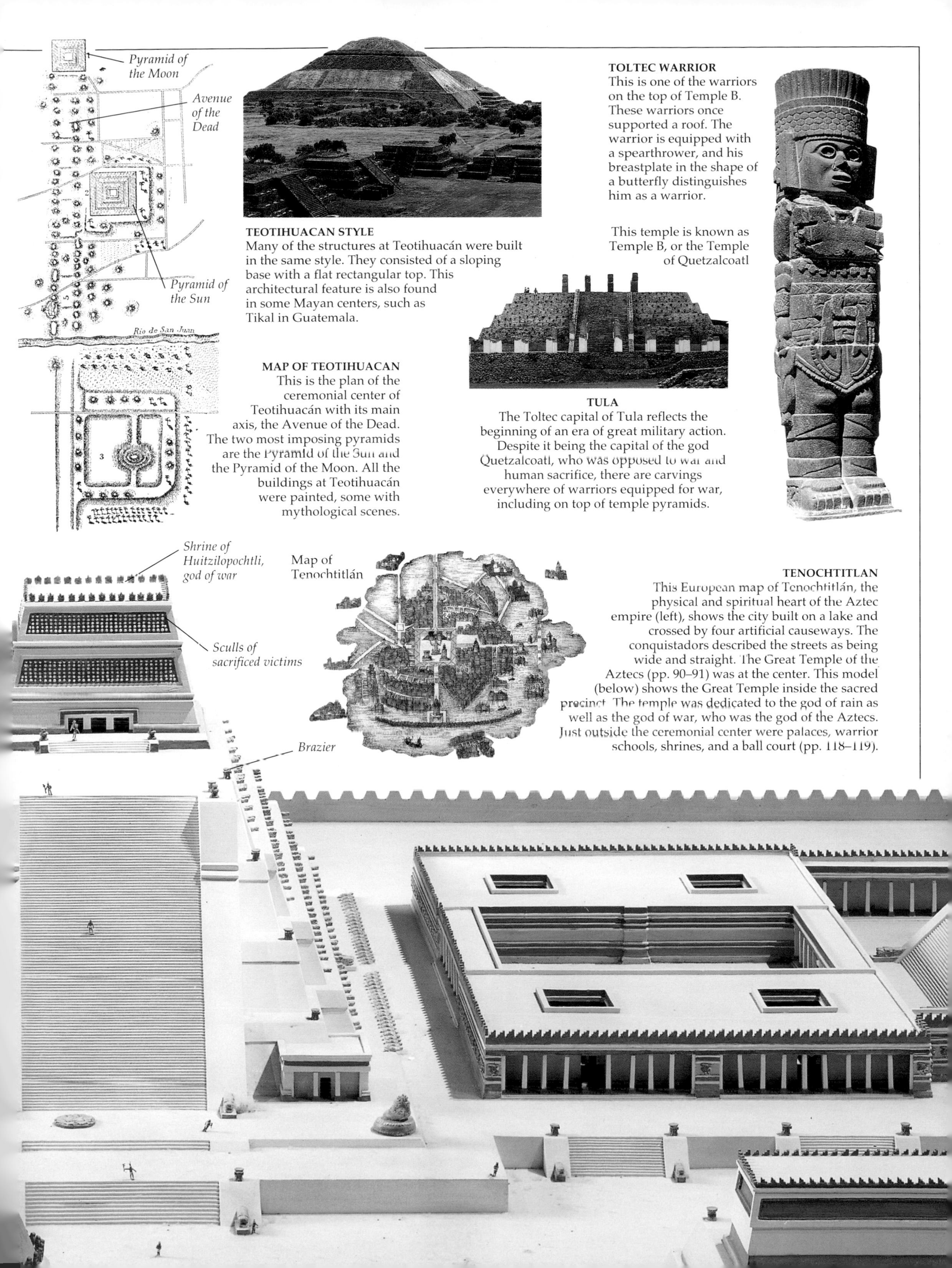

TEOTIHUACAN STYLE
Many of the structures at Teotihuacán were built in the same style. They consisted of a sloping base with a flat rectangular top. This architectural feature is also found in some Mayan centers, such as Tikal in Guatemala.

MAP OF TEOTIHUACAN
This is the plan of the ceremonial center of Teotihuacán with its main axis, the Avenue of the Dead. The two most imposing pyramids are the Pyramid of the Sun and the Pyramid of the Moon. All the buildings at Teotihuacán were painted, some with mythological scenes.

TOLTEC WARRIOR
This is one of the warriors on the top of Temple B. These warriors once supported a roof. The warrior is equipped with a spearthrower, and his breastplate in the shape of a butterfly distinguishes him as a warrior.

This temple is known as Temple B, or the Temple of Quetzalcoatl

TULA
The Toltec capital of Tula reflects the beginning of an era of great military action. Despite it being the capital of the god Quetzalcoatl, who was opposed to war and human sacrifice, there are carvings everywhere of warriors equipped for war, including on top of temple pyramids.

TENOCHTITLAN
This European map of Tenochtitlán, the physical and spiritual heart of the Aztec empire (left), shows the city built on a lake and crossed by four artificial causeways. The conquistadors described the streets as being wide and straight. The Great Temple of the Aztecs (pp. 90–91) was at the center. This model (below) shows the Great Temple inside the sacred precinct. The temple was dedicated to the god of rain as well as the god of war, who was the god of the Aztecs. Just outside the ceremonial center were palaces, warrior schools, shrines, and a ball court (pp. 118–119).

Cities of the Andes

Gateway of the Sun at Tiahuanaco

THE PEOPLE OF THE ANDEAN REGION lived in either highland or coastal areas. They built their cities to suit the location, from materials that were locally available. The typical highland building had a sloping thatched roof and stone walls. On the coast, buildings tended to have mud-brick (adobe) walls with painted mud plaster, and flat roofs. Highland cities such as Machu Picchu could not be built on a regular grid plan, in contrast to the cities in flat coastal areas, such as Chan Chan. The first buildings to be lived in as homes date to the 4th century B.C. Public constructions such as government buildings, storehouses, bridges, and canals were built by taxpayers as a kind of labor tax, with the state providing the materials.

OLLANTAYTAMBO
The Inca town of Ollantaytambo has some of the most impressive architectural remains in Peru. This doorway was built with rectangular blocks of stone. Each stone was precisely cut and fitted to a specific position.

INCA STONEMASONS
The Incas are renowned for their fine stonework. Huge stone blocks were cut by masons using just a stone hammer, and wet sand to polish them. The blocks fitted so closely that no mortar was needed.

TIAHUANACO
The city of Tiahuanaco (p. 70) is situated on a high plain nearly 13,100 ft (4,000 m) above sea level, rimmed by the mountains of the Andes. The stunning architecture of its ceremonial center included an impressive number of stone sculptures. The Gateway of the Sun (above) was carved from a single block of stone. A carving above the doorway portrays a sun god.

Bird motif on adobe wall of compound, Chan Chan

ADOBE DECORATION
The Chimu decorated their thick adobe (mud) walls with molded animals, usually associated with the sea – birds, fish, and men in boats.

Royal compound at Chan Chan, capital of the Chimu kingdom

CHAN CHAN
The Chimu people built urban centers; Chan Chan, the coastal capital of the Chimu empire, is a good example of this. The city was organized on a grid plan, and covered approximately 2.3 sq mi (6 sq km). It contained ten compounds, each enclosed by a high adobe (mud) wall. These are thought to be the royal residences and administrative centers of Chimu kings. Each king lived, died, and was buried in his secluded compound.

European map of Cuzco

CUZCO
The religious and political capital of the Incas is situated at the heart of the Andes with the mountains encircling it. The town was divided into sections by narrow paved streets, designed to represent the four quarters of the Inca empire. It had ceremonial plazas, palaces, and temples. Only the rulers and nobility lived in the city center. This European drawing wrongly portrays Cuzco as a walled town. Much of Cuzco was destroyed by the Spanish, who built their city on Inca ruins.

Stone walls of Sacsahuaman fort

SACSAHUAMAN FORT
Cuzco was protected from the enemy by the fortress of Sacsahuaman, built on a steep hill overlooking the city from the north. The fort was built with locally quarried stone, and each giant block was individually shaped. These three impressive stone walls – standing 52 ft (16 m) – guarded the fortress.

Inca baths at Tambo Machay

INCA BATHS
Inca palaces sometimes had sunken stone baths for the kings to relax and bathe in. Water ran along stone channels into the bath. These baths at Tambo Machay, near Cuzco, were built at the site of a sacred spring. They were used by the Inca kings.

Machu Picchu

MACHU PICCHU
Strategically positioned on the edge of the Inca empire, the remote city of Machu Picchu was probably built at the end of the 15th century. It was not discovered by the Spanish conquistadors, nor by other Westerners until 1911. The site is an outstanding example of Inca architecture – a natural fortress protected by steep slopes, surrounded by high mountain peaks, and approachable from only one point. Of its 143 granite buildings, about 80 were houses, the rest being ceremonial buildings such as temples. Many mummies were found at Machu Picchu, most of them of women.

COUPLE EMBRACING
In both Mesoamerica and the Andean region, a wife's role was to obey her husband. Even in art, women were often depicted in a passive position, and men in a more active position. This Mayan clay statue shows a man embracing a woman. Both wear elaborate headdresses, earplugs, and necklaces, which indicate that they were wealthy.

Family life

THE MESOAMERICAN MAN, as a husband and father, was responsible for the well-being of his household. He was expected to support his family, as well as his government, through hard work and by paying taxes. The woman, as a wife and mother, devoted her time and energy to running her household and caring for her children. Girls were taught domestic chores such as weaving and cooking, and sons followed their fathers while they worked. Children had free schooling, and nobles had their own schools. Family life was similar in the Andean region. The father worked to support the family and pay taxes; the mother worked in the home, helped her husband with his work, and cared for the children. Inca commoners had to educate their own children.

Figure has eyes and teeth inlaid with shell.

Aztec couple during marriage ceremony

JUST MARRIED
One of the rituals in an Aztec wedding ceremony was to tie the young man's cloak and the girl's blouse together. The wedding party followed, with dancing and singing.

FERTILE BLESSING
Both the Mesoamericans and the Incas considered it important for a married couple to have children. The Aztecs worshiped goddesses of fertility. This wooden Aztec sculpture is of a young woman dressed in a skirt and bare-breasted. She may be a goddess of fertility.

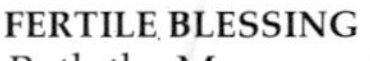

CELEBRATION
There were great celebrations when an Aztec baby was born. They lasted for days, during which astrologers checked to see when would be a favorable day for the baby to be named.

Stirrup handle

Woman giving birth, helped by two women

CHILDBIRTH SCENE
Women in the Andes were helped in childbirth by women who had given birth to twins, as well as by neighbors. There were no midwives. After birth the mother and baby washed in a river. The umbilical cord was not thrown away, but was kept in the house.

BRINGING UP BABIES
Family scenes are common in Aztec art, and show women performing various activities. This woman is carrying two children, one under each arm. One of the main roles of an Aztec woman was to bring up her children until they were ready to leave home and marry.

STEAM BATHS

Bathing was a part of the daily family routine of the Aztecs, both for keeping clean and for purification. Almost every home had a steam bath alongside it. The bathhouse was a small building that was heated by a fireplace. When water was thrown on the hot inside walls, the room filled with steam.

WOMAN CARRYING LOAD

The duties of women in the Andean region varied according to their rank. The woman depicted in this Moche vessel was probably a commoner's wife and was expected to help her husband when necessary. This included carrying heavy loads on her back. She wears a strap that passes around her forehead to hold the load on her back.

PUNISHMENT

From the age of 11 years, disobedient Aztec children were punished in various ways by their parents. Punishments included pricking their skin with spines and making them inhale chili smoke by holding them over a fire with chili peppers.

CHILD'S PLAY

Until they reached an age where they had to help their parents with their work, young children played in and around the home. This clay "toy" is in the form of a dog on wheels. "Toys" such as this one show that the Mesoamericans knew about the wheel. However, they used it for decorative purposes only. They did not use the wheel for practical purposes, such as on wagons to help them carry loads. "Toys" with wheels have been found mainly in graves in parts of the Gulf of Mexico. Toys in the form of dogs may have been thought to help the soul of the deceased to find his or her resting place in the afterlife.

At home

Maize cob used as cork

WATER GOURD
The gourd, a vegetable with a hard shell, was frequently used as a container after being dried out. Gourds were mainly used for carrying water. This type of gourd grows in most parts of the Americas.

THE AZTECS, MAYAS, AND INCAS lived in simple houses, many with only one main room and very little furniture. Inca houses were made of stone blocks or of mud (adobe), while most Aztec and Mayan houses were made of adobe. For the Aztecs, furniture was simply a few beds made of reed mats. There were also low tables, and reed chests for clothes. The Aztec home had an inside courtyard with a kitchen, and a small shrine to the gods. The bathroom was in a separate building. The homes of wealthy nobles and dignitaries had more rooms, more elaborate furniture, and a bigger garden.

Sharp wooden teeth

HANDY TOOL
Combs were made of bone or wood. They were used for hairdressing and, in South America, for preparing wool. Some were even used to make patterns on pottery.

INSIDE AN AZTEC HOUSE
An Aztec woman's home meant almost everything to her. She spent most of her day in the house, looking after the children, cooking, or weaving.

REED MAT
In Mesoamerica people sat, played, and slept on reed mats. This type of mat would have been used as a "rug" on the floor of most houses. It is thinner than the mats used as "beds." Both the rich and poor had mats such as this one.

MULTIPURPOSE POT
This pot was used to store liquids and food. It was often kept upright with a ring made of reeds.

Bowl has three sturdy legs

TRIPOD BOWL
Potters working in Teotihuacán often made three-legged bowls like this, sometimes with a lid. Everyday pots were usually plain, but others had a pattern cut into the surface, or painted on like this one.

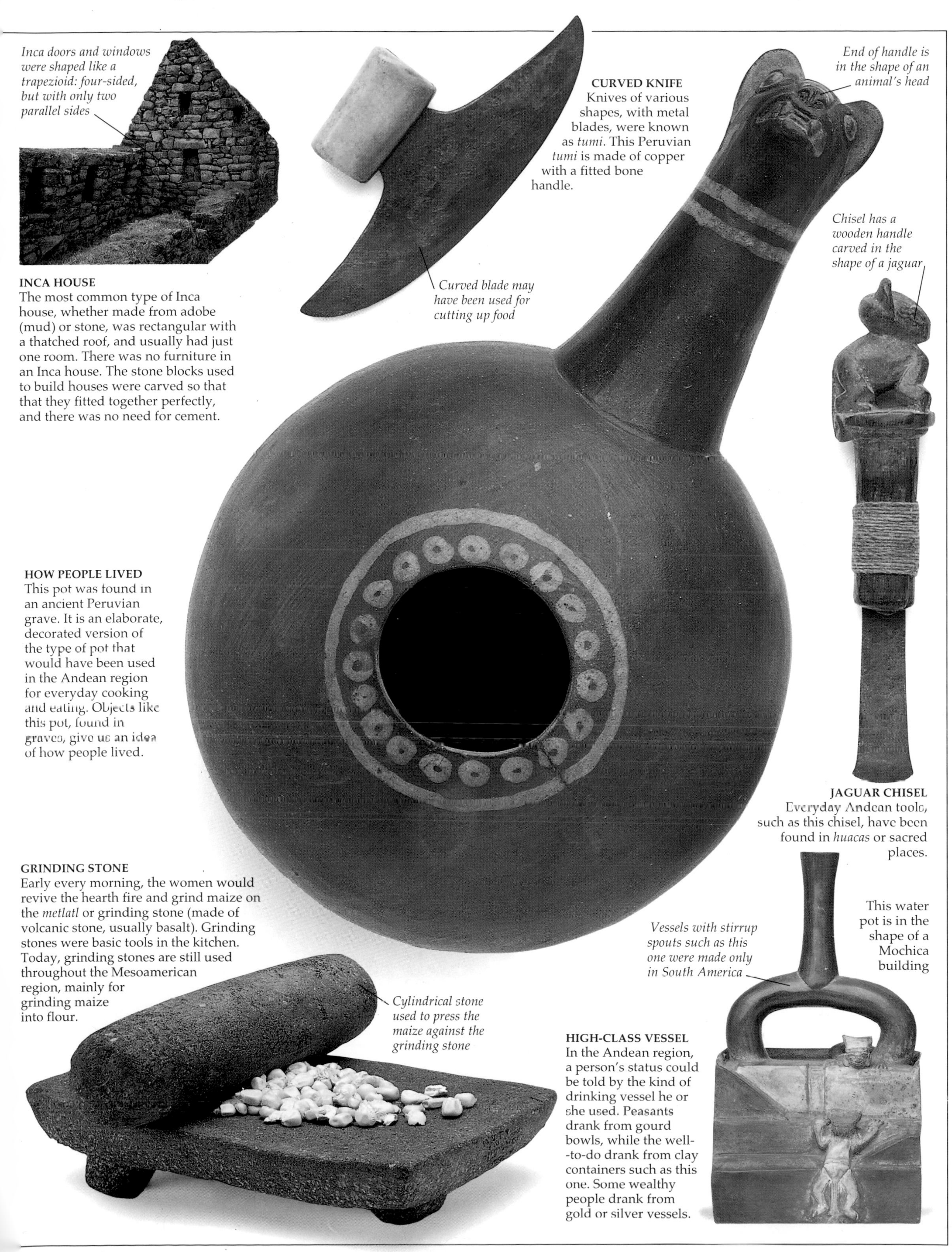

Inca doors and windows were shaped like a trapezoid: four-sided, but with only two parallel sides

INCA HOUSE
The most common type of Inca house, whether made from adobe (mud) or stone, was rectangular with a thatched roof, and usually had just one room. There was no furniture in an Inca house. The stone blocks used to build houses were carved so that that they fitted together perfectly, and there was no need for cement.

CURVED KNIFE
Knives of various shapes, with metal blades, were known as *tumi*. This Peruvian *tumi* is made of copper with a fitted bone handle.

Curved blade may have been used for cutting up food

End of handle is in the shape of an animal's head

Chisel has a wooden handle carved in the shape of a jaguar

HOW PEOPLE LIVED
This pot was found in an ancient Peruvian grave. It is an elaborate, decorated version of the type of pot that would have been used in the Andean region for everyday cooking and eating. Objects like this pot, found in graves, give us an idea of how people lived.

JAGUAR CHISEL
Everyday Andean tools, such as this chisel, have been found in *huacas* or sacred places.

GRINDING STONE
Early every morning, the women would revive the hearth fire and grind maize on the *metlatl* or grinding stone (made of volcanic stone, usually basalt). Grinding stones were basic tools in the kitchen. Today, grinding stones are still used throughout the Mesoamerican region, mainly for grinding maize into flour.

Cylindrical stone used to press the maize against the grinding stone

Vessels with stirrup spouts such as this one were made only in South America

This water pot is in the shape of a Mochica building

HIGH-CLASS VESSEL
In the Andean region, a person's status could be told by the kind of drinking vessel he or she used. Peasants drank from gourd bowls, while the well-to-do drank from clay containers such as this one. Some wealthy people drank from gold or silver vessels.

Food and drink

THE MESOAMERICANS AND ANDEANS ate simply. Maize was the central food in their diet, supplemented by other vegetables, such as beans and squashes, grown in both regions. Not all foods were grown in both regions, however. Potatoes and quinoa (a grain) came from the Andean region, while avocados and tomatoes were mainly consumed in Mesoamerica, along with all kinds of fruit. Maize was made into a sort of porridge called *atole* in Mesoamerica and *capia* in Inca territory. Maize cakes were often eaten in both regions, but only the Mesoamerican peoples ate maize *tortillas* (pancakes) with every meal. A favorite dish among Aztecs and Incas was *tamales*, a kind of envelope of steamed maize stuffed with vegetables or meat. In Mesoamerica the main meal was eaten during the hottest part of the day. In both regions, it was customary for everyone to eat twice a day.

Guinea pig meat was the only meat regularly eaten by the Andeans.

CACAO
A chocolate drink made from cacao was drunk by wealthy Mesoamericans. It was sweetened with honey and flavored with vanilla.

MORTAR AND PESTLE
Chilies and tomatoes were used for making sauces. They were crushed with a stone called a pestle in a mortar, which was a carved cylindrical stone with three little feet.

GRIDDLE WITH *TORTILLAS*
Once the *tortillas* have been made, they are cooked over the fire on a clay disk called a *comal*. *Tortillas* are still the central part of the Mesoamerican diet.

WOMEN PREPARING MAIZE
The preparation of maize was a daily task for the Mesoamerican housewife. This section of a painting by Mexican artist Diego Rivera shows a woman grinding the corn kernels into flour between a stone roller and slab. The flour is made into a dough, which another woman pats into *tortillas*.

LLAMA
The tender meat of the llama was eaten by the Incas and their ancestors. However, they ate it with moderation, as the llama was useful in many other ways.

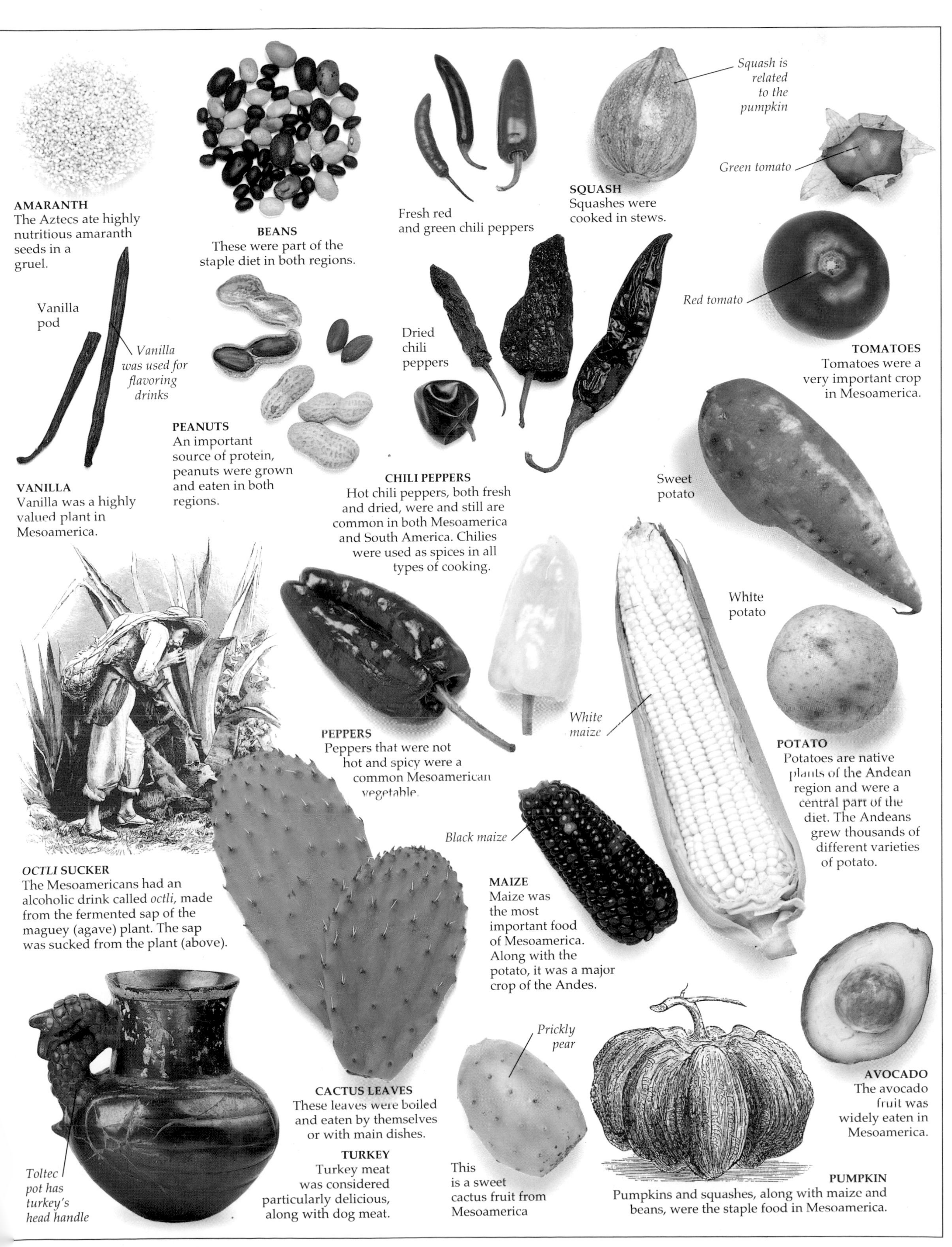

AMARANTH
The Aztecs ate highly nutritious amaranth seeds in a gruel.

BEANS
These were part of the staple diet in both regions.

SQUASH
Squashes were cooked in stews.

TOMATOES
Tomatoes were a very important crop in Mesoamerica.

PEANUTS
An important source of protein, peanuts were grown and eaten in both regions.

VANILLA
Vanilla was a highly valued plant in Mesoamerica.

CHILI PEPPERS
Hot chili peppers, both fresh and dried, were and still are common in both Mesoamerica and South America. Chilies were used as spices in all types of cooking.

PEPPERS
Peppers that were not hot and spicy were a common Mesoamerican vegetable.

POTATO
Potatoes are native plants of the Andean region and were a central part of the diet. The Andeans grew thousands of different varieties of potato.

***OCTLI* SUCKER**
The Mesoamericans had an alcoholic drink called *octli*, made from the fermented sap of the maguey (agave) plant. The sap was sucked from the plant (above).

MAIZE
Maize was the most important food of Mesoamerica. Along with the potato, it was a major crop of the Andes.

AVOCADO
The avocado fruit was widely eaten in Mesoamerica.

CACTUS LEAVES
These leaves were boiled and eaten by themselves or with main dishes.

TURKEY
Turkey meat was considered particularly delicious, along with dog meat.

PUMPKIN
Pumpkins and squashes, along with maize and beans, were the staple food in Mesoamerica.

Trade and tribute

IN MESOAMERICA and in the Andean region, it was the commoners who mainly supported the state by paying taxes. People of high rank did not pay taxes, nor did the sick and disabled, for example. In Inca territory, each province had to pay specific amounts of tribute to the government. At Tenochtitlán, the Aztec capital, the residents of each borough belonged to an institution called a *calpulli*, whose leader made sure that taxes were paid. Goods of all kinds were exchanged in both regions, and in Mesoamerica all the products of the land were sold in busy marketplaces. Aztec merchants went on long expeditions to distant lands to trade for such items as tropical feathers, gold, fine stones, and jaguar skins.

CODEX TRIBUTE
The goods paid as tribute to the Aztec rulers were recorded in books such as the Codex Mendoza.

Pottery bowl

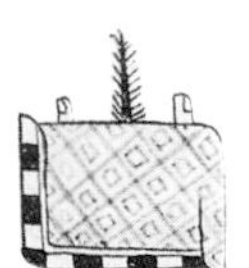

Simple cotton blankets

Heavily decorated cotton blankets

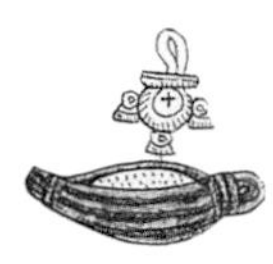

Bundle of copal incense

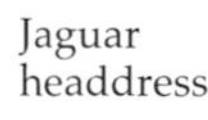

Pots of honey

Jaguar headdress

Bin with maize and chia seeds

Jaguar warrior's suit

Feather shield

RUNNER
This Moche pot depicts a runner. Runners, or *chasquis*, ran from one place to the next, usually carrying messages. The Incas had an excellent road system, which was essential for controlling the empire, for trade, and for communication.

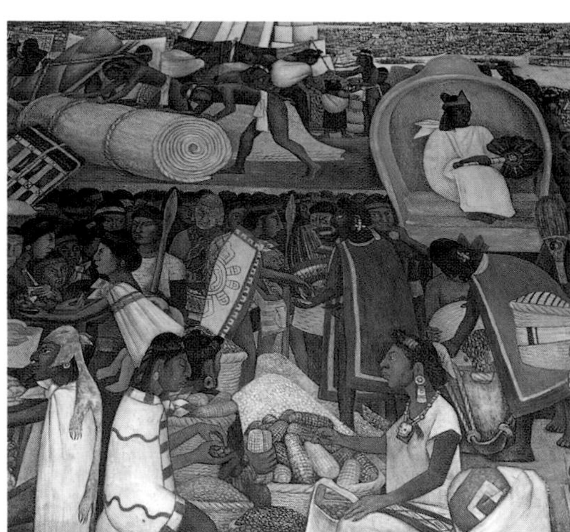

THE SALE OF MAIZE
Much can be learned from the murals of Diego Rivera about how the ancient Mexicans lived. Rivera, one of the most remarkable modern Mexican muralists, was well-read about life in Tenochtitlán. This detail of a busy market scene shows women selling various types of maize.

WARRIOR'S SUIT AND SHIELD
Tunics and shields were very expensive items of tribute. Tunics were either made of feather-covered material or of animal pelts. The jaguar helmet (left) was the warrior's insignia as well as his protection. According to the Codex Mendoza, tribute of this kind had to be paid once a year.

Ocelot skin

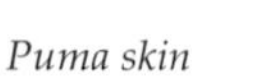

Puma skin

Jaguar skin

FUR TRADE
Animal skins were sold in the market at Tlatelolco. The skin of the puma was particularly valued by the Mayas, as its tawny color reminded them of the sun. Jaguar skins were equally valued. The black spots were thought to symbolize the night sky. Jaguar skins were used as seats for the rulers, as book covers, and as cloaks.

TLATELOLCO MARKET
When the Spanish arrived in Mexico, they found that the market at Tlatelolco (the sister city of Tenochtitlán) was bigger and better stocked than any market in Spain. Supervisors regulated prices, and judges were present in case of disputes or theft. Much of the buying and selling was done by barter – exchanging products – although copper axes sometimes served as money in both Mesoamerica and the Andes.

Inca treasurer records goods in storehouses on *quipu*.

Cacao beans

Melon seeds

Ax heads

Quetzal feather

Jade beads

Tropical bird feather

TRADING
Items such as cacao beans and feathers were in great demand, as vast quantities of each were used to pay tribute. The merchants from Tenochtitlán and neighboring major cities exported and traded luxury objects made from imported raw materials or materials obtained by tribute. In return for their goods they obtained other goods such as tropical feathers (especially quetzal feathers), cacao beans, animal skins, and gold.

INCA STOREHOUSES *left*
The Incas kept all kinds of supplies in storehouses used by government officials and those who were in need due to an illness, or after a crisis or a siege. They kept them full of items such as weapons, cloth, wool, potatoes, and maize.

Storing agricultural produce in government granaries

Simply decorated clay vessel for everyday use

All the pottery stalls were placed together in the market

Simple clay bowl

The market was a place where people exchanged news and goods

The warrior

WARFARE was a normal part of life in both Mesoamerica and the Inca region of South America, and city-states frequently fought each other. In Mesoamerica, youths had to join the army at the age of 17 for a period of intensive training. The Inca and Mesoamerican peoples were educated in the arts of war, and the fighting spirit was encouraged. Among the Aztecs the best and most common way to climb the social ladder was by showing courage in battle. One of the main aims of going to war was to capture enemy warriors for sacrifice. Aztec warriors were in a constant "sacred war," as they believed that human sacrifice kept the sun in motion (pp. 96–97). Both the Incas and the Aztecs added newly conquered areas to their empires. As power and wealth grew, they developed a thirst for more conquests that would enrich the state and add to the glory of the emperor.

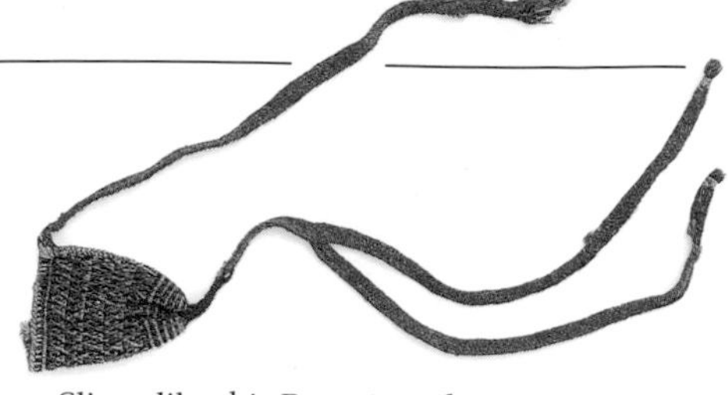

Slings like this Peruvian Chancay woven one, made from wool and cotton, were used in warfare. Warriors used stones as missiles.

TOLTEC WARRIOR
This sculpture shows a richly attired Toltec warrior wearing a feather headdress, earplugs, and a butterfly breastplate. In one hand he carries an *atlatl*, or spearthrower, and in the other a sheaf of darts.

CAPTURED
Aztec warriors who took captives were awarded costumes with distinctive designs, such as jaguar costumes and mantles. The more captives they took, the more elaborate was the costume.

AZTEC WEAPONS
A warrior usually carried spears of wood, with the blade edged with chert or obsidian, and a *maquahuitl* or war club made of wood, also, which was about 30 in (76 cm) in length. It had grooved sides set with sharp obsidian blades. Warriors also carried stabbing javelins and round shields with protective feather fringes. Flint and obsidian knives such as these (left) were also used for human sacrifices.

Flint knife has a sharp serrated edge

Long, razor-sharp knife made from obsidian

OBSIDIAN WOODEN CLUB *below*
One of the main weapons used by the Aztecs was a *maquahuitl*, a wooden club edged with obsidian blades. Obsidian is a volcanic glass that is sharp enough to sever a horse's head.

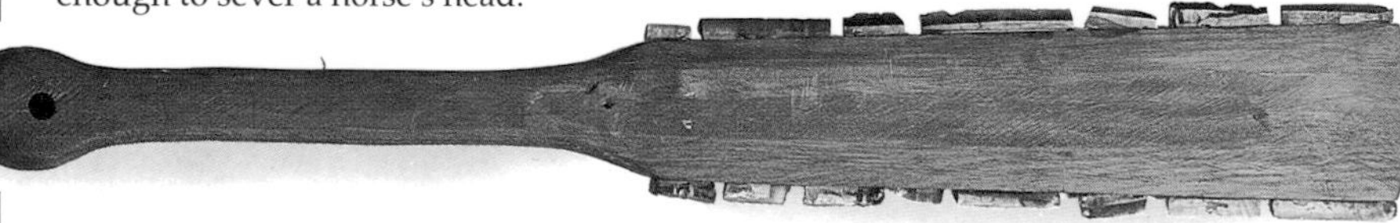

Club

EFFIGY POT
The Moche culture from the north coast of Peru often depicted warriors, such as this warrior holding a club, on clay vessels. Shields were often shown strapped to the wrist.

OBSIDIAN SPEAR *below*
A warrior usually carried one or two throwing spears of wood, the blades edged with flakes of sharp stone capable of inflicting deep cuts.

Obsidian blades around edge of spear

The Aztec Warrior

The ideal Aztec warrior was noble and brave, and had to serve and respect the gods. Warriors were so important in Aztec Mexico that the Aztec ruler had to start his rule on the battlefield, adding cities and provinces to the empire, and capturing prisoners for ritual sacrifice, an essential part of the Aztec religion.

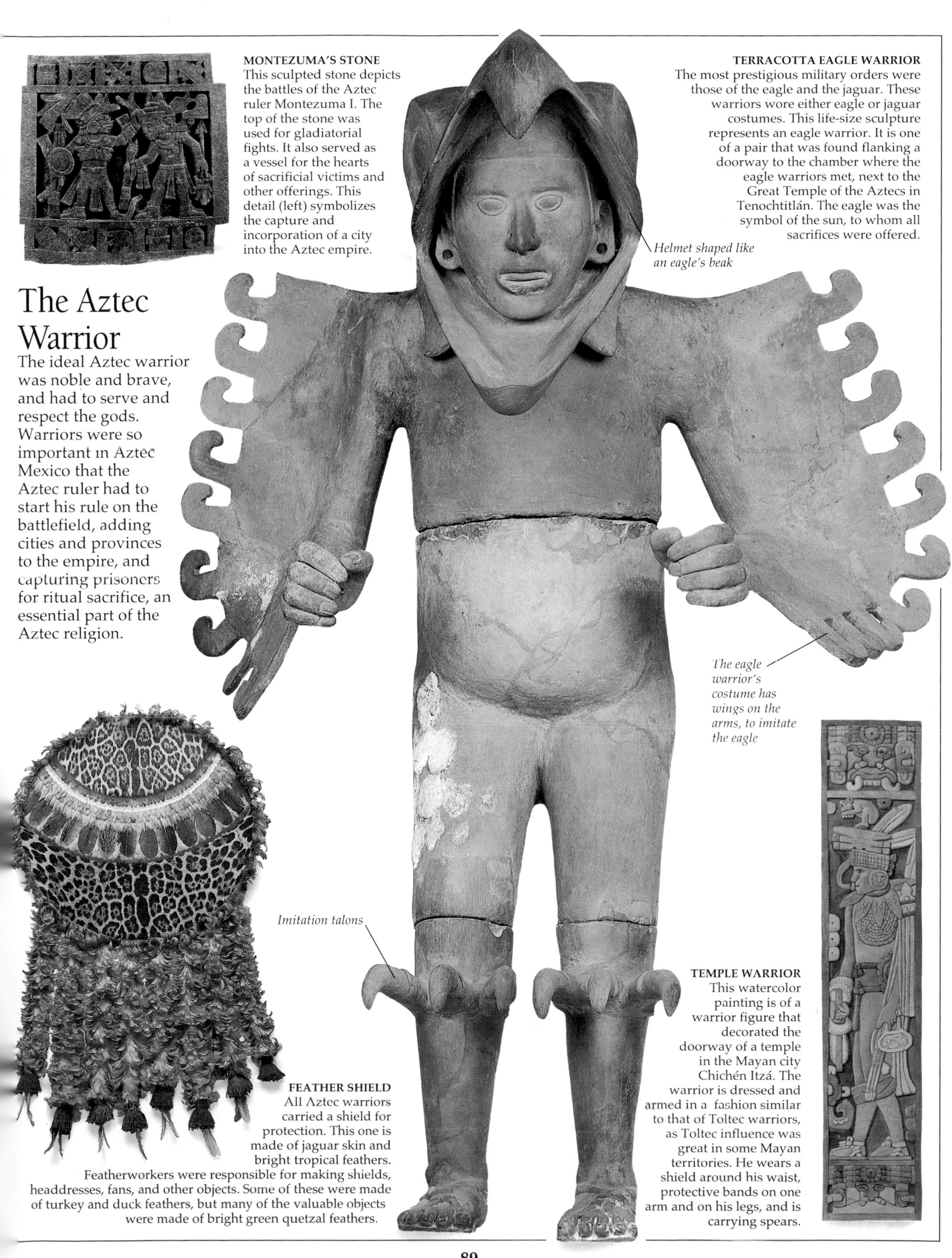

MONTEZUMA'S STONE
This sculpted stone depicts the battles of the Aztec ruler Montezuma I. The top of the stone was used for gladiatorial fights. It also served as a vessel for the hearts of sacrificial victims and other offerings. This detail (left) symbolizes the capture and incorporation of a city into the Aztec empire.

TERRACOTTA EAGLE WARRIOR
The most prestigious military orders were those of the eagle and the jaguar. These warriors wore either eagle or jaguar costumes. This life-size sculpture represents an eagle warrior. It is one of a pair that was found flanking a doorway to the chamber where the eagle warriors met, next to the Great Temple of the Aztecs in Tenochtitlán. The eagle was the symbol of the sun, to whom all sacrifices were offered.

Helmet shaped like an eagle's beak

The eagle warrior's costume has wings on the arms, to imitate the eagle

Imitation talons

FEATHER SHIELD
All Aztec warriors carried a shield for protection. This one is made of jaguar skin and bright tropical feathers. Featherworkers were responsible for making shields, headdresses, fans, and other objects. Some of these were made of turkey and duck feathers, but many of the valuable objects were made of bright green quetzal feathers.

TEMPLE WARRIOR
This watercolor painting is of a warrior figure that decorated the doorway of a temple in the Mayan city Chichén Itzá. The warrior is dressed and armed in a fashion similar to that of Toltec warriors, as Toltec influence was great in some Mayan territories. He wears a shield around his waist, protective bands on one arm and on his legs, and is carrying spears.

Religious life

Codex illustration of an Aztec temple at Tenochtitlán

RELIGION TOUCHED almost every aspect of Mesoamerican and Inca life. One of the many focal points for the religious rites was sacred buildings, or temples, dedicated to the gods. In the Andean region people worshiped a variety of shrines and objects and the natural forces associated with them, known as *huacas*. The Aztecs also worshiped sacred places. Within the official Inca state religion the sun was the most important god. It was a dominant force and a symbol of prestige and power. The Incas worshiped the sun mainly so that they would have abundant crops. The Aztec religion was also concerned with the sun. The Aztecs believed that they lived in the era of the fifth sun and that one day the world would end violently. In order to postpone their destruction, men performed human sacrifices. Their duty was to feed the gods with human blood, thereby keeping the sun alive.

TEMPLE OF THE GIANT JAGUAR
To worship their gods, the Mayans built magnificent ceremonial centers filled with temples, courts, and plazas. This majestic temple in Tikal stands in the middle of its ceremonial center. It is a giant temple-pyramid with nine sloping terraces. The ornamental roof comb perched on the temple roof soars to a height of 528 ft (161 ft).

Intihuatana *means "hitching post of the sun"*

STONE OF *INTIHUATANA*
The principal Inca temples for the cult of the sun were built by the government throughout the Inca empire. This stone in Machu Picchu worked as a solar clock and allowed people to calculate the winter solstice (21st of June) for the important festival of the sun god.

Priests performing rituals in a temple during "new fire" ceremony

AZTEC "NEW FIRE" CEREMONY
This religious event took place in temples every 52 years. When the day arrived, people extinguished all fires, and discarded idols and household utensils. The new "century" began when the sun's rays appeared again at dawn.

After sacrifice, bodies of sacrificial victims thrown down stairs

MODEL OF THE GREAT TEMPLE AT TENOCHTITLAN
At the heart of the city of Tenochtitlán was a walled precinct. Within it, sharing a single tall pyramid, were the twin shrines dedicated to Tlaloc, the god of rain, and Huitzilopochtli, god of war and the tribal god of the Aztecs. The Great Temple was the physical and symbolic center of the Aztec world, where human sacrifices and offerings to the Aztec gods took place. Each Aztec ruler tried to make a bigger and more impressive new temple. This model shows the many temples that were built, one above the other. The oldest, inner temple has a chacmool (a statue with a receptacle for hearts and blood) on the left and a sacrificial stone on the right. The excavators of the site found more than 6,000 objects buried as offerings to Tlaloc and Huitzilopochtli.

SKULL PANEL
Real skulls were placed outside temples in skull racks, or *tzompantlis*. This panel of skulls is from the Great Temple of the Aztecs. They were usually the skulls of people sacrificed to the gods.

RECLINING CHACMOOL
This reclining figure was found at the entrance of the shrine to Tlaloc at the summit of the Great Temple of Tenochtitlán. He holds a container for the hearts and blood of people sacrificed to the gods of rain and agriculture.

Gods and goddesses

Aztec god from Codex Florentino

THE MESOAMERICAN and Inca people both worshiped many gods. They had similar religions – based mainly on the worship of agricultural gods – even though the gods' names and the symbols for them were different. People asked their gods for good crops and good health or for their welfare. The main Inca god was the creator god Viracocha. His assistants were the gods of the sun, moon, stars, and thunder, as well as the gods of the earth and the sea. As farming occupied such an important place in both regions, the "earth mother," or earth goddess, was particularly important. The Aztecs adopted many gods from other civilizations. As with the Incas, each god was connected with some aspect of nature or natural force.

God of springtime, wearing the skin of a sacrificial victim

RAIN GOD
Many Mesoamerican vessels and sculptures are associated with Tlaloc, the god of rain and agricultural fertility. It is likely that this water vessel depicts the face of the god of rain, as it contains the vital liquid necessary to fertilize the earth.

Tlaloc had "goggle eyes"

GOD OF THE SPRINGTIME
The Aztec god of the springtime and of vegetation was called Xipe Totec (Our Flayed Lord). He was also the patron of metal workers. The victims sacrificed in honor of this god were flayed (skinned alive). After flaying the victim, priests would wear the victim's skin. This symbolized the annual spring renewal of vegetation – in other words, the renewal of the "earth's skin."

Xipe Totec, god of springtime and of vegetation

Feathered serpent, Quetzalcoatl

Rain god, Tlaloc

Reconstruction of temple of Quetzalcoatl in Teotihuacán

GOD OF NATURE
Quetzalcoatl, whose name means feathered serpent, was a god of nature – of the air, and of earth. The temple of Quetzalcoatl at Teotihuacán is decorated with large sculptures of feathered serpents, as this reconstruction shows.

Chicomecoatl wore a four-sided paper headdress with pleated rosettes at the corners

AZTEC MAIZE GODDESSES
There were three goddesses associated with maize. This statue is of Chicomecoatl, the goddess of mature maize. This was the best seed corn of the harvest, which was put away for sowing. There was also a goddess of tender maize, and one who was the personification of the maize plant.

Double maize cobs

WAR GOD
Huitzilopochtli (the Hummingbird of the left) was the tribal god of the Aztecs. In this illustration we see him armed with his serpent of fire and his shield.

GOD OF THE DEAD
Mictlantecuhtli was god of the dead in Aztec Mexico. Those who died a natural death went to the Mictlan, where he lived, in the cold and infernal region of the fleshless.

The Inca people worshiped the moon and the sun

SEPTEMBER FESTIVAL
The Incas celebrated different religious festivities every month of the year. Here we see the celebrations for September dedicated to female goddesses. This festivity was celebrated under the protection of the moon and the sun gods.

WORSHIPING THE SUN
The Incas worshiped the sun, Inti. Most agricultural religions included worship of both the sun and the rain, as they are both essential for good harvests. The sun was the most important god of the Inca royal dynasty. Inca kings believed that they were descendants of Inti.

Gold disk

SKY OR MOON GOD
The handle of this Peruvian ceremonial knife is decorated with the image of either the sky or the moon god. His arms are opened wide, and he is holding two disks. He wears a beautiful filigree headdress with turquoise inlay.

Turquoise was used for the inlays of the eyes, necklace, earplugs, and the clothing

Chac carries a bowl in his right hand and a ball of smoking incense in his left.

MAYA GOD OF RAIN
The Maya god of rain was called Chac. One of the sacrifices in honor of this god was to drown children in wells. In some Maya regions the god of rain was so important that the facades of buildings were covered with masks of Chac.

Chancay "doll" found in grave

Life after death

THE PEOPLE OF Mesoamerica and South America believed that after they died they would go on living in another world. They were buried with goods of all descriptions that would be of use to them. By studying the goods found in graves, pre-Hispanic codices, and early colonial manuscripts, archaeologists have pieced together some of the beliefs about death and the afterlife. It was the way that Aztecs died, rather than the way they lived, that decided what would happen to them in the afterlife. If a person died a normal death, his or her soul had to pass through the nine levels of the underworld before reaching Mictlan, the realm of the death god. Warriors who died in battle and women who died in childbirth, however, joined the sun god in the sky.

DOLL COMPANION
Colorful figures found in Chancay tombs, such as this one, are called "dolls" because it is believed that they were used in daily life. They were placed with the deceased to serve them in the afterlife.

ALL WRAPPED UP
Many mummy bundles such as this one have been discovered in the Andean region. The corpse was placed in a flexed position and bound with cord to help maintain the pose. It was then wrapped in textiles and seated upright. Goods were placed around the mummy in the grave.

MUMMY OF DEAD KING
In Andean society, mummies were looked after as if they were alive. The living often consulted their dead in important matters. At special festivals, the mummies of emperors were paraded in the streets.

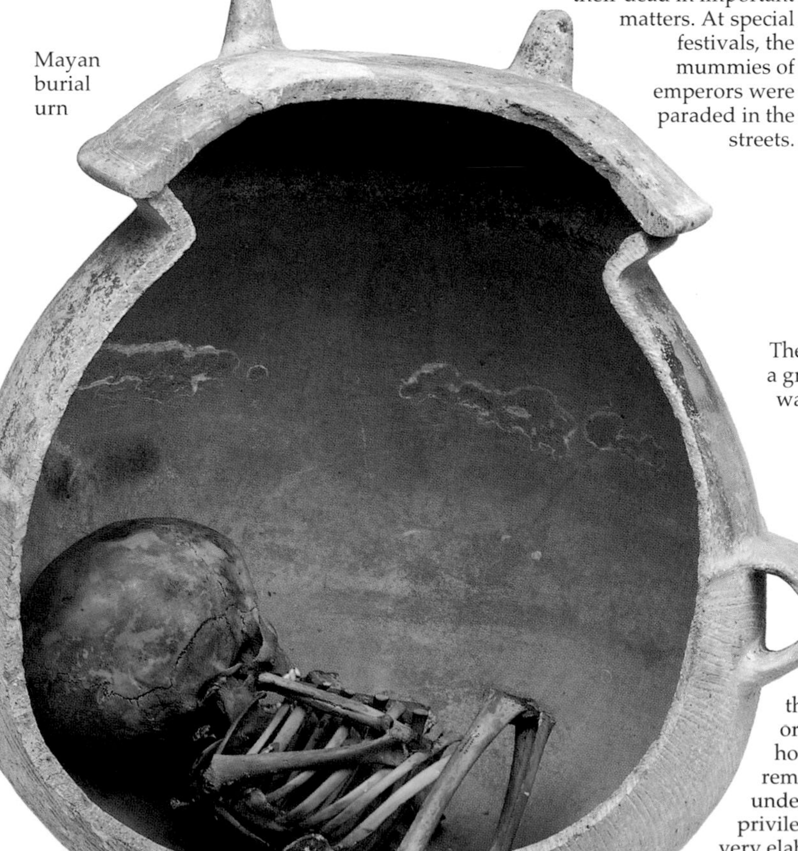

Mayan burial urn

THE RICH AND THE POOR
The more goods that were placed in a grave, the better-off the individual was. Wooden figurines such as this one of a man have been found in many Andean tombs. But tombs filled with golden objects, and more elaborately prepared corpses, indicate that everyone was not equal.

MAYAN BURIAL
The Mayas usually buried their dead under house floors or in the ground. Sometimes, however, they cremated the remains or buried them in caves, underground tanks, or urns. The privileged classes were buried in very elaborate tombs. One common type of burial for children was to place the corpse in a large urn, covered by a tripod (three-legged) vessel or pot fragment.

ALL DRESSED UP
Some corpses were much better prepared and dressed than others, depending on the person's status. The bodies of people of high status were wrapped in beautiful textiles.

Peruvian mummy bundle from Ancón

MIXTEC MUMMY BUNDLE
Mesoamerican mummies were wrapped in a similar way to those from South America. A mask was attached to the face of the mummy. The mask was usually made of stone but some masks were made of wood. People thought these masks would protect the deceased from the dangers of the afterlife.

RITES OF DEATH
This codex illustration shows an Aztec ritual in which the limbs of a sacrificial victim are being eaten by the victim's captor. This is being carried out in the presence of a mummified body.

MUMMY CLOTH
Due to the dry climate of the north coast region of Peru, all the paraphernalia attached to mummies found in this region has been beautifully preserved. This woolen mummy cloth bearing the figure of a god with arms outstretched is a typical Peruvian mummy adornment.

Human sacrifice

SACRIFICE WAS A RELIGIOUS RITUAL in Mesoamerica and in the Inca region of South America. The Incas and the Aztecs held special ceremonies that involved sacrifice in temples or on mountaintops. The Mayas sometimes sacrificed victims in wells. Priests performed the sacrifices, which took place at important festivals throughout the year. The Incas practiced human sacrifice in serious crises and for special events. For the Aztecs, sacrifice was more widespread and more frequent. The victims were men, women, and children – and sometimes animals. It was common for the Incas to ritually strangle women, while the Mayas sometimes drowned their victims and the Aztecs removed the victim's heart. Most sacrifices were performed in honor of the sun, rain, and earth gods. Human sacrifice was a communion with the gods: it was necessary to feed them to keep the cosmic order. People believed that just as the gods sacrificed themselves during the creation of the sun and the moon, they had to do the same.

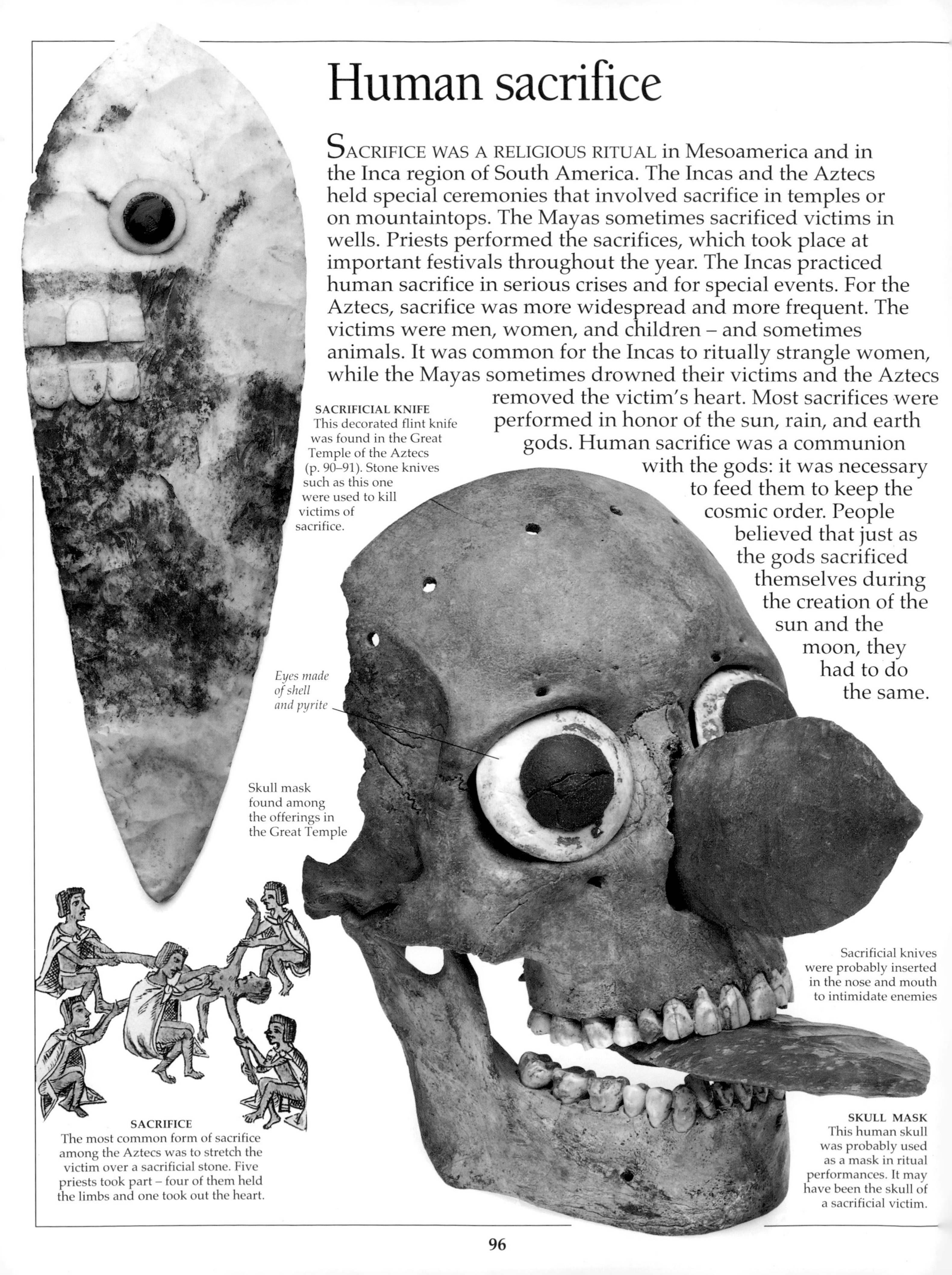

SACRIFICIAL KNIFE
This decorated flint knife was found in the Great Temple of the Aztecs (p. 90–91). Stone knives such as this one were used to kill victims of sacrifice.

Eyes made of shell and pyrite

Skull mask found among the offerings in the Great Temple

Sacrificial knives were probably inserted in the nose and mouth to intimidate enemies

SACRIFICE
The most common form of sacrifice among the Aztecs was to stretch the victim over a sacrificial stone. Five priests took part – four of them held the limbs and one took out the heart.

SKULL MASK
This human skull was probably used as a mask in ritual performances. It may have been the skull of a sacrificial victim.

AFTER SACRIFICE
Once an Aztec priest had taken the heart out, it was placed in a receptacle, such as the one below. The victim was then thrown down the temple stairs. The body was picked up and part of it, such as the thigh, was given as a reward to the victim's captor. The Aztecs practiced cannibalism in some religious ceremonies under strict regulations. For example, enemy captives were ritually eaten, but only legs or arms could be consumed.

Illustration from Codex Magliabecchiano

The skull symbol often appears in Aztec art

PRECIOUS HEART
This beautifully carved greenstone heart represents the most precious organ that the Aztecs could offer to their gods. Likewise, jade was considered the most valuable stone and the most precious material, far more so than gold. Jade was the symbol for life and agriculture.

SACRIFICIAL STONES AND VESSELS
This ritual vessel (right) may have been intended to contain the blood or the hearts of sacrificial victims. The outer surface is decorated with skulls. The skull was a symbol for fame, glory, or defeat depending on the situation. The stone below is one kind of stone that was used for the act of sacrifice. The victim would have been stretched over this stone while having his heart plucked out.

MOUNTAIN TOP SACRIFICE
This ornate Moche water pot depicts men sitting high up in the mountain peaks. Mountaintops were sacred places. Here people worshipped the earth gods, who were the providers of water and agriculture, and made human sacrifices to them. Water was considered to be the blood of agricultural life. Human sacrifices were performed for many reasons. They were generally considered a present to the gods in exchange for a favor requested – such as a good harvest. Those who were sacrificed were thought to be fortunate, since they were guaranteed a life of ease in the world to come.

High mountains and volcanoes were important places for sacred rituals

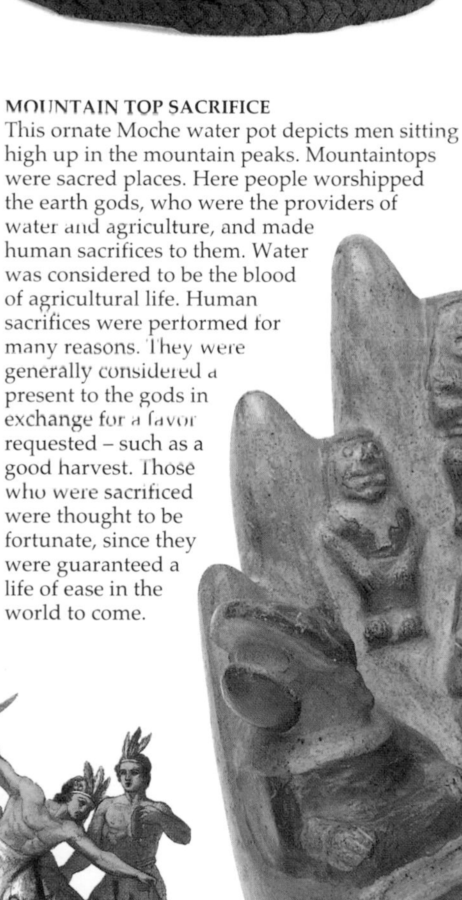

FLAYED ALIVE
This 19th-century illustration shows human sacrifice by flaying, or skinning a man alive. The ancient Peruvians performed this kind of ritual sacrifice. Skinning was also practiced by the ancient Mexicans during agricultural festivities. Like the ancient Mexicans, the ancient Peruvians had many sacrificial victims dedicated to the sun Inti or to the creator god Viracocha.

Medicine

Bather resting in steam bath

Taking a steam bath was part of the treatment to cure the sick in Mesoamerica.

In Mesoamerica and in the Andean cultures, treatments for illnesses were based on a mixture of magic and a certain knowledge of the body. Mesoamerican midwives, healers, and physicians were often women who were well versed in the use of herbs. The Andeans believed that disease had a supernatural cause. They treated the sick with herbs for both magical and medicinal reasons. The Aztecs used certain minerals for medicine, as well as the flesh of some animals. The Incas used urine for treating fever, and often bled themselves. Inca surgeons bored holes in the skull and amputated limbs when necessary. Both Mesoamericans and Andeans used obsidian knives and lancets for surgery.

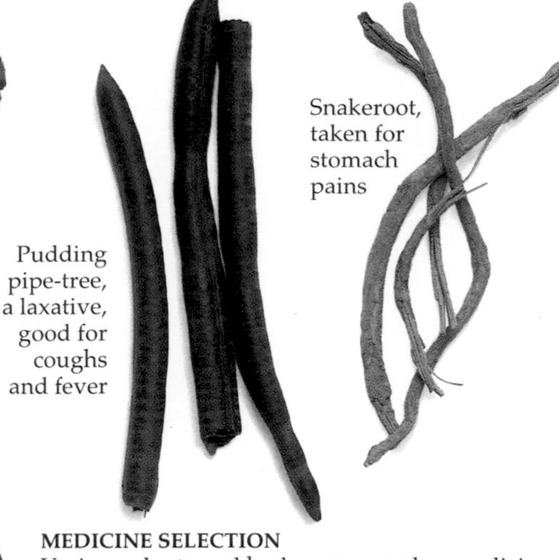

Pudding pipe-tree, a laxative, good for coughs and fever

Snakeroot, taken for stomach pains

MEDICINE SELECTION
Various plants and herbs were used as medicine. This root (left) was taken for rheumatism, and to treat bites of poisonous animals. Some roots were particularly useful for treating kidney complaints, and round beans (below) were taken for circulation ailments. Quinine (from the bark of a Peruvian tree), despite its bitter taste, was taken to prevent and treat malaria.

Rabbit fern, good for treating rheumatism

Palm nuts, good for circulation

Quinine, taken for malaria

BANDAGING A LEG
Physicians had a good knowledge of the body, and they were often right in their diagnoses. This Aztec surgeon is bandaging an injured leg.

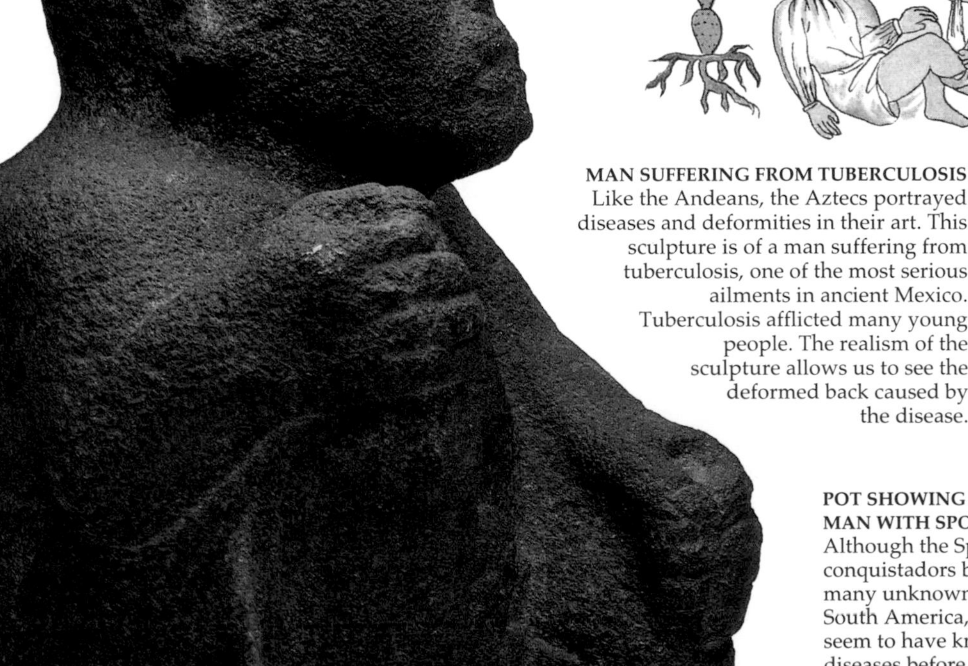

MAN SUFFERING FROM TUBERCULOSIS
Like the Andeans, the Aztecs portrayed diseases and deformities in their art. This sculpture is of a man suffering from tuberculosis, one of the most serious ailments in ancient Mexico. Tuberculosis afflicted many young people. The realism of the sculpture allows us to see the deformed back caused by the disease.

POT SHOWING MAN WITH SPOTS
Although the Spanish conquistadors brought many unknown diseases into South America, the Andeans seem to have known some serious diseases before their arrival. Examples of some diseases were *uta* (a kind of leprosy) and syphilis. The man portrayed on this Chancay vessel may have suffered from either disease.

MARKET MEDICINE STALL

In Mesoamerica, wild plants and herbs were cultivated in botanical gardens for medicinal purposes and sold in markets. There were roots, seeds, maguey leaves, *copal* resin, and all kinds of plants for treating a range of ailments from snake bites to gout and fever. The ancient Mexicans believed that *copal* smoke cured diseases. Tobacco powder was inhaled by the Andeans to help clear the head, but in Mesoamerica it was also smoked for pleasure. Many seeds and roots were combined with vanilla, cocoa, and maize to make the medicine more palatable although many of these flavorings were considered medicinal in their own right.

CACTUS TOPS

Some plants and seeds, such as *ololiuhqui* seeds (morning glory), were taken by the ancient Mexicans for medicinal purposes. These seeds as well as *peyote* (above), or cactus tops, from northern Mexico were widely taken as drugs. People who ate them experienced colorful hallucinations. Drugs causing hallucinations were also consumed in order for people to communicate with the gods.

Writing and counting

ANCIENT AZTEC GODS
According to Aztec mythology the most ancient gods and the creators of the universe were "Lord and Lady of our sustenance". They are associated with time and the calendar.

BOTH THE MESOAMERICAN people and the ancient Peruvians kept records. However, what they recorded and how they did this was very different. Mesoamerican cultures had a picture-writing system and kept details of their history and administration; the Peruvians had no written records. The Incas recorded information about tribute (p. 87) and goods in storage upon the *quipu*, an arrangement of knotted strings. Many Mesoamerican pictures (or glyphs) were pictograms, where an object was represented by a drawing. These glyphs also described ideas; for example, a shield and a club signified war. This kind of writing has been kept in books (called codices), painted on walls and vases, and carved into objects ranging from stone monuments to tiny pieces of jade. The Mesoamericans were obsessed by counting, and the passage of time. Both the Aztecs and the Maya devised a *vigesimal* counting system, based on the unit 20, and had two calendars, the solar calendar and the sacred almanac.

HIGH SOCIETY
Only the elite, a small fraction of Mesoamerican society, could read and interpret written records. This Maya woman is reading a book on her knee.

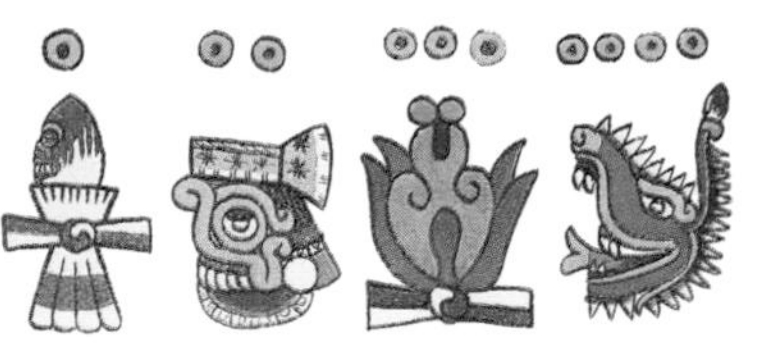

AZTEC DAYS OF THE MONTH
The Aztec solar calendar year was 365 days long. It consisted of 18 months of 20 days and five extra days that were thought to be unlucky. This illustration shows four days of the month – flint knife, rain, flower, and alligator.

Quipus were used to record the census and for taxation purposes

Numbers recorded with knots of varying sizes

INCA COUNTING DEVICE
The *quipu* was a length of cord held horizontally, from which knotted strings of various thicknesses and colors hung vertically. The information recorded varied according to the types of knots, the length of the cord, and the color and position of the strings.

MAYA PAINTED BOOK
There are four Maya codices in existence. This one, the Codex Tro-Cortesianus, contains information about divination (predicting the future) and rituals for Maya priests. Codices were made of carefully prepared paper, cloth made from fibres of the maguey plant, or animal skin. The Maya codices were written or painted with fine brushes on long strips of bark paper, folded like screens and covered with a layer of chalky paste (gesso).

INCA ACCOUNTANT
A special accountant was in charge of keeping records. He was skilled in recording figures, whether of people, llamas, or what tribute was to be paid.

Facsimile copy of original Codex Tro-Cortesianus

AZTEC SUN STONE
This stone is the largest Aztec sculpture ever found, measuring 13.2 ft (4 m) in diameter. At the center of the stone is the face of the sun, or that of the lord of the earth. This carving is sometimes called the "Calendar Stone". In fact, it represents the Aztec belief that the universe had passed through four world creations, which had been destroyed. We are now in the fifth, doomed to be destroyed by earthquakes. According to Aztec mythology, the sun, the moon, and human beings were successfully created at the beginning of the fifth era.

BUNDLE OF YEARS
The Aztecs divided time into "centuries" of 52 years. At the end of each cycle and the beginning of a new one an Aztec ceremony called "the binding of the years" took place. In sculpture each cycle is represented by a bundle of "reeds" accompanied by dates. This sculpted stone bundle symbolizes the death of an Aztec century.

RIDDLE OF THE GLYPHS
The study of Maya hieroglyphic writing started in 1827. By 1950, names of gods and animals had been identified. In 1960, researchers realized that Maya inscriptions were primarily historical. They deal with the births, accessions, wars, deaths, and marriages of Maya kings. This Maya stone carving was placed over doors and windows. It has a glyph that dates it to the sixth century.

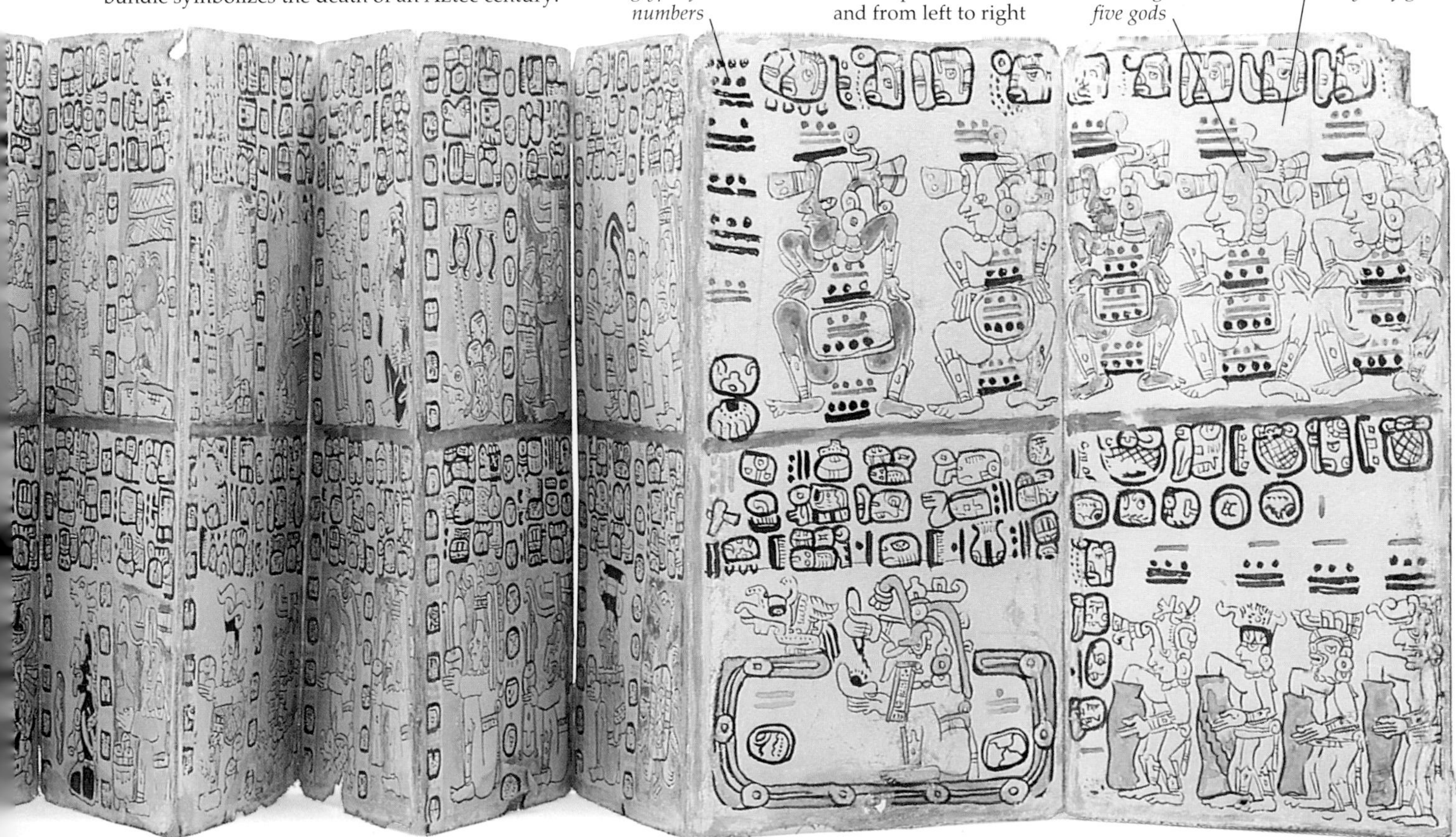

Weaving and spinning

Much of the sophisticated Andean weaving was made on the back-strap loom

Nazca textile with fringed border

NO OTHER PEOPLE in the Americas have left such a wealth of marvelous woven textiles as the ancient Peruvians have. Their exquisitely worked textiles have survived in graves in areas of Peru that have a desert-like climate. The tradition of weaving and spinning was practiced by all women, both in Mesoamerica and in the Andean region. Women were expected to spin and weave for their families' needs, and to contribute woven goods as payment of tribute and taxes to the rulers. Textiles were woven mainly from cotton and maguey fiber in Mesoamerica, while alpaca and llama wool were widely used in the Andean region.

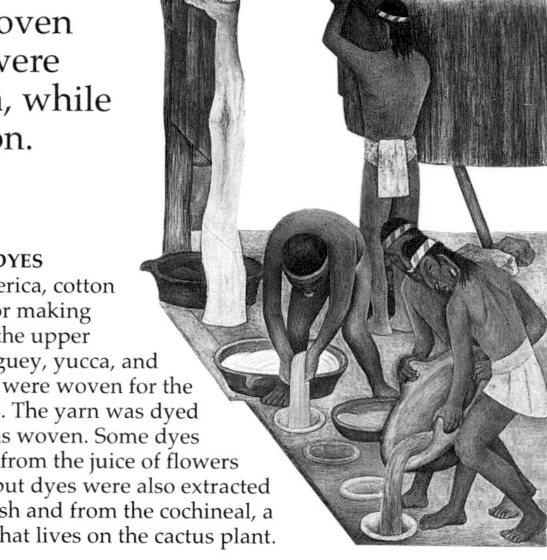

NATURAL DYES
In Mesoamerica, cotton was used for making textiles for the upper classes; maguey, yucca, and palm fibers were woven for the commoners. The yarn was dyed before it was woven. Some dyes were made from the juice of flowers and fruits, but dyes were also extracted from shellfish and from the cochineal, a tiny insect that lives on the cactus plant.

BACK-STRAP LOOM
The most common loom used throughout the Americas was the back-strap loom (left). It is still widely used today. The loom consists of two loom bars, poles holding the warp, which are hooked to a support at one end, and pulled taut by a belt around the weaver's back at the other end. The weft (horizontal) thread is passed under and over the strands of the warp (vertical) threads using a heddle stick and a shed rod to lift up alternate strands. To alter the pattern or introduce more color, more heddles are used, or different groups of warp threads are lifted up.

Figurine may be of Mayan goddess Ixchel, *patroness of weaving*

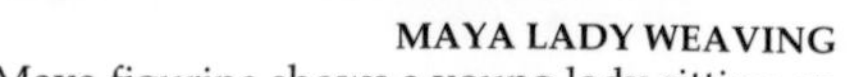

MAYA LADY WEAVING
This Maya figurine shows a young lady sitting on the ground, weaving with a back-strap loom.

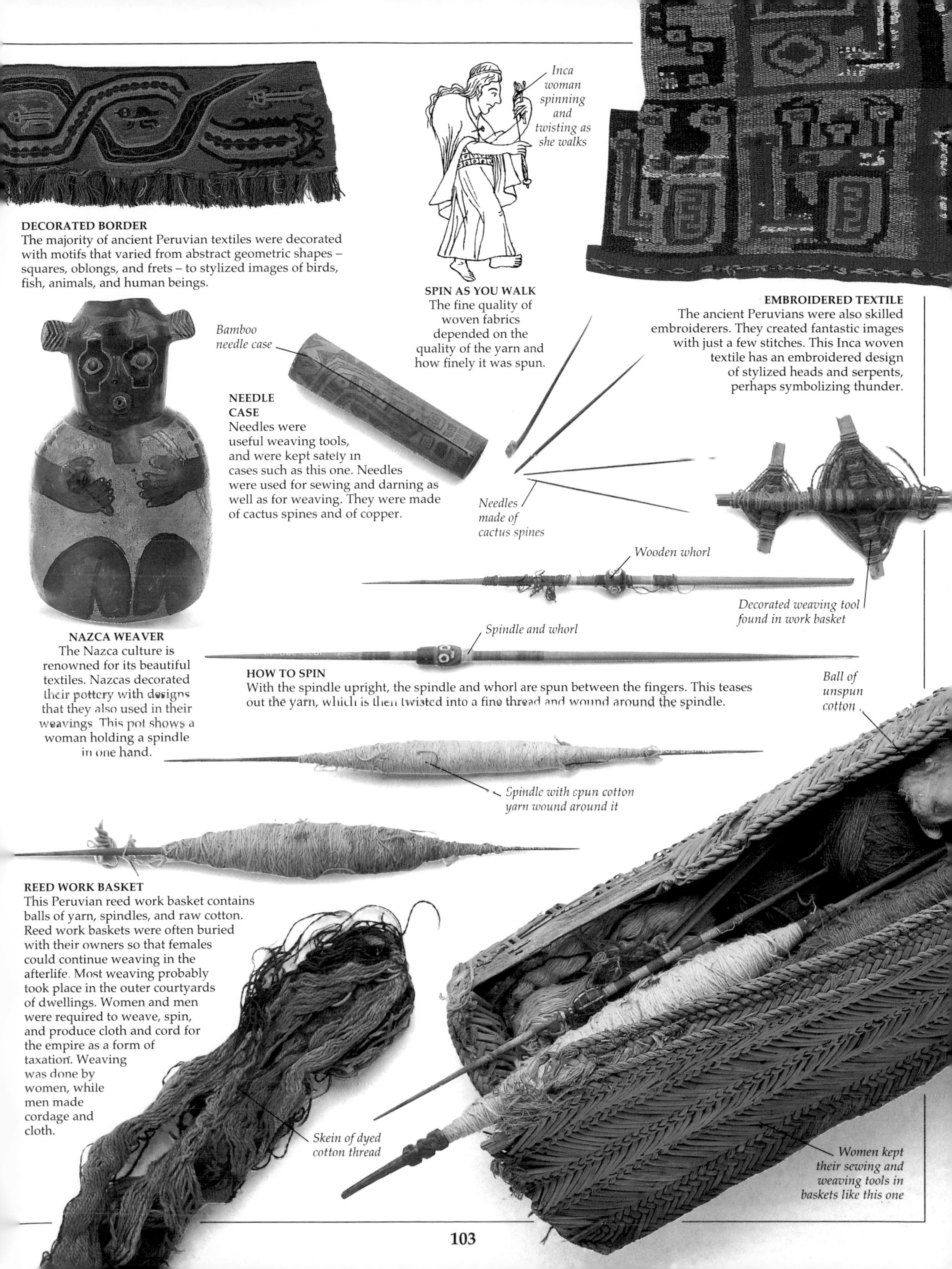

DECORATED BORDER
The majority of ancient Peruvian textiles were decorated with motifs that varied from abstract geometric shapes – squares, oblongs, and frets – to stylized images of birds, fish, animals, and human beings.

SPIN AS YOU WALK
The fine quality of woven fabrics depended on the quality of the yarn and how finely it was spun.

EMBROIDERED TEXTILE
The ancient Peruvians were also skilled embroiderers. They created fantastic images with just a few stitches. This Inca woven textile has an embroidered design of stylized heads and serpents, perhaps symbolizing thunder.

NEEDLE CASE
Needles were useful weaving tools, and were kept safely in cases such as this one. Needles were used for sewing and darning as well as for weaving. They were made of cactus spines and of copper.

NAZCA WEAVER
The Nazca culture is renowned for its beautiful textiles. Nazcas decorated their pottery with designs that they also used in their weavings. This pot shows a woman holding a spindle in one hand.

HOW TO SPIN
With the spindle upright, the spindle and whorl are spun between the fingers. This teases out the yarn, which is then twisted into a fine thread and wound around the spindle.

REED WORK BASKET
This Peruvian reed work basket contains balls of yarn, spindles, and raw cotton. Reed work baskets were often buried with their owners so that females could continue weaving in the afterlife. Most weaving probably took place in the outer courtyards of dwellings. Women and men were required to weave, spin, and produce cloth and cord for the empire as a form of taxation. Weaving was done by women, while men made cordage and cloth.

Clothes and accessories

CLOTHING styles were very different in Mesoamerica and South America, but in both regions they reflected a person's social class. People who wore clothes of fine material with colorful and elaborate decoration were of high status. The Incas made their clothes from wool, although on the coast cotton was preferred. Alpaca wool was worn by ordinary people and silky vicuna wool by the nobles. In Mesoamerica, garments were made from cotton or other plant fibers. All items of clothing were very simple. Many were just a piece of material draped around a part of the body. Men from both regions wore loincloths. Aztec women wore a skirt wrapped around the hips. Men wore cloaks draped over the shoulder. Some items of clothing – ponchos and tunics – slipped over the head and were sewn at the sides.

CAPPING IT ALL
In the Andean region people wore knitted wool or cotton caps. This handsome Chimu cap with colorful panels is unusual because it is made from woven wool.

SANDAL
The Incas made sandals with leather from the neck of the llama. In other regions sandals were made of wool or, as in this case, the fiber of the aloe plant.

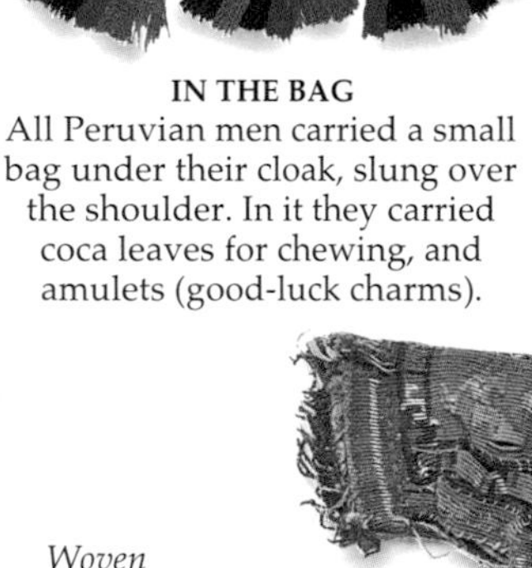

IN THE BAG
All Peruvian men carried a small bag under their cloak, slung over the shoulder. In it they carried coca leaves for chewing, and amulets (good-luck charms).

SLEEVELESS PONCHO *right*
Some ponchos were decorated with fine patterns. They were such important garments that the dead were buried with ponchos. In the highland regions of Peru, both men and women wear ponchos to the present day.

ANDEAN WOMAN'S DRESS
Although this is an 18th-century impression of a Peruvian woman, her clothing is similar to that worn by an Inca woman: a long dress of woven rectangular cloth, with a long cloak and sandals.

CHILD'S PONCHO *left*
Finely woven ponchos covering mummies have been discovered in some ancient Peruvian graves. This small poncho was discovered in a child's grave. It is woven from wool, with a design of birds in diagonal bands.

SHELL NECKLACE
In Mesoamerica, only the ruler and nobles could wear jewelry such as headbands, armbands, or nose, lip, and earplugs. Even necklaces made of shells like this one could not be worn by everyone.

DIFFERENT CLOTHES, DIFFERENT JOBS
Aztec people wore clothes that suited their role in society. The lavish headdresses and rich materials worn here show that these are people of high rank.

COORDINATED CLOTHES
This Mayan woman is wearing a matching turban, skirt, and shawl. Her beautiful long hair is tied back with white ribbons. She wears a feather ornament in one ear and a bracelet probably made of leather.

SOPHISTICATED LADY
This richly attired figure is obviously a high-ranking Mayan woman. She wears a headdress with two folds, and blue earplugs that perhaps represent turquoise. Her beaded necklace, is similar in shape to Mayan jade necklaces and she wears bracelets on both arms. With one hand she protects her face with a parasol.

FANCY CAPE
Capes like this one were worn throughout Mesoamerica. This army commander is of high rank, so his cape is finely decorated.

MALE FASHION
This life-size head of a Mixtec man shows what adornments they wore. He has a headband tied around his forehead, with a bird's head at the center, and blue disks at the sides. His hair is loose, and he wears round blue earplugs. His mouth is painted with black and white spots, resembling a mouth ornament.

Master potters

THE DECORATED CERAMICS of ancient Andean cultures are one of their most striking achievements. The Mesoamericans also had a rich and varied pottery tradition. Potters did not use a potter's wheel in either region.They produced a wide range of shapes, which they painted, carved, or stamped for decoration. The finest ceramics were for the rich or for ritual use. Pottery for everyday use was more simple. Because the Andean cultures had no writing system, pottery is a valuable source of information about the societies that made it, and their religious ideas and cultural influences.

MAYAN FRESCO VASE
This cylindrical pot, decorated with the figure of a jaguar, was a common shape among the Mayas. It was covered with stucco and then painted over while still wet.

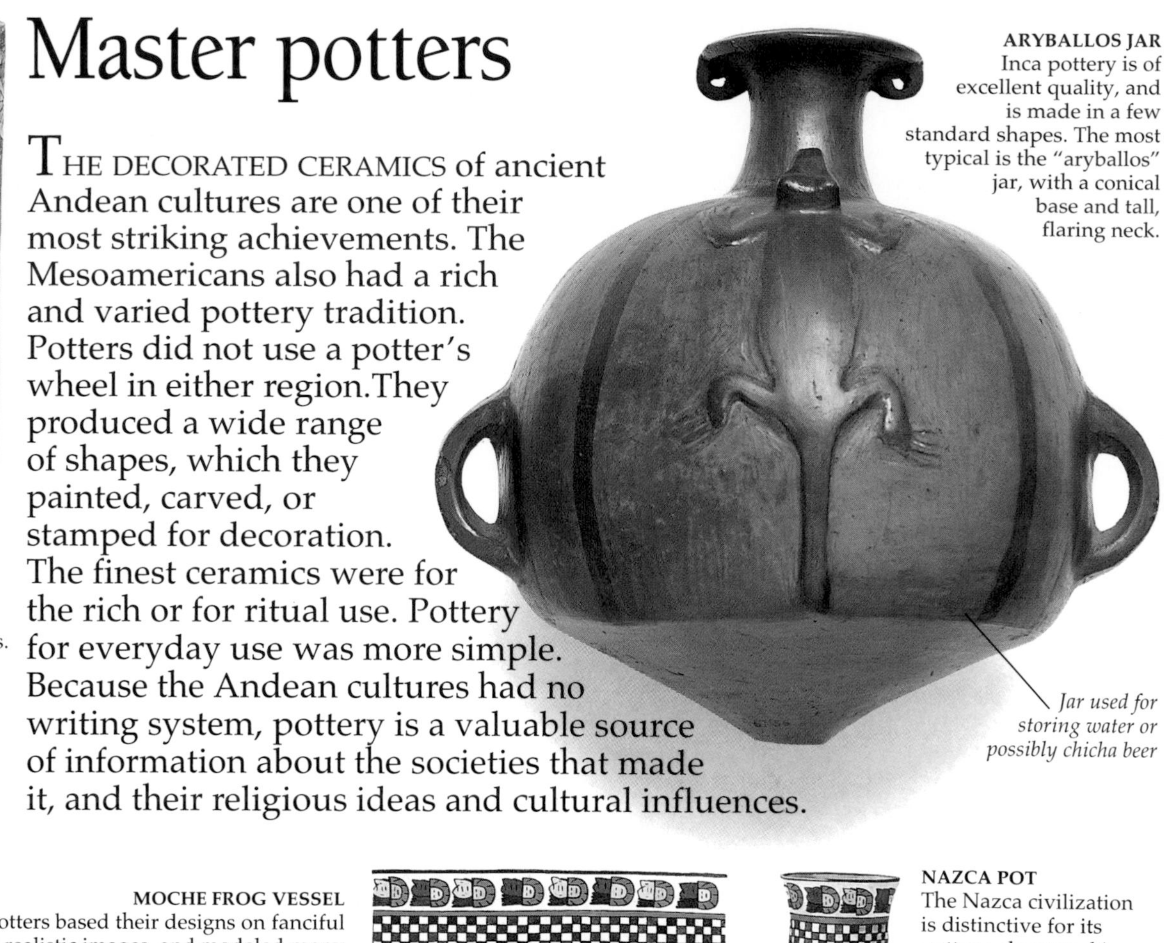

ARYBALLOS JAR
Inca pottery is of excellent quality, and is made in a few standard shapes. The most typical is the "aryballos" jar, with a conical base and tall, flaring neck.

Jar used for storing water or possibly chicha beer

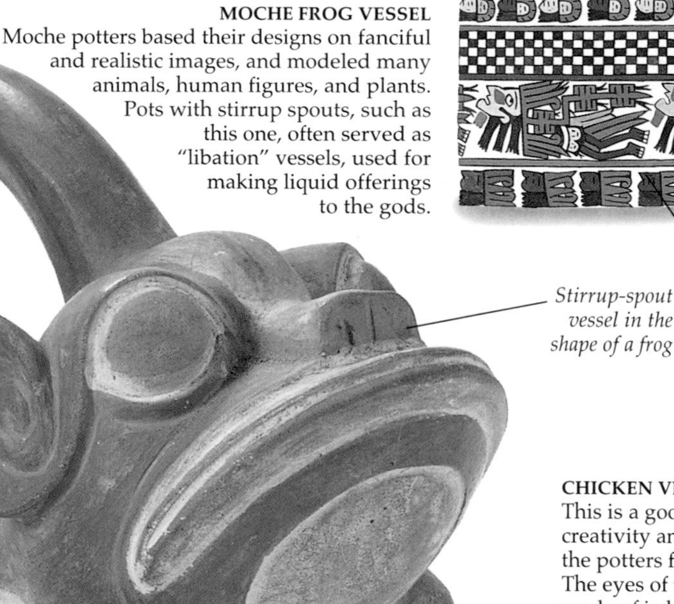

MOCHE FROG VESSEL
Moche potters based their designs on fanciful and realistic images, and modeled many animals, human figures, and plants. Pots with stirrup spouts, such as this one, often served as "libation" vessels, used for making liquid offerings to the gods.

Stirrup-spout vessel in the shape of a frog

Nazca vessel unrolled to show decoration

NAZCA POT
The Nazca civilization is distinctive for its pottery, decorated in many colors with both realistic and mythological creatures, such as this demon with a human body.

CHICKEN VESSEL
This is a good example of the creativity and imagination of the potters from Teotihuacán. The eyes of this "chicken" are made of jade and shell, and the body is decorated with conch shells.

Jade and shell eyes

Pieces of shell

How a pot was made, its shape, and the motifs decorating it help researchers discover when it was made

PAINTING PALETTE
It is very likely that the Teotihuacán potters used some kind of palette to mix pigments. They used both vegetable and mineral colors. This pottery object may have been used as a palette for the pigments.

FIGURINE AND MOLD
This figurine of a goddess with two children was modeled using a clay mold. It may have been placed on the altar in a peasant house, as peasants could not afford anything bigger or of better material.

AZTEC BOWL
The decoration on this bowl is based on an abstract pattern of zigzag lines. Painted decoration was usually only in two colors, as on this bowl.

MIXTEC CUP
This beautiful Mixtec cup is decorated with a hummingbird perched on the rim. The base has the characteristic "step fret" motif often used by Mixtec artists.

FUNERARY URN
Some clay vessels were not painted, but rather the decoration was cut into the surface. The picture on one side of this urn is of a bearded god wearing a necklace. He holds a spearthrower in one hand, and spears in the other.

Featherwork

THE BRIGHT COLORS and natural sheen of tropical bird feathers made them a valuable item for trade and tribute in Mesoamerica and in the Andean region of South America. Tropical birds were hunted and raised in captivity for their feathers, which were worked into stunning patterns and designs. For the Mesoamericans, the iridescent green feathers of the quetzal were the most prized. The Incas used feathers as part of their dress and wove them into clothing for special occasions. They also used them to decorate headdresses and tunics, and to make mosaics (a design of feathers glued to a backing to decorate hard items such as shields). Skilled Aztec featherworkers made beautiful garments only for the nobility, while the Mayas made superb items such as headdresses that were extended at the back and made the wearer look like a bird that had just landed.

FEATHER MOSAICS
Ancient Mexico had a guild of expert featherworkers who used intricate methods of gluing and weaving feather mosaics. These methods were studied and illustrated by a Spanish friar called Bernardino de Sahagún.

Tall feather headdress

FEATHER SHIRT AND HEADDRESS
This type of feather shirt is known as a *poncho*. Each of the feathers has been carefully stitched to a cotton cloth to make up the design of stylized owls and fish. Several Peruvian cultures, such as the Chimu and the Inca, had expert featherworkers.

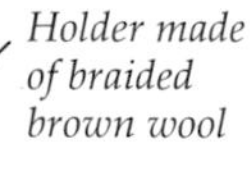

Fan made of macaw feathers

Holder made of braided brown wool

WAVE OF COLOR
The ancient Peruvians made very colorful fans using feathers from tropical birds. These fans were useful for keeping cool in hot climates. The Peruvians made many practical objects with feathers, especially from parrots and macaws, as these were their favorite birds.

FEATHER HEADDRESS
This simple Peruvian headdress was made from feathers possibly taken from birds in the Amazon region. Items made from the feathers of exotic birds were status symbols.

MONTEZUMA'S HEADDRESS
This is a replica of a headdress said to have belonged to Montezuma, the last Aztec ruler. The headdress was part of the booty sent by Cortés to Spain (pp. 122–123). It is made of green quetzal feathers, blue cotinga feathers, and gold disks.

MEXICAN FAN
This fan was made with the feathers of several kinds of bird. Sumptuous fans such as this one were used by dignitaries.

WARRIOR OUTFIT
An Aztec warrior's rank was reflected in the kind of feather suit he wore. This elaborate feather suit, complete with shield and headdress, was worn by a high-ranking warrior.

...oak of ...llow and ...een feathers

FEATHERS IN STONE
This carved stone Atlantean figure from a temple at Chichén Itzá was originally painted all over. The watercolors show two views of it as it would have been. The figure is dressed in a full-length feather cloak and a feather headdress.

REBUILDING THE PAST
Watercolors like this one by British artist Adela Breton give us an idea of how pre-Columbian sculptures were painted, and what the buildings at Chichén Itzá looked like originally.

Precious metals

LIP ORNAMENT
Eagle heads like this one made by the Mixtecs were popular as decoration for lip plugs, or labrets. The Mixtecs produced most of the gold work for the Aztec elite. Labrets were inserted through a hole made below the bottom lip.

THE PERUVIAN TRADITION of crafting magnificent artifacts from precious metals began 3,500 years ago, the age of the oldest piece of precious metalwork found in the Andes. Methods of metalworking gradually developed, and metals were widely worked in South America before the Christian era. They were introduced to Mesoamerica about 850 B.C. Some of the most common precious metals in the Americas are gold, silver, and platinum. These were mostly used for making objects for ritual use, trinkets, and jewelry. Combinations of gold and silver, and gold and copper (called *tumbaga*), were also used. Because of the value attached to gold, wearing gold jewelry was a sign of a person's wealth and power. When a wealthy person died, his or her tomb would be filled with precious gold and silver objects, encrusted with precious stones.

GOLD CREATURE
The ancient South American goldsmiths produced many and fantastic creatures. This figure is a mixture of human and animal forms.

PORTRAIT CUP
This cup is called a "portrait cup," as it seems to portray the face of a real person. Portrait cups were often made of pounded silver.

Almond-shaped eyes

Aquiline nose

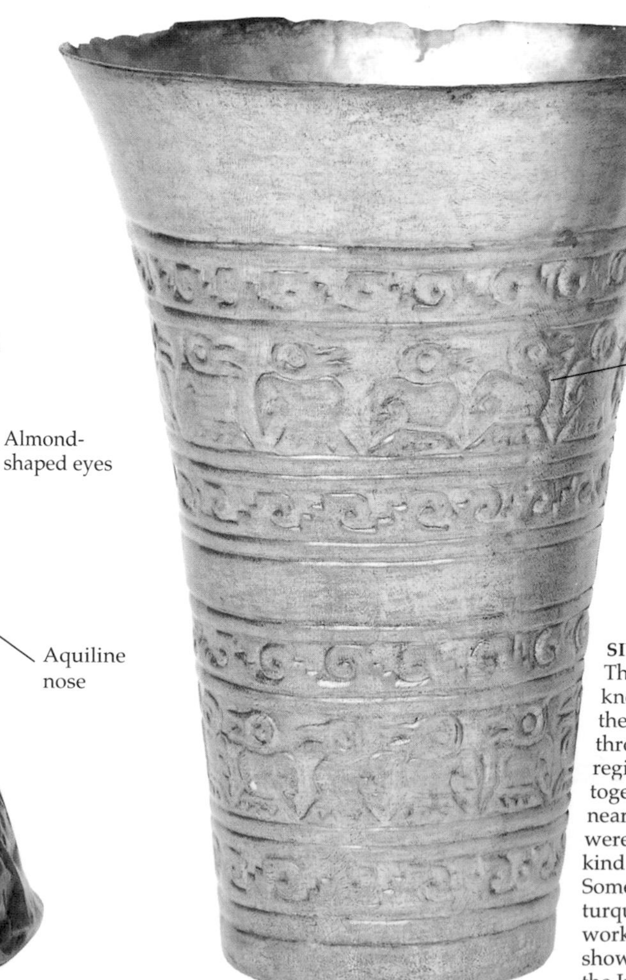

Cup has hammered bird design

SILVER DRINKING CUP
These cups are usually known as *keros*. Many of them have been found throughout the Andean region, placed in cemeterie together with other objects near the corpses. Some *keros* were used to drink *chicha*, a kind of beer made of maize. Some cups were inlaid with turquoise. This cup is the work of a Chimu metalsmit showing it was made before the Inca period.

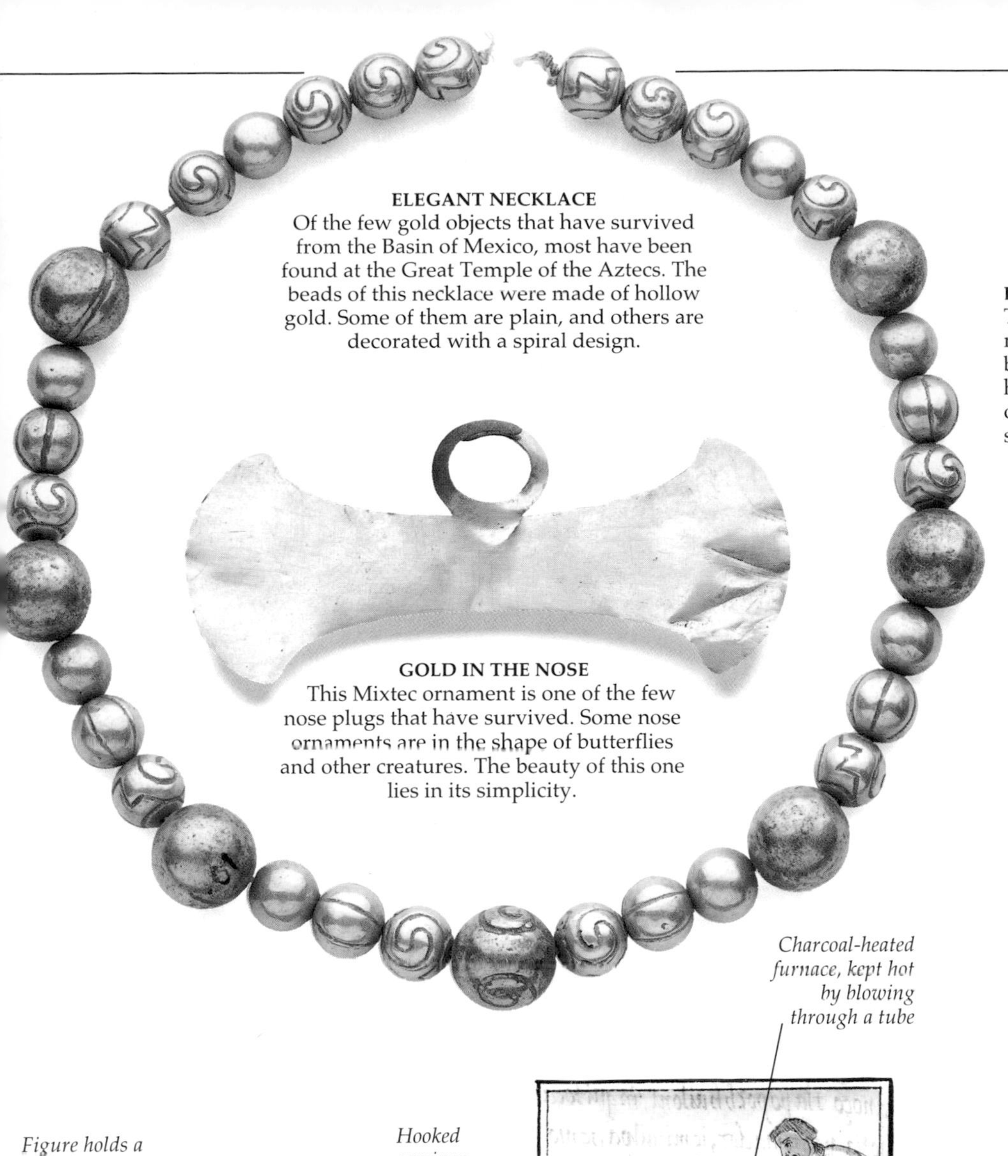

ELEGANT NECKLACE
Of the few gold objects that have survived from the Basin of Mexico, most have been found at the Great Temple of the Aztecs. The beads of this necklace were made of hollow gold. Some of them are plain, and others are decorated with a spiral design.

GOLD IN THE NOSE
This Mixtec ornament is one of the few nose plugs that have survived. Some nose ornaments are in the shape of butterflies and other creatures. The beauty of this one lies in its simplicity.

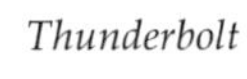

BAT RATTLE
This cast gold rattle represents a bat god. The god is holding a thunderbolt in one hand and a throwing stick in the other.

PANNING FOR GOLD
Most of the gold used by the Peruvian Indians was obtained from "placer" mines in rivers, where the gold is near the surface. They used fire-hardened digging sticks to break up the earth, and shallow trays in which to carry and wash it.

Charcoal-heated furnace, kept hot by blowing through a tube

GOLDSMITH
The goldsmith had a high status in Aztec society. He made the most intricate objects using the "lost wax" method. First he made an intricately carved beeswax mold, and carefully covered it with a layer of clay. When it was heated, melted wax flowed out and the mold was filled with molten metal. In this illustration, the goldsmith is about to pour molten gold into a mold.

Handle has figure of a hummingbird

LIME SCOOPS
These tiny lime scoops were used in the preparation of a drug called *coca*. Powdered lime was scooped onto a coca leaf, made into a ball, and chewed.

Figure holds a standard or banner

Hooked earrings

ZAPOTEC GOLD FIGURE
Many gold items seem to depict important people or gods. The items they wear and hold may have had a symbolic meaning for the Mesoamerican people, but we can only guess what it symbolizes. This standing gold figure was probably the work of a Zapotec goldsmith. The figure is wearing a pendant around its neck. Three bells hang from the pendant's head.

Llamas were highly valued in the Andean region. Many stylized llama figurines were made

GOLD LLAMA
The Incas made vessels and figures using the casting method, by pouring molten metal into a mold. Items like this llama figure were sometimes partly soldered together too.

Precious stones

THE INCAS, MAYAS, AND AZTECS had a taste for all kinds of stones, and their skilled craftsmen fashioned exquisite objects from them. The Incas favored turquoise, which they used as inlay in gold and silver objects. The Mesoamericans favored stones of different colors with shiny surfaces, such as jade and green stones in general, turquoise, onyx, rock crystal, and porphyry (a dark red rock), among others. They made jewelry and a variety of containers, masks, and sculptures. Jade was the most precious material, according to the Mesoamerican people. It was associated with water, the life-giving fluid, and with the color of the maize plant, their staple food. Turquoise was also highly valued and was laboriously worked both in Mesoamerica and in the Andean regions.

TURQUOISE NECKLACE
In the Andean region, turquoise was used for making jewelry and for decorating objects such as pots and statues. This necklace was probably made by the Incas.

Necklace made of thick turquoise disks

Red shell beads

TURQUOISE AND GOLD NECKLACE
Turquoise was highly valued in the Andean region. Only a few artifacts, like this delicate Inca necklace, have survived.

Pieces of turquoise

Hollow gold bead

CHIMU WOMAN
This Chimu figurine (left) is of a woman wearing a headdress and a necklace strung with various beads, perhaps shells and stones.

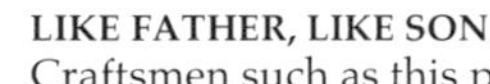

LIKE FATHER, LIKE SON
Craftsmen such as this precious-stone cutter (called a lapidary) passed their skills on to their sons, who took up their trade on reaching manhood. The Aztecs believed that the arts of the lapidary and the goldsmith came from the Toltecs, who had received their skills from the god Quetzalcoatl.

Detail from Codex Mendoza

VAMPIRE BAT
This Zapotec mosaic mask is made of 25 pieces of jade. It is in the shape of a human head covered by a bat's mask. The bat was an important symbol in the art of the Zapotec people.

Eyes made of shell

ONYX CUP
In Mesoamerica, onyx was used for making objects for the elite. The craftsman would begin with a large lump of onyx, cutting out the center with obsidian tools (above). Many onyx objects are rounded, like this cup (below), as this was the easiest shape to produce.

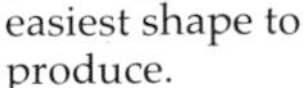

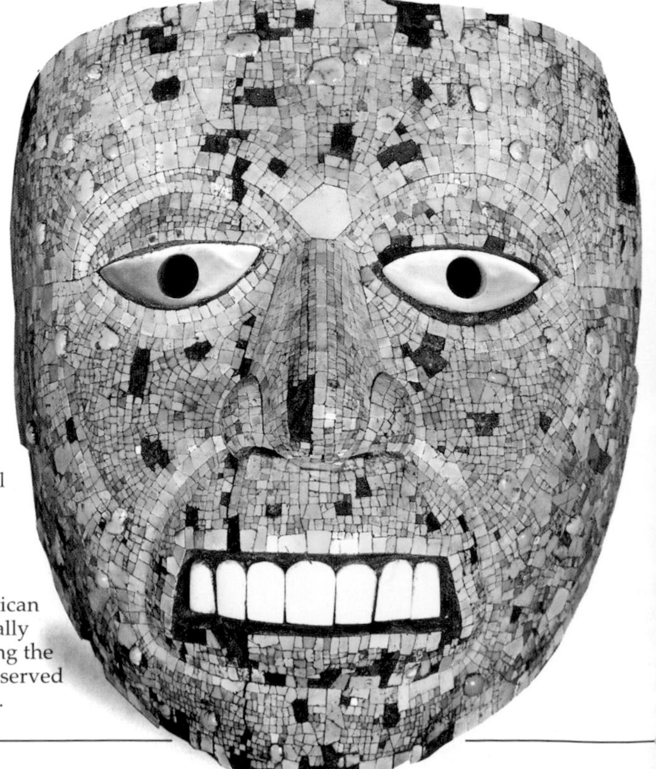

Eyes and teeth made of shell

TURQUOISE MASK *right*
One of the most remarkable Mesoamerican arts was that of mosaic making, especially using turquoise. This mask, representing the god Quetzalcoatl, is one of the best preserved examples of Mexican turquoise mosaic.

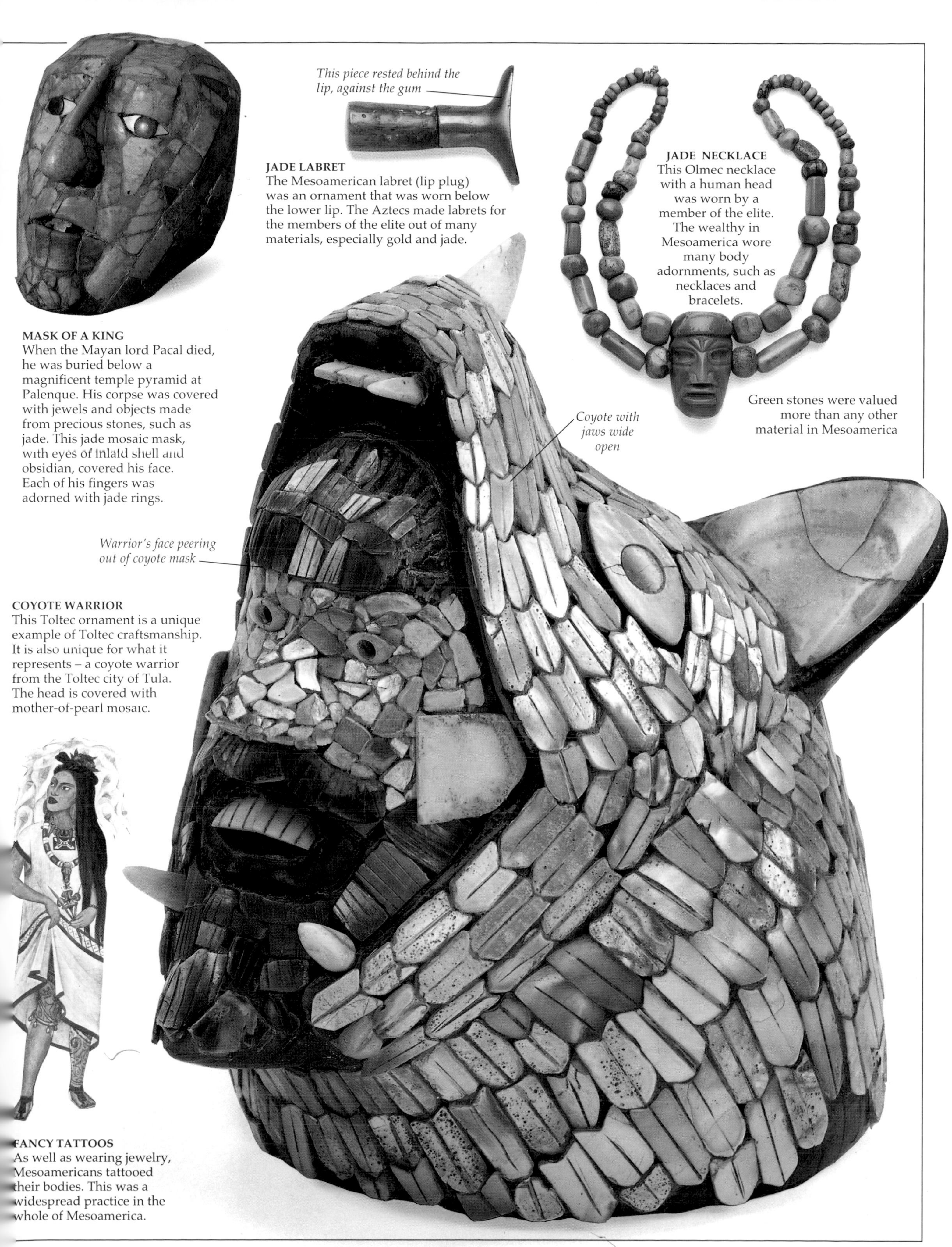

This piece rested behind the lip, against the gum

JADE LABRET
The Mesoamerican labret (lip plug) was an ornament that was worn below the lower lip. The Aztecs made labrets for the members of the elite out of many materials, especially gold and jade.

JADE NECKLACE
This Olmec necklace with a human head was worn by a member of the elite. The wealthy in Mesoamerica wore many body adornments, such as necklaces and bracelets.

Green stones were valued more than any other material in Mesoamerica

MASK OF A KING
When the Mayan lord Pacal died, he was buried below a magnificent temple pyramid at Palenque. His corpse was covered with jewels and objects made from precious stones, such as jade. This jade mosaic mask, with eyes of inlaid shell and obsidian, covered his face. Each of his fingers was adorned with jade rings.

Coyote with jaws wide open

Warrior's face peering out of coyote mask

COYOTE WARRIOR
This Toltec ornament is a unique example of Toltec craftsmanship. It is also unique for what it represents – a coyote warrior from the Toltec city of Tula. The head is covered with mother-of-pearl mosaic.

FANCY TATTOOS
As well as wearing jewelry, Mesoamericans tattooed their bodies. This was a widespread practice in the whole of Mesoamerica.

Masks

Jade earplug

HUMAN MASK
This finely carved greenstone mask, found at the Great Temple of the Aztecs, was an offering to the gods. It is inlaid with shell and obsidian, and its earlobes are pierced to attach earplugs.

FOR HUNDREDS OF YEARS, masks fashioned from materials such as gold, obsidian, jade, and wood – some inlaid with turquoise and coral – have been worn in the Americas. Masks were commonly placed over mummy bundles to protect the deceased from the dangers of the afterlife. They were also worn for festivals. Among the Incas and the Aztecs, for whom music and dance (pp. 116–117) were a form of religious expression, masks and costumes had a symbolic meaning. Even today in Mesoamerica and in the Andean region, people still wear masks during festivals.

HAMMERED COPPER MASK
Masks such as this copper one (left) have been found on mummies in many Andean burial sites. The wealthier the individual the more elaborate was their burial and the more expensive the fabrics that wrapped and decorated the mummy bundle.

Holes in mask may have had hair threaded through them

Mask made of stone

FACE VALUE
Many objects from the Mezcala region, including masks, were found at the Great Temple of the Aztecs. This mask was paid as tribute to the Aztecs (pp. 86–87).

MAYAN HEAD
Many heads and masks give an idea of what people looked like. This head shows that the Mayas practiced cranial deformation, which means that they forced the top of the head to grow taller and slope backward.

Eyes decorated with emerald beads

JEWELED MASK
This Chimu funerary mask is made of thin sheet gold. It would have been placed over a mummy's face. The nose ornament, decorated with gold disks, was made separately.

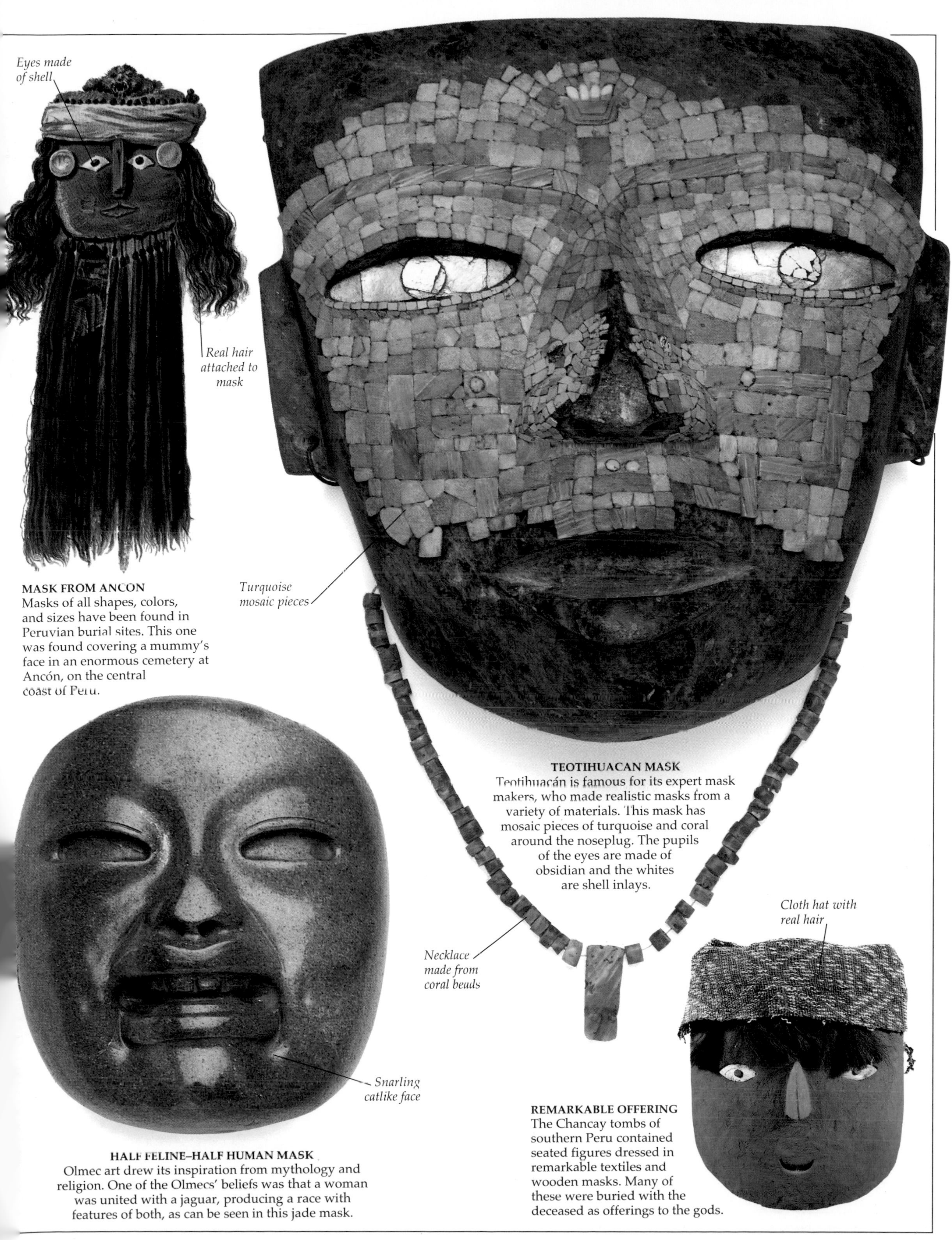

MASK FROM ANCON
Masks of all shapes, colors, and sizes have been found in Peruvian burial sites. This one was found covering a mummy's face in an enormous cemetery at Ancón, on the central coast of Peru.

TEOTIHUACAN MASK
Teotihuacán is famous for its expert mask makers, who made realistic masks from a variety of materials. This mask has mosaic pieces of turquoise and coral around the noseplug. The pupils of the eyes are made of obsidian and the whites are shell inlays.

HALF FELINE–HALF HUMAN MASK
Olmec art drew its inspiration from mythology and religion. One of the Olmecs' beliefs was that a woman was united with a jaguar, producing a race with features of both, as can be seen in this jade mask.

REMARKABLE OFFERING
The Chancay tombs of southern Peru contained seated figures dressed in remarkable textiles and wooden masks. Many of these were buried with the deceased as offerings to the gods.

Music and dance

MOCHE FLUTIST
Many Moche vases are realistic portraits of people and their pastimes. This one shows that flutes were played in the Andean region.

Music, song, and dance were an important part of Mesoamerican and South American life. Scenes of people playing music and dancing decorate many clay vases, especially those produced by Moche potters. The most common instruments in both Mesoamerica and South America were rattles, whistles, trumpets, flutes, copper bells, and shells. String instruments were practically unknown in the Americas. The music in South America was not very varied, and often musical instruments played only one tone. For these civilizations, music and dance were closely linked to religion. Everyone, from rulers to peasants, took part in dances performed especially for their gods.

End of rattle in shape of a dog's head

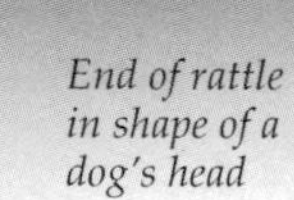

CLAY TRUMPET
Moche trumpets came in straight and coiled shapes. This one ends in two catlike heads, which may represent a god. This shape of coil is typical of Moche trumpets.

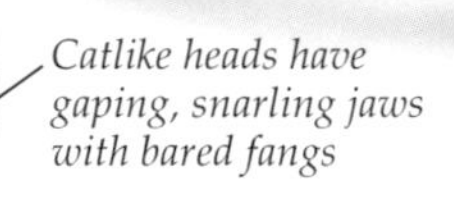

Catlike heads have gaping, snarling jaws with bared fangs

In Aztec times two types of drum were played – the *huehuetl* or *tlapanhuehuetl* (vertical drum) and the *teponaztli*, or horizontal drum

Pole decorated with paper sheets and flags

Drum covered with a feline's pelt

FEAST FOR THE DEAD
Dance and music were an important part of feasts and ritual occasions. This illustration shows men holding hands, dancing around a pole, at a feast for the dead. The pole is festooned with paper sheets and three big flags, one of which has a feather decoration. The Aztecs adorned an image of the dead person with flags. This feast lasted all day, and people danced to the beat of the drum, played by a priest. The dancers in this illustration were captives who were later burned as sacrifice.

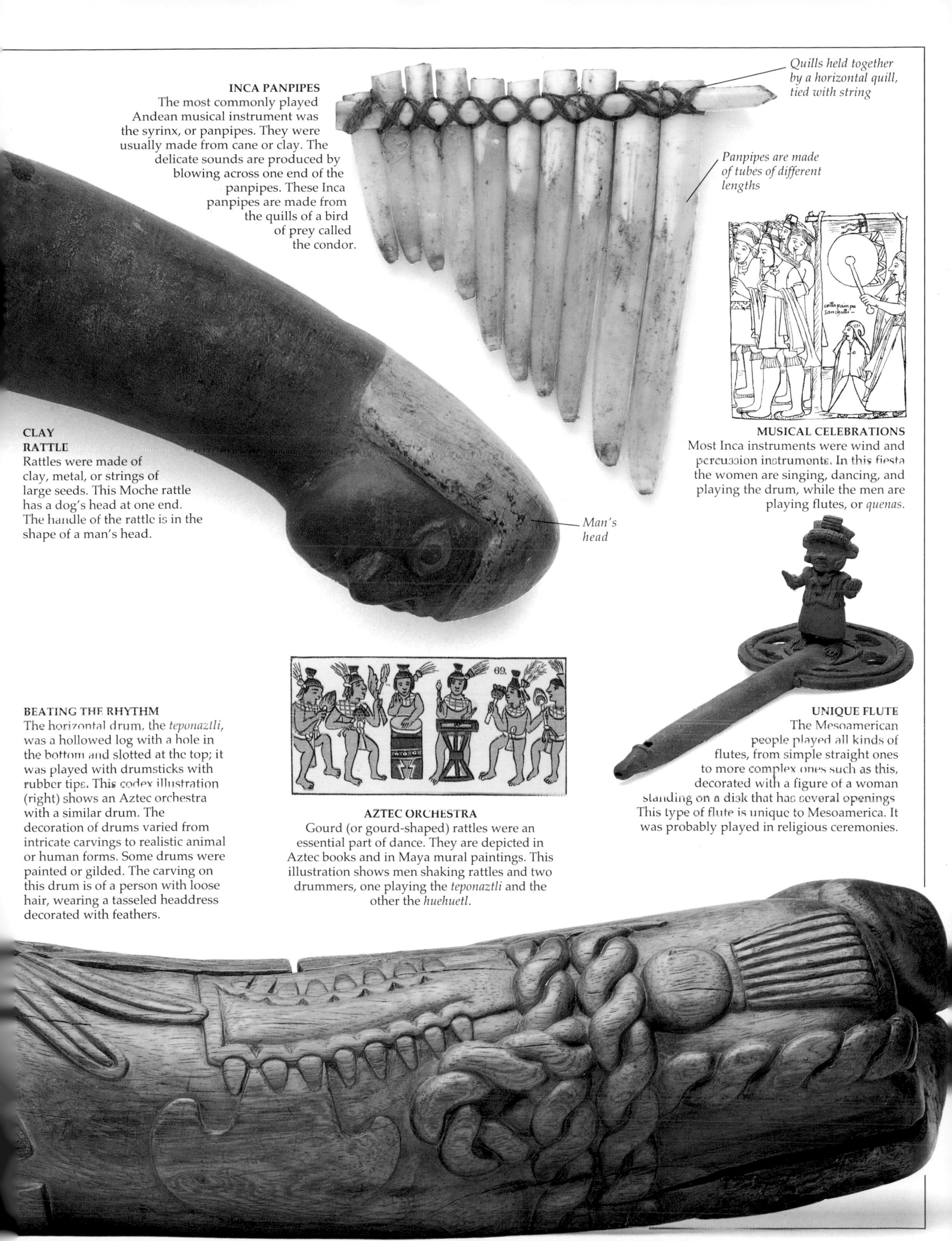

INCA PANPIPES
The most commonly played Andean musical instrument was the syrinx, or panpipes. They were usually made from cane or clay. The delicate sounds are produced by blowing across one end of the panpipes. These Inca panpipes are made from the quills of a bird of prey called the condor.

MUSICAL CELEBRATIONS
Most Inca instruments were wind and percussion instruments. In this fiesta the women are singing, dancing, and playing the drum, while the men are playing flutes, or *quenas*.

CLAY RATTLE
Rattles were made of clay, metal, or strings of large seeds. This Moche rattle has a dog's head at one end. The handle of the rattle is in the shape of a man's head.

BEATING THE RHYTHM
The horizontal drum, the *teponaztli*, was a hollowed log with a hole in the bottom and slotted at the top; it was played with drumsticks with rubber tips. This codex illustration (right) shows an Aztec orchestra with a similar drum. The decoration of drums varied from intricate carvings to realistic animal or human forms. Some drums were painted or gilded. The carving on this drum is of a person with loose hair, wearing a tasseled headdress decorated with feathers.

AZTEC ORCHESTRA
Gourd (or gourd-shaped) rattles were an essential part of dance. They are depicted in Aztec books and in Maya mural paintings. This illustration shows men shaking rattles and two drummers, one playing the *teponaztli* and the other the *huehuetl*.

UNIQUE FLUTE
The Mesoamerican people played all kinds of flutes, from simple straight ones to more complex ones such as this, decorated with a figure of a woman standing on a disk that has several openings This type of flute is unique to Mesoamerica. It was probably played in religious ceremonies.

Sports and games

Every aspect of Aztec life, including sports and games revolved around religion. The two main games played by the Aztecs were *patolli*, a board game similar to backgammon, and the ball game *ulama*. *Ulama* was played in Mesoamerica long before the Aztecs by other ancient Mexican civilizations, such as the Mayas. As well as being a sport, the ball game had a religious meaning. The ball court represented the world, and the ball stood for the moon and the sun. Bets were placed on the outcome of the game, and some players lost everything they had – including their lives.

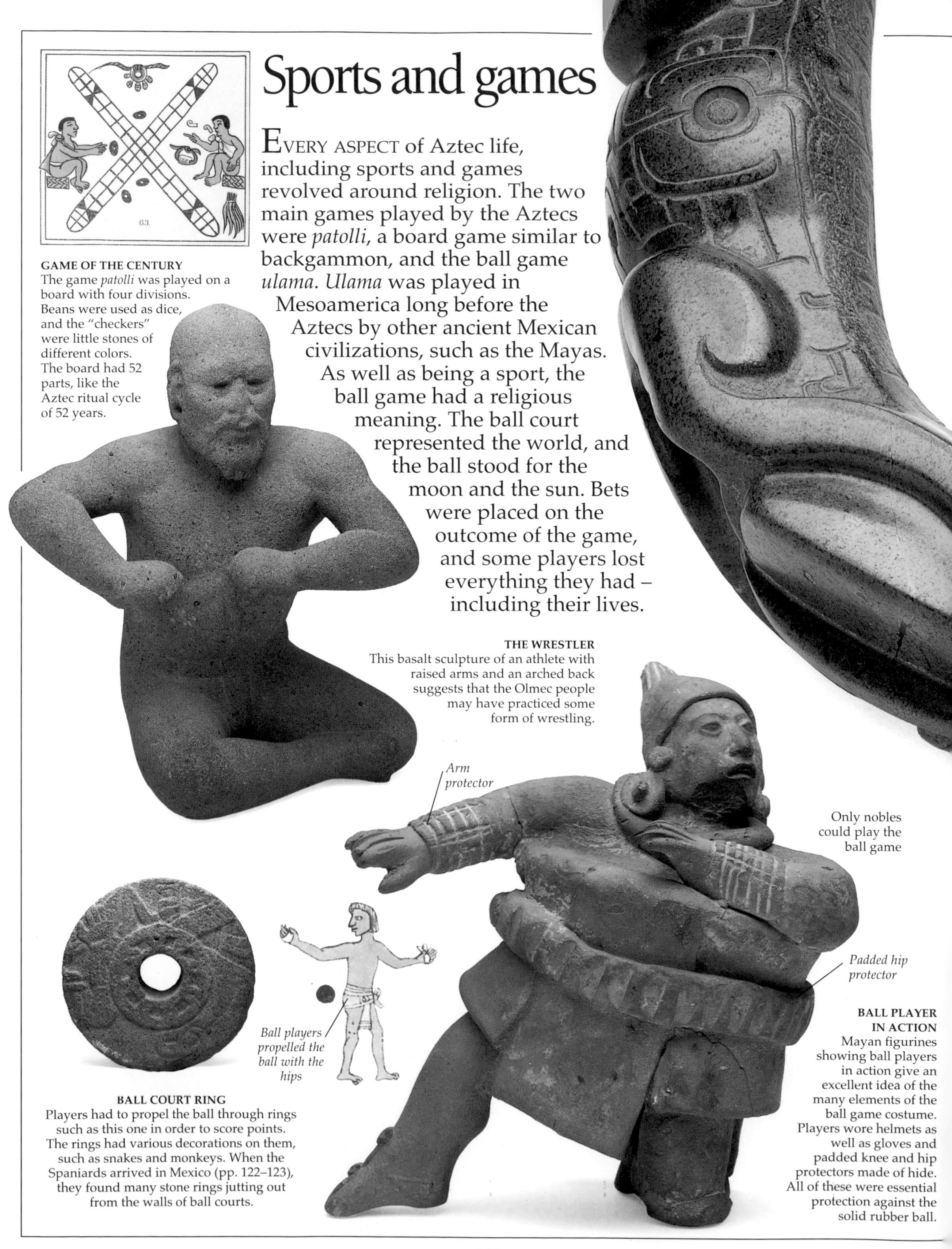

GAME OF THE CENTURY
The game *patolli* was played on a board with four divisions. Beans were used as dice, and the "checkers" were little stones of different colors. The board had 52 parts, like the Aztec ritual cycle of 52 years.

THE WRESTLER
This basalt sculpture of an athlete with raised arms and an arched back suggests that the Olmec people may have practiced some form of wrestling.

BALL COURT RING
Players had to propel the ball through rings such as this one in order to score points. The rings had various decorations on them, such as snakes and monkeys. When the Spaniards arrived in Mexico (pp. 122–123), they found many stone rings jutting out from the walls of ball courts.

BALL PLAYER IN ACTION
Mayan figurines showing ball players in action give an excellent idea of the many elements of the ball game costume. Players wore helmets as well as gloves and padded knee and hip protectors made of hide. All of these were essential protection against the solid rubber ball.

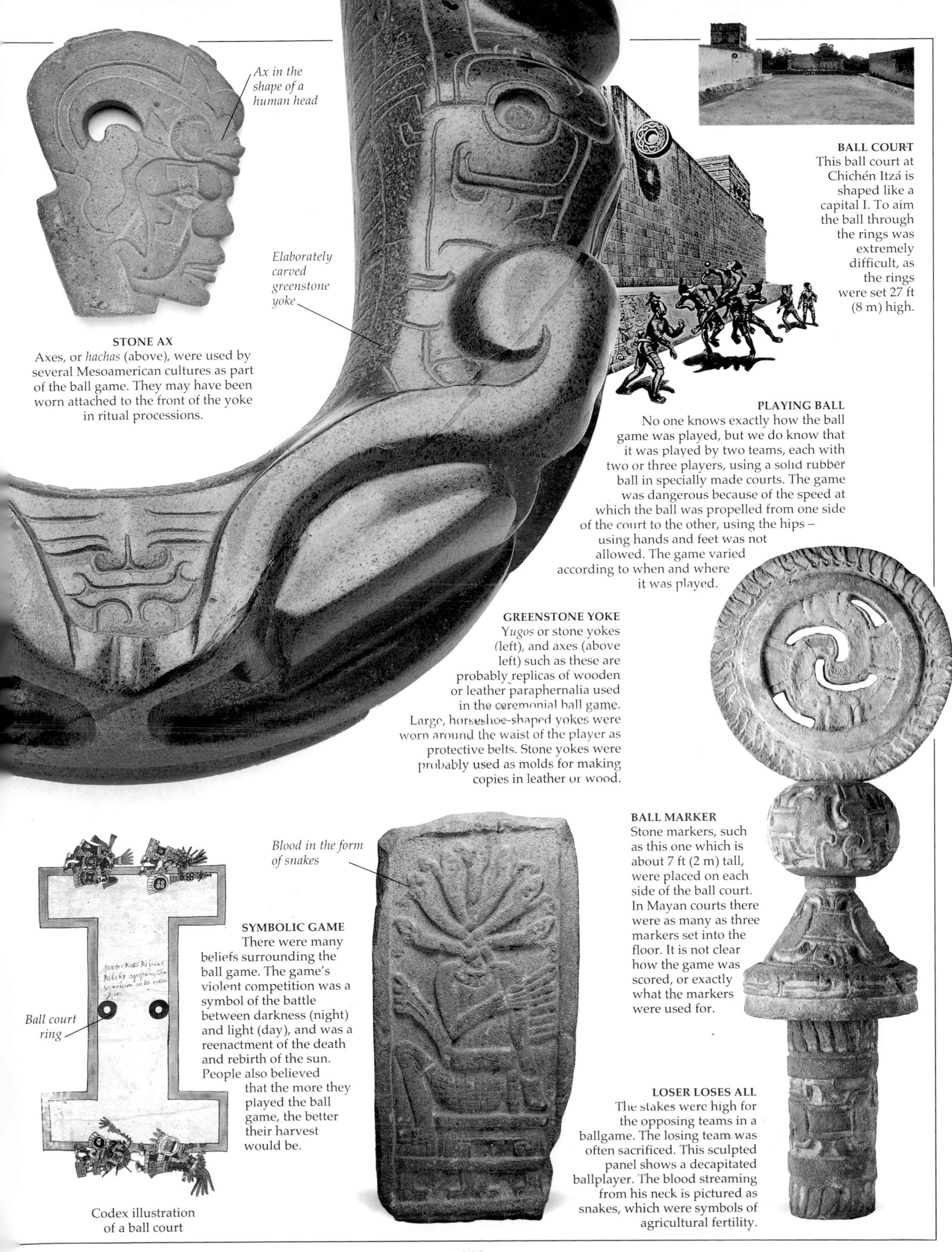

STONE AX

Axes, or *hachas* (above), were used by several Mesoamerican cultures as part of the ball game. They may have been worn attached to the front of the yoke in ritual processions.

BALL COURT

This ball court at Chichén Itzá is shaped like a capital I. To aim the ball through the rings was extremely difficult, as the rings were set 27 ft (8 m) high.

PLAYING BALL

No one knows exactly how the ball game was played, but we do know that it was played by two teams, each with two or three players, using a solid rubber ball in specially made courts. The game was dangerous because of the speed at which the ball was propelled from one side of the court to the other, using the hips – using hands and feet was not allowed. The game varied according to when and where it was played.

GREENSTONE YOKE

Yugos or stone yokes (left), and axes (above left) such as these are probably replicas of wooden or leather paraphernalia used in the ceremonial ball game. Large, horseshoe-shaped yokes were worn around the waist of the player as protective belts. Stone yokes were probably used as molds for making copies in leather or wood.

BALL MARKER

Stone markers, such as this one which is about 7 ft (2 m) tall, were placed on each side of the ball court. In Mayan courts there were as many as three markers set into the floor. It is not clear how the game was scored, or exactly what the markers were used for.

SYMBOLIC GAME

There were many beliefs surrounding the ball game. The game's violent competition was a symbol of the battle between darkness (night) and light (day), and was a reenactment of the death and rebirth of the sun. People also believed that the more they played the ball game, the better their harvest would be.

Codex illustration of a ball court

LOSER LOSES ALL

The stakes were high for the opposing teams in a ballgame. The losing team was often sacrificed. This sculpted panel shows a decapitated ballplayer. The blood streaming from his neck is pictured as snakes, which were symbols of agricultural fertility.

Bestiary

ANIMAL LIFE in the Americas was very rich and varied. Animals played an important part in everyday life as well as in the religions of both regions. Many works of art are decorated with images of animals that had religious significance – foxes, owls, hummingbirds, jaguars, eagles, and llamas. Some animals were domesticated – the turkey and the dog in Mesoamerica, and the llama and the alpaca in the Andean region. With their relatives, guanacos and vicunas, llamas and alpacas were valued for their wool, meat and as beasts of burden. In both regions, deer, rabbits, ducks, and many other kinds of edible bird, abounded. Animal life in the tropical forests included the largest cat in the world, the jaguar, which was worshipped and feared along with snakes.

BIRD ASSORTMENT
Mesoamerica had a variety of brilliantly colored tropical birds such as parrots, macaws, and quetzals. Their feathers were used to decorate many objects and clothes (pp. 108–109).

QUETZAL BIRD
This bird was greatly valued by the ancient Mesoamericans, for whom its long, deep green feathers were as precious as jade or gold. Some of their gods were covered in quetzal feathers, and they were also used to make the headdresses of rulers and kings.

BIRD TAPESTRY *above*
The Paracas culture is renowned for its abundant, ornate textiles that were placed alongside the dead. This textile fragment is decorated with a typical Paracas design of stylized birds.

This Toltec vessel is an example of plumbate pottery – lead in the clay gives the pot a metallic finish

TOLTEC CERAMIC DOG
Some breeds of dog were fattened and eaten by the Aztecs and the Mayas, but the Incas found eating dog meat a disgusting habit. The Mesoamericans used dogs as companions in hunting expeditions. According to their religion, dogs were also necessary for the journey to the afterlife, as they helped the dead cross rivers.

Figure has catlike claws and ears and a monkey's tail

FABRIC "DEVIL"
Many textiles from Paracas are woven or embroidered with animal images, often in a stylized form. Sometimes it is difficult to identify the animal in question, because of the geometric forms.

FOX
Animals such as the fox, that hunted and killed other animals, were in turn hunted by the Aztecs and the Incas. This Moche vessel is in the shape of a snarling fox.

Stirrup-spouted Moche vessel in form of a fox's head.

ARMADILLO

The Aztecs ate the meat of the armadillo, which is white and tastes like chicken. Among the Mayas, the armadillo was associated with the afterlife.

Some armadillos grow to a length of 4 ft (120 cm)

The armadillo is a nocturnal mammal that lives in tropical areas

Vicunas live on the grasslands of the Andean mountains

Vicunas reach a height of 30 in (80 cm) at the shoulder

ALPACA

The alpaca lives in the Andean highlands. It was kept in herds by the ancient Peruvians because, along with the vicuna, its long wool was ideal for weaving. Its relatives the guanaco and the llama were killed for food, though the llama was mostly used for carrying loads. The ancient Andean people made offerings to this animal as it was an important contribution to their livelihood.

VICUNAS

Like the alpaca, the vicuna (above) was a good wool-producing animal. Vicunas had the most elegant silklike wool. Garments woven from vicuna wool were worn by the Inca nobility.

Zapotec vessel probably used as an incense burner

Ocelot

OCELOT

This wild cat is sometimes known as the Mexican tiger. The ocelot was a greatly feared creature. Some warriors wore ocelot skins when going to battle.

Jaguars, ocelots, and pumas lived in tropical forests

PUMA

The puma is a native animal to the Americas. It was hunted for its skin.

Puma

Jaguar

SACRED JAGUAR

The jaguar was one of the most powerful symbols in Mesoamerica and South America. Its strength, ferocity, cunning, and hunting ability were greatly admired. This Zapotec vessel (far right) is in the shape of a jaguar standing on three legs.

Leg decorated with head of baby jaguar

The Spanish conquest

WHEN THE SPANISH ARRIVED in the Americas, they knew nothing about the Andean and Mesoamerican cultures with their powerful empires, elaborate palaces, magnificent engineering works, and religions that reached into every part of their life. Neither did the inhabitants of the Americas have any knowledge of the Spanish. Many omens had forewarned Montezuma, the Aztec ruler, of an imminent disaster. The Inca ruler Huayna Capac, too, had heard that strange, bearded men had appeared on the coast. When Cortés entered Mexico in 1519 and Pizarro arrived in Peru in 1532, they easily overpowered resistance. Despite being few in number, the Spanish armies, with their horses and cannons, were stronger. Cortés had the added advantage that the Aztecs believed him to be the king and god Quetzalcoatl. Within a short time, the world of the Aztecs and the Incas was destroyed, their temples razed to the ground, and their emperors murdered. The Mayas resisted until 1542, when the Spanish established a capital at Mérida.

MONTEZUMA GREETS CORTÉS
When they first met, Cortés greeted Montezuma with a bow, and Montezuma handed him splendid presents of gold, precious stones such as jade, and feather objects. Cortés was on horseback, and Montezuma was carried in a litter. The Spanish soldiers were dressed in steel armor, while the Aztecs wore simple cotton cloaks. This meeting would prove decisive in the conquest of Mexico. Montezuma at this point was in two minds about the true nature of Cortés – was he human or god, their enemy or their savior? The events that followed proved Cortés to be the former.

MASSACRE
The conquistadors went in search of riches. If they met with resistance from the native people, the conquistadors killed them. This illustration depicts an expedition to Michoacán in the west of Mexico, where many local noblemen were killed for refusing to say where their treasures were hidden.

Warriors from the state of Tlaxcala supported the conquistadors

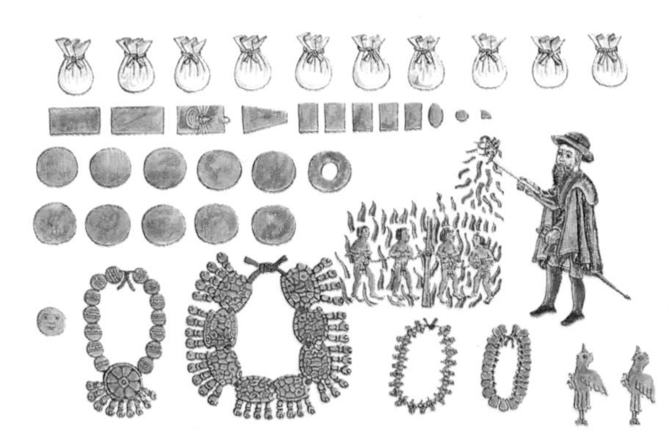

GOLDEN DEATH
This scene from Codex Kingsborough shows a Spanish tribute collector punishing the Mexican Indians at Tepetlaoztoc. A Spanish tribute collector was known as an *encomendero* (privileged Spanish colonist). The Indians being burned were late in paying their tribute. The tribute consisted of bundles of maize and gold jewelry.

Gold doubloons made from gold mined in South America

A DISEASE THAT ONLY GOLD COULD CURE
To coerce the people of Middle and South America to give them their gold, the Spanish often told them that they suffered from a disease that only gold could cure. Cortés and Pizarro both went to the Americas in search of gold and they found much of it. At the start of the conquest, Cortés sent booty to King Charles V of Spain consisting of gold and silver objects and many other goods. Over the years, huge quantities of gold were shipped to Spain. Today the ceilings of many Spanish churches are gilded with gold from the Americas.

PUNISHMENT
This illustration shows some of the punishments used by the Spanish on the Inca people, which included beating the Incas and hanging them upside down. The cruelty of many of the conquistadors made some Spanish friars devote their life to denouncing the behavior of their compatriots.

Francisco Pizarro, conquistador of Peru

Wooden Inca cup made for Pizarro

GREED FOR GOLD
This caricature shows a greedy Francisco Pizarro, contemplating gold from his new Peruvian mine. Pizarro did not understand the civilization that he helped to destroy.

CONQUISTADOR'S CUP
This wooden *kero* (p. 110) portrays the conquistador of Peru, Francisco Pizarro. Under Pizarro, Spanish control was established over the Inca empire. The Spanish forced people to abandon their irrigated lands and demanded that they mine more precious metals. Christianity was imposed upon the Incas, but they were slow to accept the new religion and continued their old practices. The Incas continued some crafts, such as weaving and making wooden *keros* like this one.

Ceremonial dress for a Dakota elder

Checklist of tribes

Tribes mentioned in this book are grouped according to their geographical location.

Ancient tribes

Adena (Northeast)
Anasazi (Southwest)
Clovis (Southwest)
Folsom (Southwest)
Hohokam (Southwest)
Hopewell (Northeast)
Mimbres (Southwest)
Mogollon (Southwest)
Temple Mound Builders (Southeast)

Northeast

Cayuga
Delaware
Erie
Fox
Huron
Iroquois
Malecite
Menominee
Miami
Micmac
Mohawk
Ojibwa
Oneida
Onondaga
Penobscot
Potawatomi
Powhatan
Sauk
Secotan
Seneca
Shawnee
Wampanoag
Winnebago

Southeast

Catawba
Cherokee
Chickasaw
Choctaw
Creek
Natchez
Seminole
Timucua
Yuch

Plains

Arapaho
Blackfeet
Cheyenne
Comanche
Crow
Dakota (Sioux)
Gros Ventre
Hidatsa
Mandan
Omaha
Plains Cree

Southwest

Apache
Bonito Pueblo
Havasupai
Hopi
Navajo
Papago
Pima
San Ildefonso Pueblo
Taos Pueblo
Zuni

Plateau

Nez Perce
Thompson

Great Basin

Kaibab
Northern Paiute
Southern Paiute
Ute
Washoe

California

Maidu
Modoc
Mohave
Pomo

Tolowa
Yahi
Yuman

Northwest
Bella Coola
Chilkat
Haida
Kwakiutl
Quinault
Tlingit
Tsimshian

Subarctic
Chipewyan
Naskapi
Northern Cree
Northern Ojibwa
Slavey

Arctic
Baffin Inuit
Copper Inuit
North Greenland Inuit
Southampton Inuit
West Alaska Inuit

Mesoamerica
Aztec
Maya
Mixtec
Olmec
Teotihuacán
Toltec
Zapotec

South America
Chancay
Chimu
Huari
Inca
Moche
Nazca
Paracas
Tiahunaco

Gods and Goddesses of Mesoamerica and South America

Aztec
Chicomecoatl
(goddess of mature maize)
Huitzilopochtli
(god of war and tribal god of the Aztecs)
Mictlantecuhtli
(god of the dead)
Tlaloc
(god of rain)
Xipe Totec
(god of vegetation and of spring)

Inca
Inti
(god of the sun)
Viracocha
(creator god)

Maya
Chac
(god of rain)
Ixchel
(goddess of weaving)

Toltec
Quetzalcoatl
(god of nature)

Mayan pottery figurine of powerful man

Index

Acknowledgments

Dorling Kindersley would like to thank:

For Chapter 1 – North American Indian:

The American Museum of Natural History, especially Anibal Rodriguez and Judith Levinson (Anthropology); John Davey (Publications); Deborah Barral, Mark Gostnell, Lize Mogel, Alan Walker, Marco Hernandez, and Rob Muller (Exhibitions); Joe Donato, Tony Macaluso, Martin Daly, Eadwinn Brookes, and Aldwin Phillip (Electricians); Eddy Garcia (Maintenance). Leslie Gerhauser, photographic assistance. Sally Rose, additional research. Helena Spiteri, Tim Burton, Sophy D'Angelo, Ivan Finnegan, Kati Poynor, and Susan St. Louis for editorial and design assistance.
Index: Marion Dent
Artwork: John Woodcock
Extra photography: Dave King, and Kate Warren, Museum of Mankind.

For Chapter 2 – Aztec, Inca & Maya:

Dra. Mari Carmen Serra Puche and all those who helped with photography at Museo Nacional de Antropologia, Mexico City; Profesor Eduardo Matos Moctezuma and all those who helped with photography at the Great Temple Museum, Mexico City (INAH.-CNCA.-Mex); Phil Watson at the Birmingham Museum; Maureen Barry at the Royal Museum of Scotland; British Museum; Pitt Rivers Museum; Cambridge University Museum of Archaeology and Anthropology; Reynaldo Izquierdo (Mexico) and Eugene Staken for photographic assistance; Sue Giles at the City of Bristol Museum; Jabu Mahlangu, Manisha Patel, Jill Plank, and Sharon Spencer for design assistance; Katharine Thompson; Lic. Victor Hugo Vidal Alvarez and Lic. Javier García Martínez at the Tourist Office, Mexico City.
Index: Lynn Bresler
Artwork: John Woodcock and Andrew Nash
Extra photography: Geoff Dann (84tr); Steve Gorton (99tl); Peter Hayman (120cl, 120c); Dave King (121bc); James Stephenson (74bl, 122–123t, 123bl); and Jerry Young (121tr, 121cl).

Editorial Co-ordinator: Marion Dent
Assistant Editors: Julie Ferris & Nicola Waine
Assistant Designer: Iain Morris

Picture credits
(t=top b=bottom c=center l=left r=right a=above)

American Indian Contemporary Art: Larry McNeil, 62bl.
American Museum of Natural History: 36tl (no. 335493), 43cb (no. 2A342), 52cbr (no. 44309), 56cbr (no. 121545); E.S. Curtis 39tr (no. 335534), 46tl (no. 335553A); J.K. Dixon 28b (no. 316642).
Archaeological Museum, Lima / e.t. archive: 80bl, 98br, 111br, 115br.
The Arizona Historical Society, Tucson 48tr.
Arteaga Collection, Lima / e.t. archive: 75cr.
Biblioteca Medicea Laurenziana, Florence: 74tcl, 108tl, 111c.
Biblioteca Nacional, Madrid / Bridgeman Art Library: 122cl.
Biblioteca Nazionale Centrale, Florence: 81tl, / Photo - Scala: 95cl, 97tl.
Bibliothèque de l'Assemblée Nationale, Paris: 90bl, 116bl, 119bl.
Bristol Museums and Art Gallery: 89br, 106c, 109bl, 122br.
Bridgeman Art Library: D.F. Barry, Bismarck, Dakota 31c;
British Museum 18c; Private Collection 32c;
Royal Ontario Museum, Toronto 59cbr.
British Library / Bridgeman Art Library: 77c, 79tl.
Trustees of The British Museum: 9cl, 9c; / Bridgeman Art Library 114bl.
J.L.Charmet: 97bl, 104bl.
Bruce Coleman Ltd: 76tr, 79tr, 120tr, 121tl, 121tc.
Colorific! / Black Star: J. Cammick 63cl; P.S. Mecca 62r.
Comstock: Georg Gerster 45cb.
Dorig / Hutchison Library: 67tr, 90cl, 94tr.
e.t. archive: 82c, 92tl, 93tcl, 98c, 100cr, 111br, 117c, 118tl.
Mary Evans Picture Library: 93cl, 105tc, 122bl.
Explorer: 100tl.
Robert Harding Picture Library: 71bl, 77tc, 78cr, 78bl.
Michael Holford: 76c, 77tr, 93bl, 114br, 116tl.
Hutchison Library: / Moser: 63br; 119tr.
The Image Bank: Marvin Newman 63tl.
Ann Ronan Image Select: 16tr.
Kimball Morrison, South American Pictures: 78tr.
Tony Morrison, South American Pictures: 73tl, 73br, 75bc, 78cl, 87tl, 87tcl, 90tr, 93tr, 100bc, 102tl, 103tc, 117tr.
Collections of the Library of Congress: 30cr.
Magnum Photos: E. Arnold 63tr.
Mansell Collection: 25cbr, 25b, 49cr.
Minnesota Historical Society: 33c.
Montana Historical Society, Helena: 34tr.
Museo Ciudad Mexico / Sapieha / e.t.archive: 72tc.
Museo d'America, Madrid / Photo Scala: 66br.
Museum Für Vülkerkunde, Vienna: 109cr.
Museum of Mankind / Bridgeman Art Library: 86tcl, 112br.
National Palace, Mexico City / Giraudon / Bridgeman Art Library: (detail, Diego Rivera 'La Civilisation Zapotheque') 69bl, (detail, Diego Rivera 'Cultivation of Maize') 84bc, (detail, Diego Rivera 'The Market of Tenochtitlan') 113bl, / e.t. archive 86c, (detail, Diego Rivera 'Tarascan Civilisation') 102 cr.
Nevada Historical Society, Reno: 40cra, 41tr.
Peter Newark's Western Americana: jacket, 10ca, 10cb, 12ca, 14tl, 19tr, 21br, 23tl, 27cr, 28c, 33tl, 34c, 37bl, 40tl, 46clb, 119tcr.
NHPA / Bernard: 73tcl, / Woodfall: 79b.
Pate / Hutchison Library: 77tcr.
Private Collection / Bridgeman Art Library: 123br.
Rietberg Museum, Zurich: 70bl.
Rochester Museum and Science Center, Rochester, NY: (*Formation of the League*, Ernest Smith) 14cr.
Royal Ontario Museum, Toronto: (detail from *Hunting Moose Deer in Winter*) 59tr.
Nick Saunders / Barbara Heller: 78c, 79tcl, 83tl, 91tr, 123tr.
Service de la Marine, Vincennes: (detail from *Culture & Stationis Ratio*, de Bry) 17br.
Ronald Sheridan / Ancient Art and Architecture Collection: 111tcr.
Smithsonian Institution: Department of Anthropology 30/31 (cat. no. 358425); National Anthropological Archives 19br, 26bc, 27tcr, 30tr, 35tr, 41tl, 42cra, 50cra, 60bcr.
South American Pictures: 94c.
Courtesy of The Southwest Museum, Los Angeles: 22c.
Frank Spooner Pictures / Gamma: A. Ribeiro 63cr.
University Museum, Cuzco / e.t. archive: 70tr.
Werner Forman Archive / Anthropology Museum, Veracruz: 69tr, / Edward H. Merrin Gallery, New York: 105tr, / National Museum of Anthropology, Mexico City: 113tl.
Trip / Eye Ubiquitous: L Fordyce 63bc.
Michael Zabé: 90–91, 96bl, 107tcl, 109c, 110tl, 111tr, 112bl, 112c, / NMA, Mexico City: 89tl.

Every effort has been made to trace the copyright holders of the photographs. Dorling Kindersley apologizes for any unintentional omissions and would be pleased, in such cases, to add an acknowledgment in future editions.

Catalog numbers of artifacts photographed at the AMNH (Chapter 1):
1. 50.1/2448. **2.** tl 50.1/1331; tc E/2565; tr 50/3084; cl 50.1/1205; c 50.1/316; CR 60–53; cb 50/3808; bc 50/9789AB. **3.** tl 50/7649; tr 16/902; b 50/5545, 5546. **4.** tl 50/355; tc 50/7388; tr 50/3045; cl 1/2082; clb 50.1/954; bl 50/8405; bc 50/8196; br 50/9485, H/15179. **5.** tr 50/5719. **6.** cl 20.2/2778; tr 20.2/5865, 20.1/8577; c DN/756; br T/2448, 20/6871, T/914, 20/6795. **7.** tl H/5144; tc 29.1/6070; cl H/10426; cr 29.1/7105; bl 29.1/341. **8.** l 50.2/1182A; br 50/9173. **9.** t E/419; br 50/7649. **10.** l 16/4921; cl 50.1/5418; br 16/535, 16.1/769, 16/534. **11.** tl 50/5449A; br 50.1/5466A–H. **12.** tr 50.1/7475; cl 50.1/6443; b 1/4133. **13.** tl 50.2/1320; cr 50/7388; cbr 50.1/7607AB. **14.** l 50.1/1696; ct 50.1/1768. **15.** tl 50.1/1744; r 50.1/1528. **16.** ctr 50.1/5651, 50.1/1544; c 50/3706, 50/6870; bl 50.1/5632A, 50/6188H; br 50.1/5648, 50.1/1852. **17.** tl 50/6486; cr 50.1/1908; bl 50.1/1786, NAE/0064, 50.1/1886. **18.** tr 50.1/1942; cbl 50.1/1943, 50.1/1595; bl 50.1/1603; br 50.1/7572. **19.** tl 50.1/1613AB, 50.1/1614AB. **20.** tr 50.1/6609; cl NN1–4; b T/833. **21.** tl 50.1/8657; tc 50.1/7038; tr 10/34. **22.** tr 50/2232; cl 50.1/7174AB; bl 50/9950, 50/9949, 50/572; br 50.2/1378. **23.** tr 50.1/6625; br 50/4695AB. **24.** cr 50/5336; b 50.1/7215. **25.** tl 20.0/713; tc D/N116; tr 50/5816; ct 50/5363; cb 50/5364. **26.** l 50/3808; tr 50.2/6405, 50.2/6407; c 50/7306. **27.** tl 50/5323. **28.** l 50.1/516, 50.1/507, 508. **29.** tl 50.1/5768AB; cl 50.2/2878; tr 50/311, 50/301A–C. **30.** cl 50.1/7515. **31.** tl 50/5740; bl 50/5756; r 50.1/392, 50.2/6554, 50.1/301, 50.1/323AB, 50.1/8035AB. **32.** l 50.1/5432. **33.** cr 50.1/6012; r 50.1/7894. **34.** cl 1/4606; br 50/5545. **35.** tl 50/5760; br 50/5546. **36.** tr 50/5719; bl 50.1/5652AB; br 50.1/4011A. **37.** tr 50/6166D. **38.** t 16/8648; c 16/8649, 8650A–F; cr 16/9076, 16/9077A; bl 50/3768. **39.** l 16/1285; c 16/8666; br 50/2515. **40.** cb 50/9268; bl 50.2/6786. **41.** l 50.1/5991; cr 50/1275AB; br 50.2/3470AB. **42.** cl 50/3132; bl 1/4681, 4682; r 50/2612. **43.** tl 50/565; tr 50/2588; cr T/18243; br 50/3178, 50/3431, 50.1/2038B. **44.** l 50.1/9232; c 50.2/4760; cr 50.1/4049; b 50.1/9218. **45.** t 50.1/2448. **46.** l 50/9485, H/15179; cl H/15199; tr 50.2/5664; r 50/9523. **47.** tr 50.2/6593; l 50/9433; r 50/9318. **48.** tl 50.2/4817; bl 50/8629; c 50.1/6213AB; cr 50/8405; r 50.1/954. **49.** l 50.2/4819A–D; tr 50.2/4819E; br 50/8196.**50.** tr 50.1/4191; bl 50.1/4776; br 50.1/4889; r 50.1/4182. **51.** c, bl 50.1/4592. **52.** tl E/1525; cl 16/16B; b 16/949. **53.** tr E/806; l 16.1/558B; r 16/8686. **54.** tr, cl 16/6770; cr 16/308; bc E/348; br 19/803. **55.** br 16/1507. **56.** tr 16/245; bl 16.1/404. **57.** l 19/1000; tr 19/1048; c 19/1086; br 19/1239. **58.** tr 50.2/3008; c 50/7028; bl 50.1/7722; br 50/7108, 7109. **59.** tl 50.2/2736B; cr 50/7018B. **60.** l 60/2477, 60/2478A; cl 60.2/5371, 60/6975D; cr 60.1/5361; cb 60/1133–4; br 0/63ABC. **61.** t 60.2/5500; cr 60/5269, 60/3336B, 60/1355; cbr 60.1/3996; b 60.1/3773.